Places We Share

Program in Migration and Refugee Studies

Program Advisors:
Elzbieta M. Gozdziak and Susan F. Martin, Institute for the Study of International Migration

Places We Share

Migration, Subjectivity, and Global Mobility

Edited by Susan Ossman

LEXINGTON BOOKS
A division of
ROWMAN & LITTLEFIELD PUBLISHERS, INC.
Lanham • Boulder • New York • Toronto • Plymouth, UK

LEXINGTON BOOKS

A division of Rowman & Littlefield Publishers, Inc.
A wholly owned subsidiary of The Rowman & Littlefield Publishing Group, Inc.
4501 Forbes Boulevard, Suite 200
Lanham, MD 20706

Estover Road
Plymouth PL6 7PY
United Kingdom

British Library Cataloguing in Publication Information Available

Library of Congress Cataloging-in-Publication Data

Places we share : migration, subjectivity, and global mobility / [edited by]
Susan Ossman.
    p. cm.
  Includes bibliographical references.
  ISBN-13: 978-0-7391-1708-8 (cloth : alk. paper)
  ISBN-10: 0-7391-1708-4 (cloth : alk. paper)
  ISBN-13: 978-0-7391-1709-5 (pbk. : alk. paper)
  ISBN-10: 0-7391-1709-2 (pbk. : alk. paper)
  1. Transnationalism. 2. Cosmopolitanism. 3. Immigrants—Cultural assimilation.
I. Ossman, Susan.
  JV6035.P63 2007
  304.8—dc22   2006030168

Printed in the United States of America

⊗™ The paper used in this publication meets the minimum requirements of American
National Standard for Information Sciences—Permanence of Paper for Printed Library
Materials, ANSI/NISO Z39.48-1992.

Contents

Acknowledgments

The project that led to this book has been generously supported by many individuals and institutions. A conference on serial migration in March 2004 in Washington, D.C., was made possible by the Center for Contemporary Arab Studies and the Institute for the Study of International Migration at Georgetown University and the Cultural Services of the French Embassy in Washington, D.C. Naila Sherman, Rania Kiblawi, and Chantal Manès were instrumental in making that event a success. Rabia Bekkar and Rajae Nami contributed to our discussions, while James Faubion, Elzbieta Gozdziak, and Nabiha Jerad critically responded to our talks on that occasion: a daunting task given that our meeting was more as a socio-critical experiment than a presentation of the results of a standard research program. I owe special thanks to Elżbieta, whose involvement with the project extended to critically reading the manuscript. Katie Funk has also been especially helpful during the editorial process.

I would personally like to thank Georgetown University's School of Foreign Service for awarding me a grant for the summer of 2003 that enabled me to carry out research in Montreal in collaboration with Leila Abouhouraira. I was able to continue my research thanks to a fellowship from the John Simon Guggenheim foundation in 2005–2006. Goldsmith's College, University of London, has been an ideal place to complete the first stage of this work and prepare this book for publication. Many thanks to all of those involved in these institutions and especially, to the people who have been willing to talk to me and my colleagues about what life is like for people on the move.

Editor's Note on Transcriptions and Translations

I have not developed a standardized method of transcription throughout this book. Given the importance attached by several authors to the variability within any given language, I judged it best to let each author provide a simplified transcription of important terms. Where foreign words or neologisms have been defined in the text, I have italicized their first appearance in each chapter. When foreign spellings have been used by the author, I have maintained them as long as they can be easily understood by an English-speaking audience. For example, I write "Fez" in the introduction, while Justin McGuinness prefers the French, Fès in chapter 7.

Introduction

Susan Ossman

The truth is that the folks that we've scooped up have, on a number of occasions, had multiple identifications from different countries, Defense
Secretary Donald H. Rumsfeld said today at a briefing in Washington.
They're quite skilled at confusing people as to what their real nationality
is or where they came from or what they're doing.

—Fisher 2003

Who are these elusive people beholden to no nation, who, like Satan himself,
can take any bodily form, speak every tongue and cross borders undetected? In
the wake of the attacks on New York and Washington on September 11, 2001,
the figure of the nomadic chameleon came to symbolize a kind of evil that is
difficult to locate and strangely volatile in its form. Mohammed Atta and his
co-conspirators were not simply criminals, nor were they portrayed at run of
the mill terrorists. Instead, they appeared as malevolent changelings whose
ability to blend in to any environment allowed them to threaten security and
civilization. Unlike a girl wearing a *hijab* (veil) in Europe, or a cleric representing his community at meetings for interfaith understanding, this figure
challenges prevalent conceptions of the relationship between identity and appearance, belief and representation. This man of all nations mocks the certi-
tudes of settled society through the ease with which he blends in everywhere.
Were it not for his treacherous intentions, he would be perceived as a consum-
mate cosmopolitan, the ideal subject of a world in the throes of globalization.

An increasingly global economy facilitates mobility and logically works to
produce more adaptable, moveable people. Yet, people with multiple national
identifications challenge how we think about stability. Their movements
demonstrate contradictions between political and economic orders. They ask

1

us to rethink issues of loyalty and patriotism at a time when both increased attention to national borders and the opening of wider regions to transnational circulation are affecting the lives of millions of people. For every Mohammed Atta there are scores of engineers and managers, petty thieves and housewives whose lives are unfolding in spaces that include several countries (Robbins 2001). Are these peripatetic subjects chameleons or cosmopolitans? Are they nomads or sojourners, would-be terrorists or exemplary late modern subjects? These questions are being posed by philosophers and exploited by politicians. But what do we actually know of lives in motion? This book seeks to answer these questions by addressing debates about cosmopolitanism and mobility, immigration and personal stability based on the authors' experiences as migrating would-be cosmopolitans. As social scientists who have studied immigration and philosophers well versed in discussions about perpetual peace, we explore the life-worlds, literature, and dreams of people who have had many homes in several countries. Drawing on our expertise in socio-linguistics, anthropology, or literary criticism, we offer interpretations of how subjectivity, modes of action, and strategies for social visibility are shaped in the process of moving from one place to another. Collectively, we develop an understanding of mobility that is not predicated on notions of integration into a fixed community, yet might not be described in terms of a cosmopolitan practice that naturally emerges from thinking of oneself as a citizen of the world.

Our project opens up a space of dialogue between discussions of cosmopolitanism and the study of migration. Along with theories of globalization, these domains share a common tendency to conceive of the world in terms of binary oppositions. Even the most sophisticated research on immigrant communities tends to focus on the social and political dynamics set in motion by contrasts of host to home countries (Brettell 2000). In spite of demands to pay attention "actually lived cosmopolitanism," the figure of the world citizen is also generally pulled between some local earth and a global sky, conceived as a part of a general process of "ungrounding." Cosmopolitan perspectives tend to be imagined in terms of a particular kind of relationship between any place on earth and a second space of global consciousness. Critiques of these positions have tended to point to their elite assumptions (Calhoun 2002). We suggest that even the way we imagine elites must be reworked according to how mobility shapes social differences of all kinds (Ossman 2002). We extend critiques of what understanding mobility or globalization in terms of a simple back and forth motion obscures by following the very different paths open to people as they make lives across nations. By focusing on individual stories of lives lived in several countries we show that the nomad is not a romantic hero who escapes detection, but an individual who desperately seeks to be given a name. We call attention to how the histories of people who have spent time in several countries are repeatedly denied by processes of identification that only take into account bloodlines or birthplace. Theories of social reproduction that focus primarily on our earliest experiences or *habitus* participate in this erasure (Bourdieu 1977). We recognize that even these early sites of self-making are often infused with tensions and contradictions because they themselves include coexisting and sometimes contradictory ways of life. Experience of life in places where different ideologies or modes of thinking compete might provide the linguistic and mimetic propensities required to adapt to a more mobile world. But only by recognizing and exploring the individual trajectory can we see how and why these qualities are activated. Only in this way can we begin to recognize what having "multiple identifications from different countries" really means in world where the relationship between mobility and subjectivity, identity and place are changing, and in which the ability to move and to engage in different kinds of motion over time are increasingly important to the making of society.

A SOCIO-REFLEXIVE ENCOUNTER

Most of those whose work you will read about in this pages first met at a conference I organized at Georgetown University in March 2004. As I was planning that occasion, I strove to think about mobility and identity in ways that would avoid the kinds of static identity corsets or assumptions about the relation of host to home countries that have all too often inhibited the study of lives in motion. I wanted to invite a group of scholars and professionals who had personal experience of living for several years in more than two countries; people I called "serial migrants" (Ossman 2004). Since the point of the encounter was to focus on paths and ways of moving, it would not have made sense to determine participation according to any ethnic, religious, or national background. Yet, some common space of reference seemed necessary if we were to highlight the ways that the passage through different territories and submission to various regimes of identification worked upon us. In conceiving of what would be a kind of socio-reflexive encounter, I thought of George Marcus's understanding of complicity as arising from the ethnographer's and informant's "mutual curiosity and anxiety about their relationship to a 'third'—not so much the abstract contextualizing world system but the specific sites elsewhere that affect their interactions and make them complicitous in relation to the influence of a 'third'—in creating the bond that makes their fieldwork relationship effective" (Marcus 1999, 122). Redrawing this idea in terms of collaboration among several people engaged both as informants and researchers, I designated Morocco as the reference point or terrain that would define our meeting.[1]

Given the importance of the nation-state in regulating where people can and cannot go, it seemed both natural and provocative to use the borders of a nation to define our group. Our different positions with respect to this third would motivate discussion, while beginning our work with reference to a particular place and nation would eliminate some of the imprecisons that arise from speaking about state and nation or modern societies in general. We might examine varieties of forms of "disembedding" instead of envisioning only a single way of moving away from a stable ground (Giddens 1991). Joined by our different connections to Morocco, our meeting would involve a measure of subjective implication not simply on the order of biographical detail, but in terms of potentially conflicting subject positions that these involved[2] (Kaplan 2003). I reasoned that as the organizer of the event, I should be the first to be vulnerable to what was a potentially conflict-ridden process. But there were further reasons for selecting my "third country" as a gathering point.

Allowing our debates to emerge from a shared experience of a particular national territory had practical advantages. We all speak French, Arabic, and English with varying degrees of proficiency. We share references to places, events, laws, and political debates in our "home country" that provide the conditions for serious conversation. We have in common references to books, places, jokes, and kinship terms. Out of this common terrain that we have each called home, the significance of other marks of identity and social position would no longer be a matter of establishing a checklist against which to measure our lives in terms of positions of gender, citizenship, and class (Glick Schiller, Basch, Blanc-Szanton 1992; Grewal and Kaplan 1994, 19). Moving out from Morocco in a dual motion, toward our other homes and toward each other, the most pertinent similarities and differences among us could become salient. Those of lesser importance would fade away. By selecting a shared point of passage, we enabled our discussions to get beyond abstractions about the thrills and threats of mobility or world citizenship. By deliberately playing on Moroccan borders we have been able to play on assumptions about migration, render our questions about contemporary forms of mobility more precise, and then, broaden the scope of our investigations to explore how Morocco is related to other political, social, and imaginary spaces.

By working out of Morocco, we also go against the grain of a series of assumptions. Morocco has generally been studied as a place that people leave. By looking at the national territory as a space that people move to or pass through, we displace its identification as a "sending country" and see it as it in fact is: an ambiguous zone where nomads shepherd their flocks, holiday making sheikhs build palaces, and people from other countries settle. As I write, the fences of the Spanish enclaves in the North of the country are being stormed by people from West Africa. People living in camps on the edges Ceuta and Melilla are being transported toward the Sahara to keep them away from "Fortress Europe" (Goldschmidt 2006). It is no longer news that thousands of others are embarking on flimsy boats each day to try to survive the dangerous voyage across the straights of Gibraltar.[3] Some of these would-be Europeans end up settling in Morocco, as do students from Senegal or France and businesswomen from Germany or New York; others, like most of us, might spend years in Morocco before moving on.

In advertising the conference that led to this publication, I wrote, "While some people study globalization, others live their lives as global experiments. This project brings together a group of people who do both." Was I just setting the stage for yet another performance of self-congratulatory rhetoric on the part of intellectuals who could easily see themselves as exemplary of some kind of protean cosmopolitan community? The educational backgrounds, linguistic faculties, and personal trajectories of those who participated in this experiment might seem to make them ideal candidates for future cosmopolitical campaigns. Yet, a closer look at where we come from and where we have gone shows that at least some of us share countries and stories that are not so dissimilar to those of the most sought after criminal-chameleons in the world. Our parents were from every income group according to any mode of classification. Some of us were born in small villages, others in global cities. We were raised in Muslim and Christian, Jewish and agnostic homes. We have in common the fact that we have all obtained advanced degrees, a fact that in and of itself might qualify us as members in a shared, universal intellectual community. The reactions of those who commented on our presentations at the Georgetown conference showed, the fact that we worked out of a common Moroccan framework toward generalities displayed the fractured and conflictual nature of that apparently cohesive, imagined whole. This was not simply because we were working "from the margins" by moving out of a small, poor nation. It has to do with the nature of the global situation.

Nabiha Jerad spoke eloquently at the conference about the kinds of rifts and *décalages* (slippages) that characterize a supposedly universal academy. In recounting her experience of adding English to her bilingual Arabic/French repertoire, she describes a kind of intellectual serial migration. Language communities continue to structure traditions of research and reflexes that structure how we come to arrive at what is real and true. The importance that attention to language assumed in our work led us to recognize that study "Morocco" might need to expand to include wider zones; in Arabic *al-maghrib* designates both the nation of Morocco and "the west," a zone including Tunisia, Algeria,

Morocco, Mauritania, and Libya. To speak of "Maghrebians" in French immediately involves a lexicon of immigration as well as colonial history. Talking out of Morocco can lead to sketching out an unconventional map of the "Arab world" or engagement with *francophonie*.

I put the accent on the willfulness of Nabiha's *démarche* (approach, way of walking) because it seems characteristic of both practical and intellectual aspects of serial migration. The concrete realities of actually trying to live with more than one nationality, in several linguistic and political spaces are too often readily forgotten when we start to think about globalization or becoming a citizen of the world. It is not easy to develop a general concept of what the cosmos or the polis is that truly involves several strands of collective thought developed in different states. Monarchies, constitutional democracies, and Islamic republics are predicated on different conceptions of the subject, his links to other people, and to the cosmos. To try to think in general about the world is perhaps less a matter of picturing utopias than trying to picture infinity: more a matter of developing a theory of limits, or *rapprochement*, or an idea of closeness (*qrib*) than conceiving of oneself as an ideal citizen in a hypothetical global polity.

MOBILITY AND VISIBILITY

All too often, migrants' willful work at becoming something other, something more, goes unrecognized. Smain Laacher writes about nameless wanderers, people who are identified only as bodies out of place. While the "immigrant" is carefully rendered in statistics and studied in-depth, even if he is an illegal alien, people who are identified as nationless nomads are the object of indifference, except in the plays and films, novels and philosophical treatises which readily adopt the global nomad as a way of speaking about the human condition. The nomad appears free of all bonds, open to all horizons in ways that are not dissimilar to the cosmopolitan. Laacher's study of people living in the French internment camp of Sangatte responds to the aestheticization of the nomad by telling us the stories of individuals who only ask for the right to settle down somewhere. His interlocutors trekked thousands of miles over the mountainous terrain of central Asia, finding occasional employment and encountering police brutality in the countries they traversed. Many dreamed of making it to England, just across the channel from the refugee center where Smain met them. Some, like Ali, tried to hitch a ride on trains heading under the Chunnel. Most of those who attempted this were caught and sent back. Ali not only didn't make it to London, he lost a leg falling off the train.

Laacher draws on his long interviews with Ali to show the impossibility of translating this young man's sense of himself and his purpose into the vocabulary of citizenship and international law. Ali was born in Afghanistan. His extended family contributed to paying for his journey. They counted on him to succeed in his quest to find a place to settle, a place to anchor the family outside of their nation: itself a mockery of the modern nation state. Now, following his ordeal, Ali cannot understand why England will not take him in. After all, he shed his blood for her. Shouldn't this sign of devotion be enough to enter the British family? He draws on notions of honor and belonging to explain his position. Laacher seeks to understand Ali, but this is not an easy process. Still, this experience leads him to conclude that we must make the effort to listen to the stories of the increasing number of global wanderers if we hope to find ethical responses to the real political and philosophical challenges their lives pose. The nomad should not be romanticized or spoken of in terms of population flows, but recognized as having the right to be recognized in his singularity.

While the people Laacher interviewed are nameless and seek only to settle down, Susan Terrio proposes a study of what might be called overidentification. In analyzing the story of Zacarias Moussaoui, she details his fruitless effort to escape his only too visible identities as an immigrant, Muslim, and Arab in France. She draws our attention to the fact that Moussaoui was not a "typical" immigrant at all. He seems to have had everything he needed to live happily in the country his mother adopted with great fervor. Hers was a story of immigrant success: In spite of a failed marriage and a limited education, she managed to land a white-collar job and raise her children in a middle-class neighborhood. She kept her children from socializing with other Maghrebis, expecting them to be upwardly mobile. When Zacarias proved to be only an average student and was routed into the technical track at school, she saw it as a sign of racism. She and her son believed that it was as an immigrant and the son of a manual worker that he was denied access to the kind of education to which he aspired and felt entitled. Terrio draws our attention to how closely Moussaoui resembles some other less internationally known cases of young Frenchmen of North African descent that have become involved in terrorist activities. These were not poor kids from the projects, but ambitious young men whose families were doing rather well. Yet, it is perhaps the very intensity of their families' dreams combined with the difficulty of feeling caught in the stigmatized position of the immigrant that led them to experience acute humiliation and develop extreme cases of *la haine* (angry rage) that is not uncommon among the second generation of immigrant children (Ossman and Terrio 2006). Perhaps Moussaoui sought to escape from his ascribed identity by moving to England to study. But by then, Terrio tells us, he was already well on the path to becoming involved in al-Qaeda. Unlike Mohammed Atta who used his chameleon powers with deadly precision, Moussaoui seems to have had little facility for fitting in. His trial led some observers to doubt his sanity. Yet, we must keep in mind that he is not an isolated madman but indicative of the darker possibilities of what mobility, free motion, and cosmopolitan belonging promise. His attempts to find escape from his status as a migrant and expectations of fulfilling the rags to riches immigrant's story led him on a path of serial migration that was smoothed by adherence to a rulebound version of Islam and the networks of an international movement bent on destruction.

Nabiha Jerad follows up on Terrio's discussion by showing how the Maghreb was both "made in France" and in relation to the space of the Mediterranean. She explores how different terms have been used to designate immigrants in France, focusing on how the term "Maghrebian" and "Arab" have been adopted in public discourse and literally turned around by those it designates; "Arab" has become "Beur" thanks to "verlan," the slang of the French suburbs. While official discourse places the emphasis on how immigrants and their children live in an in-between space between their country of origin and France, new forms of speech, literature, and music produced by people whose parent's or grandparents came from North Africa are creating a kind of expressive third space. The Mediterranean emerges as a new imaginative horizon, a space in which people living all over the world can participate. Jerad writes of her own participation in this Mediterranean world, and emphasizes that even a space that is shared is not necessarily equally open to those who inhabit it. We are still in a postcolonial context, which means that the sea looks very different for those on its southern and northern shores, in spite of the fact that recent beur literature and raï music overcome the duality assumed to characterize the lives of immigrants and their children.

COSMOPOLITAN CONTRADICTIONS

Nadia Tazi draws attention to dilemmas of identification in both aesthetic and political terms through an analysis of Salman Rushdie's *The Satanic Verses* and the French "veil affair." Is there a way of moving that escapes the namelessness of the nomad and the entrapment of pejorative ascribed identities? As a Moroccan brought up in Spain and Casablanca, who now lives in Paris, making frequent visits to her other home in India, Tazi might appear as someone who could escape the kinds of problems of in-betweeness described in the preceding articles. However, she writes about situations in which her own cosmopolitanism fails her. She sees Rushdie's writing as a way to get "beyond the logic of belonging," an ambition with which she is clearly in sympathy. She admires the fact that his art displays a cosmopolitanism that "involves giving oneself the luxury of a crossed critique that does not simply denounce each side but denounces one through the other in a series of mediations and oblique movements." Yet the interpenetration of apparently contradictory elements that Rushdie so deftly effects in the service of his art is precisely what is impossible in life. Nadia writes of her struggle to make sense of her own contradictory reactions to the banning of the hijab in French schools. Was it really possible to find a common ground between her own identities as a Moroccan and cosmopolitan, a woman living in France and a Muslim intellectual? She embraces the discomfort born of her inability to develop a cosmopolitan response to a cosmopolitical dilemma by suggesting that those who brush aside real differences and contradictions in favor of a false tolerance must be exposed (Cheah and Robbins 1998). She reserves particular criticism for intellectuals who defend Rushdie by saying that his work is "merely fiction." Rushdie knew very well that he was playing with fire in the way that he drew on the Koran and Muslim tradition, she insists. But for him, "Writing becomes a move not to find one's roots but one's wings: even if one burns them in the process." While Tazi adopts the same metaphors of roots and wings as does Ulrich Beck in his efforts to define a "rooted cosmopolitanism," to expose the contradiction at the heart of such a formulation (Beck 2001, 19).

Shana Cohen writes of how religion conceived in terms of action instead of community can provide a thread to hold together experiences and commitments that transcend and traverse nations. Jews have often been seen as the quintessential diasporic community. They have been feared and berated for their cosmopolitanism. But, Cohen writes, her experience of being Jewish is not so much about community in diaspora as the actualization of ethical principles. She writes of Emmanuel, a would-be kosher butcher from Manchester, who has decided to live in Morocco after spending time in Israel. He chose to settle in Casablanca neither because he has family there, nor because he feels integrated in Moroccan Jewish circles. It is because it is in Morocco that being a Jew becomes a meaningful action. He says that it is important for Muslims to see that Jews are not all the same, that they have personal opinions about politics and religious practice. In Morocco this is possible. Similarly, Cohen considers her own migrations have not been motivated by any particular effort to become a part of Jewish communities. It is not the archipelago of the Jewish diaspora that gives direction to her to travel, nor does she seek out affiliation with Jewish organizations. Instead, she explains that she acts out her faith by becoming involved in projects to promote development and social services in several sites with people from a variety of religious backgrounds.

Nick Mai pursues this line of thought in a different manner by asking what experiences of mobility allow people to reconcile the different real and imaginary places of their lives to become mature, adult selves. He offers an account of his efforts to situate himself between the country where he lives (England) and the country of his birth (Italy) and contrasts his situation to that of young men from Morocco, Romania, or Albania who move from one European city to another. He traces the parallels between his own struggle to construct a "third space" where his Italian and English sides could coexist alongside the development of his scholarly research. Studying the relationship of media and migration in Albania, elaborating a theory of "errance" based on research among young men who enter Europe illegally and engage in illicit activities to keep their dreams alive, Mai reflects on how television and film contribute to dreams of hedonism and individuality, materialism and sexuality freed of the constraints of any patriarchal order. Long passages from conversations he has had with youths about how they live, going home, and sexuality point to the dilemma of those who choose to wander aimlessly: they cannot reconcile their expectations of themselves with their actual lives. They dream of returning home with a car, a wife, and gifts for the family. But for most of them this is impossible, not only because they lack the financial basis to live out this dream, but because it is at odds with the very motivations that led them to begin their journey in the first place. Their action is predicted on an imaginative distinction between home as a place where the individual is repressed, and a hedonistic, wealthy, individualistic life in Europe. They steal, prostitute themselves, or deal drugs because they are literally caught in a liminal space between childhood and adulthood.

Like Mai, Justin McGuinness notes the power of the media to motivate people to undertake journeys to far-off places. He writes of people lured to life in the medina of old Fez by the exoticism of the tales from the Arabian nights. He himself was drawn to the Arab world by seeing a documentary on North Africa while growing up in England. Like his interviewees, he was entranced by the beauty of Moroccan architecture. And recently, he too has started to refurbish an old house in Fez. "Neo-Fassis" come to Morocco from Europe, North America, and the Middle East looking for a more authentic, spiritual, or relaxed way of life. While well-off Moroccans tend to prefer to live in the new parts of town, these immigrants seek to preserve and resuscitate Morocco's historic beauty. They have reinvigorated the economies of cities like Marrakech and Fez by transforming their decaying old cities. Whether they move to Morocco because they have converted to Islam, fallen in love, or seek to develop businesses that would be too costly to set up in Europe, everything from the price of property to the way that an old house "should" be furnished is transformed by their presence. McGuiness points out that their attempts to follow assumed traditions or particular notions of the authentic often lead neo-Fassis to defy the very social conventions they so passionately want to adhere to. For instance, they often engage in activities that are deemed unacceptable for people of their status, like doing their own housekeeping or woodworking. McGuinness readily calls his fellow new Fassis cosmopolitans. He says that in all likelihood, many of them will one day leave Fez behind. But in the process, their creations inspire arts and living magazines and create the conditions for enchanting other new Fassis to come and take their places.

Evelyn Early tells her life story to reflect upon the networks and spaces that structure a nomadic existence. She explains that it is because of love and family ties that Egypt and Morocco became her two countries, but her ways of arriving in each country at different times have led to different ways of engaging with each place. Writing of the years she spent in Egypt as an anthropologist and the fiancée of a Cairene intellectual, she reminds us that even scholars who are said to "go native" do so in terms of specific social milieu. By introducing the voice of her teenage daughter who was brought up in Rabat, Damascus, Maryland, and Prague, she offers an interesting picture of the native turned tourist. Although she might inhabit different positions as lover or tourist, diplomat or anthropologist, Early says that her self is not defined by these roles. Instead, she finds continuity in what she calls the "moving seminar," times and places that bring people from various moments in her life together, social spaces where she encounters people with shared interests; Abdulhai Diouri's monthly anthropology seminar in Rabat, an American Institute of Maghrebi Studies conference in Tangiers, the book fair in Casablanca. Events like these put her in touch with people she first got to know in Lebanon and Egypt, Sudan or Syria.

Leila Abouhouraira, on the other hand, writes of how the memory of a specific city leads her to relish travel and be willing to always move on. She suggests that growing up in multilingual Tangiers led her to develop a particular version of what a cosmopolitan life might resemble. While Early evoked the foreign missionaries who visited her childhood home, Abouhouraira recalls the Northern Moroccan landscape. She sees Morocco, Spain, and Gibraltar as part of a single ecosystem. She dates her decision to leave Morocco from the moment she learned that she would need a visa to visit places that she still considers to be home. She writes of how the Tangiers she experienced in a time before visas and before the spread of conservative interpretations of Islam continues to shape her life. She explains that she has progressively transposed the image of her lost city on the other places she has adopted as home: the French city of Toulouse, and Montreal. Abouhouraira goes on to describe how she "keeps Tangiers alive" by speaking its different languages to her children. She notes that other Moroccans living in Canada also integrate French, Spanish, English, and Moroccan dialects of Arabic into their daily conversations. Yet, the Egyptian or Iraqi serial migrants she interviewed did not seem to place the same importance on linguistic versatility. Unlike the Moroccans, they tend to presume a certain homogeneity of the Arab world and were mainly concerned that their children learn Arabic. Leila marks a strong attachment to Tangiers and Morocco and demonstrates this through her linguistic practices. Yet, she emphasizes her inability to converse in Egyptian or Levantine Arabic, although in Canada she is identified as an Arab by her Lebanese or Egyptian acquaintances.

Fatima Badry's research on language use among Moroccan women living in the United Arab Emirates (UAE) leads us to further explore how hierarchies of language are related to identity. She explains how she herself has progressively picked up languages, accents, and dialects in the course of her peregrinations from Morocco to France, England to the United States, and now, living in the UAE. She notes that even in Morocco, men and women eagerly address their interlocutor in the language or dialect that they imagine he speaks. This is often considered to be simply a sign of tolerance or openness, but it is in fact the result of local hierarchies related to colonial history and a marginalization of Morocco in the Arab world. While the legacy of French and Spanish rule has been carefully studied, and the ongoing necessity of knowing at least French and increasingly English to gain access to management positions is well known, Badry's research breaks new ground by detailing the ways that Moroccans also abandon their dialect in Arabic speaking contexts. Moroccan women living in the UAE perpetuate a hierarchy among Arabic speakers that favors those who speak Egyptian, Palestinian, or in this instance, Emerati dialects. This is the result of an order of dialects established by the media, literature, and political engagements. Speaking with a Moroccan accent has particularly undesirable consequences for women. Their speech identifies them with the image of the Moroccan woman that is widely circulated in the Arab world, which portrays them as prostitutes, or at least sexually available to men. In places where men's honor is still determined by keeping close watch over the sexual comportment of their female kin, Moroccan women and girls try to adopt alternatives to their native language to appear more generically Arab. In this situation, chameleon skill at moving through overlapping social and political spaces is not a sign of privilege or aesthetic play. Indeed, it could be interpreted as a sign of disempowerment. However, the women involved in

Badry's study emphasized the positive side of their linguistic adaptability. The relinquishment of an audible national identity is not experienced as a personal tragedy. Moroccan national identity appeared as hindrance to attaining status and respect, while adopting other dialects or languages brought personal and financial fulfillment.

While serial migrants born in Morocco now living in Quebec seem to make an effort to maintain the accents of the city or region of their birth in their homes, Moroccan women in the UAE suffer a stigma so strong that it alters their desire to speak their mother tongue, even with their children. Abderrahmane Lakhsassi's tale of his life as a Berber-speaking child in Tiznit remind us of the linguistic divisions that alter people's involvement in the nation, even within the national territory. In the Tiznit of Lakhsassi's youth, everyone conversed in Berber. Arabic and French were only spoken only in school. He writes of moving to Marrakech to attend high school and realizing that being Moroccan meant adapting to a new linguistic configuration that made Berber a tongue of the private realm. He recounts his moves to Lebanon, Paris, and England as efforts to explore how universalism might allow him to participate in a community beyond his village. After studying European philosophy, he sought out the universal in Islamic thought before leaving behind philosophy for anthropology and the study of Berber poetry. His story of serial migration is thus a kind of intellectual and personal quest that ultimately leads him back home. In fact, when he "returns" to live in Casablanca after many years abroad, he finds a place transformed by the work of people like himself, academics and activists with an interest in Berber cultural expressions.[4] Today, Berber languages can now be spoken in public. In parts of the country where Berber is widely spoken, schools are introducing Berber curricula. These changes and the possibility of maintaining ties to the broader scholarly communities that Lakhsassi calls his "virtual tribes" make it possible for him to envisage a cosmopolitan life in Morocco.

I end the book by asking how modes of comparative study might be inspired by the ways that serial migrants move among the places of their lives. I explore the role that my third country played in my own story of serial migration, and attempt to tease out my personal story against the background of the linked comparative approach to ethnographic fieldwork I developed to study globalization and beauty in the salons of Casablanca, Paris, and Cairo. I suggest that increased attention to how we design the pathways and not only the places of study can lead us to move beyond the idea that ethnography's promise lies in its claims to grounding. By noticing how social milieu and interactions are produced according to distinctly different relations to place and other people, the anthropologist can mimic the serial migrant to propose accounts of society rather than merely contextualzing ethnographic data in terms of static modes of sociological certainty.

EMBARKATIONS

People with several passports, who seem to fit in anywhere, are indeed a challenge to the usual ways in which we make sense of who we are, and how our identities are related to where we might hope to travel, both literally, or in terms of our social position or personal ambitions. By showing how wanderers and errant youths, immigrants, and serial migrants make their way through social and political landscapes, the essays in this book point to the limits of standard sociologies, modes of representation, measures of identity, and conceptions of loyalty. We take a small step toward moving from devising taxonomies of people who move differently across the shared background of the earth, to trying to understand how mobility produces a variety of worlds that, together, make up society (Clifford 1997; Urry 2000).

As increasing numbers of people will be unable to state their "real nationality," and some of those who can will find it increasingly irrelevant to "where they came from" or "what they are doing," those who seek to control migratory flows and shape new forms of power will surely abandon debates on assimilation (Fisher 2003). Economic and political agencies will become more and more aware of the importance of disseminating the chameleon techniques required to live successful lives of serial migration. States and international organizations will devise new ways of labeling migratory patterns and replace the potentially infinite hyphenated identity with more succinct terms. Citizens of the world will only be able to critically respond to these developments by thinking about how the way we move among the places of our lives entails specific possibilities for connecting to others. Only by thinking about the places we share and how we arrived there, by promoting future meetings on different terrains, will we be able to respond to a situation in which distinctive ways of moving through the world will become the dominant mode of generating and explaining social difference. This book provides no global vision of the subject. Instead, it alerts us to some of the ways in which forms of social and political control are no longer grounded solely in strategies of confinement, in spite of the regressive dreams of some world leaders, who suggest that acts of terror can be avoided by reinstating practices of exile.[5] Exile is still possible, but it need not entail treaties of extradition to foreign lands. Freedom has not vanished, but we must be willing to find it in a cosmos woven of our collective motion.

NOTES

1. This project thus differs from other works of collaborative anthropology in that those who are doing the interviews and examining the literature of serial migrants are themselves a part of the group. In some sense this might be likened to the kind of activist anthropology in which a member of a particular association or party engages in what is known in French as *recherche-action*. While our engagement is a kind of research in action, it was conceivable only after the fact, after those involved in it had become serial migrants. Our work tries to give a name to an experience and mode of mobility that is otherwise unrecognized. It is a foray into a kind of social reflexivity involving attention to the scholarly event as a mode of interaction and a moment of research on the theme being explored as much as a forum for reporting research results. The participants in this event represented not only those they studied, but themselves.

2. Thus, our work differed from studies of Diasporas that explore "flexible citizenship" based on the experience of a recognized ethnic group or family networks (Ong 1998).

3. People from North Africa have been trying their luck getting across the straights of Gibraltar for years. Increasingly, immigrants from the rest of Africa and even from as far away as Afghanistan travel to Morocco to try to make their way to Europe. Many of them end up in camps on the edges of Spain's African territories in the North of Morocco. In September 2005, more than 500 people tried to force their way across the Morocco Ceuta Border. 163 people succeeded in getting in, 100 were wounded, and 5 were killed. See *Le Monde*, 30 September 2005, 1.

4. *Amazigh* is the indigenous term for "Berber."

5. I am of course thinking of Tony Blair's idea of sending foreigners suspected of promoting terrorist agendas out of the country. The same tactic has been adopted by other governments, for instance, Egypt and Saudi Arabia, with the results we are all now familiar with.

REFERENCES

Beck, Ulrich. 2001. The Cosmopolitan Society and its Enemies. *Politologiske Studier*. arg. 4, NR2, May.

Bhabha, Homi. 1994. *The Location of Culture*. London: Routledge.

Bourdieu, Pierre. 1977. *Outline of a Theory of Practice*. Cambridge: Cambridge University Press.

Brettell, Caroline. 2000. Theorizing Migration in Anthropology. The Social Construction of Networks, Identities, Communities, and Globalscapes. *Migration Theory. Talking Across Disciplines*. Brettell, Caroline and Hollifield, James F. (eds). New York: Routledge.

Calhoun, Craig. 2002. The Class Consciousness of Frequent Travelers: Towards a Critique of Actually Existing Cosmopolitanism. *Conceiving Cosmopolitanism,*

Theory, Context, Practice. Vertovec, Steven and Cohen, Robin (eds).Oxford: Oxford University Press.

Cheah, P. and B. Robbins (eds). 1998. *Cosmopolitics, Thinking and Feeling Beyond the Nation*. Minneapolis: University of Minnesota Press.

Clifford, James. 1997. *Routes, Travel and Translation in the Late Twentieth Century*. Cambridge: Harvard University Press.

Giddens, Anthony. 1991. *Modernity and Self Identity: Self and Society in the Late Modern Age*. Oxford: Polity Press.

Glick Schiller, N., L. Basch, and C. Blanc-Szanton (eds). 1992. *Towards a Transnational Perspective on Migration: Race, Class, Ethnicity, and Nationalism Reconsidered*. New York: New York Academy of Sciences.

Goldschmidt, Elie. 2006. Storming the Fences: Morocco and Europe's Anti-Migration Policy. *MERIP*, 229, summer.

Fisher, Ian. 2003. Six Held in Iraq by US Claim to be American. nyt.com (accessed September 16, 2006).

Grewal, Inderpal and Caren Kaplan, (eds). 1994. Introduction. *Scattered Hegemonies. Postmodernism and Transnational Feminist Practice*. Minneapolis: University of Minnesota Press.

Hannerz, Ulf. 1992. *Cultural Complexity, Studies in the Social Organization of Meaning*. New York: Columbia University Press.

Kaplan, Caren. 2003. Transporting the Subject: Technologies of Mobility and Location in an Era of globalization. *Uprootings/Regroundings. Questions of Home and Migration*. Ahmed, Sara; Cateneda, Claudia; Fortier, Anne-Marie; Sheller, Mimi (eds). Oxford: Berg.

Marcus, George. 1997. The Uses of Complicity in the Changing Mise-en-scène of Multi-sited Ethnography. *Ethnography Through Thick and Thin*. Princeton, N.J.: Princeton University Press.

Ong, Aihwa. 1998. "Flexible Citizenship Among Chinese Cosmopolitans." *Cosmopolitics: Thinking and Feeling Beyond the Nation*. Pheng Cheah and Bruce Robbins (eds). Minneapolis: University of Minnesota Press.

Ossman, Susan. 2002. *Three Faces of Beauty: Casablanca, Paris, Cairo*. Durham, NC: Duke University Press.

———. 2004. Stories of Serial Migration. *International Migration*. October.

Ossman, Susan and Terrio, Susan. 2006. The French Riots: Questioning Spaces of Surveillance and Sovereignty. *International Migration*. June.

Robbins, Bruce. 2001. The Village of the Liberal Managerial Class. *Cosmopolitan Geographies: New Locations in Literature and Culture*. Dharwadker, Vinay (ed).London: Routledge.

Urry, John. 2000. *Sociology Beyond Societies, Mobilities for the Twenty-first Century*. London: Routledge.

Vertovec, Steven and Cohen, Robin (eds). 2002. Conceiving Cosmopolitanism, Theory, Context, Practice. Oxford: Oxford University Press.

The Power to Name and the Desire to be Named

State Policies and the Invisible Nomad

Smaïn Laacher

Translated by Kim Jones

Why is immigration policy always perceived to be the domain of the state? Why is the state's natural inclination to reduce immigration to a disciplinary matter to be dealt with by the police? The power, efficiency, and credibility of the police and the state depend on their respective capacities to discipline migrants and also to decide what kinds of people they want to allow into the country. Their power emerges through the process of exercising this disciplinary power to regulate immigration by the use of numbers and statistics that categorize people and take account how many people are extradited or turned away at the border. Issues of immigration are always perceived as fundamental to national sovereignty. Their symbolic significance goes beyond issues of bureaucracy and involves the way that policy claims to represent the will of the people. Public opinion is important to consider in examining how the state acts to preserve the country from outsiders and controls outsiders who have been granted entrance. To fulfill its role the nation-state requires a legal and practical opposition between the national and the nonnational. It requires a principle of positive discrimination for citizens (Laacher 2002).

If we want to decide who belongs to the nation or who might join it, categories of foreigners must be created. In France and Europe the ways that nonnationals are named and categorized, controlled, and allowed to circulate have been the subject of major political debates. The expansion of the European Union and the adoption of the Schengen treaty have made it ever easier for some people to move about the continent. This opening of European borders has led to the creation of new categories of wanderers: people who are not EU citizens, but who have managed to enter this vast European space and wander about it for years on end. What do we call these "floating people?"

In France the state uses words like *immigrants*, *clandestins* (literally, those who are hidden, referring to illegal immigrants), *illegal aliens* (literally, a person without papers), *migrants économiques* (economic migrants), *faux refugiés* (false refugees, or those individuals who falsely claim refugee status). However, these terms are unclear and imprecise, yet they are used in official declarations, the media, and everyday conversation (Tassin 2003, 277). Different terms are used to designate the same person on different occasions. What is clear is that in France people passing through the national territory on their way to some other destination have no formal right to recognition or protection from the state.[1] Yet, ultimately, these transmigrants act as a kind of screen against which the state projects its own image and reaffirms its power. We observe that the difference between illegal aliens and clandestine nomads has been widely developed in state discourse and the media. By playing on these appellations politicians progressively construct the social and juridical identities of two distinct groups. There are illegal aliens, people who have the goal of settling in the country, presented as a political problem deserving of public interest. Then there are the others, variously identified as nomads, transmigrants or clandestins. They are considered to be a humanitarian rather than a political problem.

Illegal aliens have a collective identity and their efforts to be recognized are generally seen as part of a larger struggle with other social and political groups. In France the movement for the legalization of illegal aliens has been supported by a wide range of progressive political and religious organizations. An illegal alien's struggle to be recognized and regularized by the state is not a solitary venture. Her desire to settle in the country is backed up by a collective project; her demands are supported by groups aiming to generate a political climate favorable to giving amnesty to illegal aliens. Thus, while people in this category may not have legal rights, they do have a public presence. Together they question the fundamental distinction between nationals and nonnationals, by *voluntarily* politicizing their condition. In doing this, they distance themselves from clandestins, who are perceived not as potential candidates for *integration* but in terms of national security and humanitarian obligations. The term *clandestine* participates in a lexicon of secret, illicit practices. Secrecy, lack of visibility, and assumption of criminal activities accompanies the very mention of the word. Someone who is in the country not only illegally, but clandestinely, seems to present a danger to the nation. Whether those grouped together under this term are people seeking political asylum, economic migrants, or people actually just wandering through Europe, they are generally perceived as a kind of floating population who are, by definition, unable to settle. Their identities are fluid, their intentions unclear. From the point of view of the state and society they have no fixed identity and no real home.

THE AESTHETICS OF NOMADISM

A clandestine nomad has no public face. Often he hides his identity for fear of being sent back to the war-torn, poverty stricken, or politically oppressive country he is fleeing. Perhaps because he hides his face, this figure has become the object of intense aesthetic experimentation in Europe over the last few years. Whether someone is a refugee, an asylum seeker, or involved in transnational networks of illicit trade is of no consequence for these aesthetic speculations. It is simply the idea of a floating being, someone at home everywhere and anywhere that is attractive. Through an aesthetic redefinition, the nomad becomes a romantic wanderer, an ideal protagonist for stage and film. He can be portrayed and described as a hero of modern times, a person on the margins, a product of a globalized society. Traveling alone, he braves the absurdity of borders and boundaries—symbolic and physical—that separate individuals and nations. Unlike the illegal alien, he has no public face and makes no collective declarations that might intervene in the artist's appropriation of his character.

In November 2002, former Washington Theater director Peter Sellars directed a show at Bobigny Theatre called "The Children of Herakles," a play originally written by Euripedes. Over 2,000 years ago, Euripedes articulated the elements of what would later be the right of asylum, presented not only as a moral imperative but also as a founding principle of democracy. Regarding this text, Peter Sellars notes: "What he described 2500 years ago is what is happening today. When I spoke of his play to theater professionals, they told me it was a 'weak text.' When I read it to experts on human rights, they told me it was a scientific description of what is happening to refugees: expulsion or escape, fear, freedom when they find asylum—but also the question of vengeance, which is always pertinent, whether in Rwanda or in Serbia" (Interview with B. Salino *Culture Théâtre*, November 21, 2002).

Another example from the theater is Ariane Mnouchkine's interpretation of *The Last Caravan Stop*, which first played in 2003 and 2004. It came out in two stages: *The Cruel River (Le Fleuve Cruel)* in 2003, and *Origins and Destinies (Origines et Destins)* in 2004. It was as an anthropologist that Ariane Mnouchkine attempted to understand the motives, the actions, the situations, and the itineraries of these millions of people who seek to enter rich countries. Shaghayegh Behesti, a young Iranian actor in her company, explained that

that it was necessary to call on art, film, and theater to understand the suffering felt by foreigners. To gain this understanding the company watched fictional films and documentaries, they looked at photos, and conducted interviews with wandering foreigners, primarily in Australia and in Sangatte, a detention center for clandestine wanderers in the North of France where I have also done research.

Another recent example of this phenomenon can be found in the cinema. In 2003, British filmmaker Michael Winterbottom released *In This World.* The director traces the secret voyage of two young Afghans from a refugee camp in Pakistan to France, where they end up in the Sangatte detention center. Winterbottom combines several techniques, from an animated map, to cartoons, to printing the date and location of the characters to show that the film "is not pure fiction." The characters are fictional heroes, but their trip is based on the lived experiences of immigrants. He said, "I allowed my actors to act as if they would have acted in reality. Jamal (the main character) actually attempted to sneak into England after making this film. He filed for political asylum and was rejected. This film forces the viewer to ask himself what is fictional and what is real" (Mandelbaum 2003).

The themes of exile and of epic voyage taken up by internationally acclaimed artists remind us that there are millions of people seeking homes all over the world. However, in reality the quest for asylum, the experience of rejection which transforms itself bit by bit into psychological instability, the ongoing, secret voyage of permanent danger, and the inability to know one's destination are not the ingredients for making a life. Still, in theater and film, the experience of seeking a home is experienced as a creative, heroic quest, a move toward liberation. This can lead us to forget that these wanderings are due to violent upheavals in the nomad's native land, the result of poverty, or exploitation. These aesethetic renditions can lead us to forget that to even become a clandestin, one has to meet a series of requirements set up by the "passers" who organize networks of illegal immigration. They are often in cahoots with members of state police forces. Most nomads are from countries and societies where there is no political culture of peaceful conflict, where the absence of a social mise en scène authorizing the existence of the "other" leads to a state where the exception becomes the rule, and where ethnic hatred leads to the end of politics.

If the clandestine wanderer has become such a riveting figure in the art of wealthy, democratic societies, it is because he allows us to develop critical analysis of the process of redefining the links between birthplace and nation, between man and citizen. At a moment when national sovereignty is put in question by the emergence of the European Union, there are millions of foreign people without rights living within European borders. If one assumes that each foreigner who remains in a country should become naturalized, this indicates a belief that the principles of nativity and of sovereignty are eternally linked in the "body of the sovereign subject" (Agamben 1997). This may be good for illegal aliens. But what of those being romanticized as eternal wanderers, people whose place of birth and social connections are obscured by their function as nomads, as people whose images are invoked only as a kind of romantic contradiction to the fundamental territoriality of the state?

THE STATE AND THE PERSON SEEKING A PLACE

A man without a name and without an identity, a being without roots, without connections to others (one might say, *without faith, without a heart, and without law*) cannot hope to become a citizen. He barely has a singular existence. We might get a glimpse of him when he appears on the television screen. But his face appears there only as evidence of an anonymous social problem. He has no personal history. His story is inextricable from that of the many others who are just part of a mass, a wave of migration. In the media we see pictures of people in camps, interacting with NGO's or state authorities. We might be served up small parts of their stories. However, these tend to be humiliating for the clandestine immigrant, since the whole point of telling the individual's story is to show that he is simply one person among many, one example of the multitude. What we see in these representations is never the tale of a singular being, but the *number* of people involved in these waves and flows. Because we pay attention to the extent of the problem by reference to numbers, the singularity of each person is forgotten. The story of each individual clandestin as one among many makes him invisible and relegates him to a position as a victim without a voice, even when he does speak out.

From this point of view, the example of the Sangatte "welcome center" is of particular interest. The center was set up in 1999. It was administered by the Red Cross. It was located in Northern France at a point where people might hope to hitch a ride on the high-speed Eurostar train heading for London. By 2002 it housed between 1,500 and 2,000 people (Laacher 2002). Many of those who lived there were Afghans and Iraqi Kurds. Most had no proof of any official identity. Many people who did have identity papers hid them out of fear of being identified to the governments of the country they had left. In fact, in some cases French public officials did not ask them to identify themselves, or, to be more precise, they did not force them to describe who they were and what they wanted. Opting for the latter would have entailed mutual recognition. It would have meant that each party was deserving of the trust of the other and able to enter into a reciprocal exchange. If the state did not deem it imperative to register them and exert administrative control over them, there were two fundamental reasons. On one hand, these people were perceived and considered to be victims, as persons without origin, without names or nationalities, without speech and without anyone to speak on their behalf. They were seen as lacking an identity other than that of victim. Their case was thus a matter of humanitarian concern. They had no place in the political arena of the nation.

The state concerns itself politically only with people who entered its territory without authorization and who have the intent of *remaining*. Many of the people at Sangatte wanted to cross the channel to England. Others said they had no clear destination: they would go anywhere except back to their country of origin. The French state was extremely reticent about exerting its power to decide what kinds of people these were, since they appeared to be just passing through its territory. The people living in Sangatte might say "now that I am here, I will stay." To which the state would respond: "According to which rights? Who authorized you to enter my nation, without my authorization? Where are you from and how long do you intend to stay? Who are you anyway?" As I met with people living in Sangatte and heard their life stories, I came to a understand why people could not answer these questions. I came to see that their inability to respond implicitly undermined the foundation of state power.

ALI'S STORY

One day in March 2000 a Red Cross mediator invited me to accompany her to the hospital where there was a group of Afghans who had each lost a leg while passing under a train during their attempt to reach England. I met each of them, all reclining in a row with their legs suspended above their beds. I saw their unhealed wounds. They had all been in the hospital for about a week. We began by discussing their accidents, then turned to other subjects. I spoke with Ali, whom I had known before the accident. His story was particularly enlightening because it put my own conceptions of the border into perspective.

Ali was in anguish. He kept asking "how it was that I traveled over more than 5,000 kilometers from Afghanistan only to fail to reach England by just a few kilometers?" In clear weather the English coast is clearly visible from Sangatte, a bird's flight away, only fifteen kilometers. Many of the people who had passed through Sangatte had successfully crossed the English Channel. Everyone in the center knows who makes it and who doesn't. Back in Sangatte, in his hospital bed, Ali could not conceal his failure to get across to

Britain from those in the center. Here, everyone knows who is lucky or unlucky, who is a hero and who is a victim. Everyone can see who is able or disabled. Ali's failure was two-fold. Not only was his passage to England now rendered impossible by his handicap, but he would also be a burden for himself and for his family. His entire extended family and even his friends made sacrifices so that he could leave home and travel to Europe. They gave their possessions—their sweat—so that he could make this journey. Their sacrifice had been in vain. This was probably the part he had the most difficulty accepting. An indelible stain of shame was starting to seep into the fundamental structure of his personality.

Ali had almost made it to the far reaches of Europe. He shed his blood and lost his leg. This is why he simply could not understand why, although he had done so much to get there, England would not accept him. He had sacrificed not only his family's wealth and his youth, but his very body for her. "Why didn't England recognize that his young, mutilated body was the most visible form, the highest and most sincere symbolic allegiance to the English nation one could give?" he asked me. He insisted in a firm and intelligent voice, now that he had one less leg, at least England should allow him to enter. He did not understand that the *price of blood* was not a means of joining a country.

My response to Ali's incredible interpretation of events was spontaneously a response typical of the state: one can enter a country, in a territory other than one's own, only if one is authorized to reside there or to visit. But for Ali, blood was more powerful than such bureaucratic matters. Listening to Ali I became aware that these were two different ways of imagining belonging. For Ali, entrance should be granted in recognition of a kind of sacrifice that demonstrated one's will to belong. Belonging was founded on relations of dependence. My ideas were the result of recognizing a series of regulations and regulators who determined entrance requirements on abstract, bureaucratic grounds. My conception related to thinking about belonging in terms of mechanisms for integrating the various functions of state and society. Our views represented two ways in which to envision the notion of frontier and of access. For Ali, his border and the borders of his group did not always correspond with those of the state-territory; instead, there were symbolic frontiers and real frontiers, insurmountable limits for some and not for others (Laacher 2004). For me, the borders separating national territories are always real and physically manifested themselves in the juridical laws of control and surveillance, laws that prevent and authorize the passage from one territory to another, independently of my will, my actions, or my desires.

My conversation with Ali revealed two competing visions of the world, each with a distinct conception of what it means to belong to a group. Ali believed that English hospitality should involve some kind of exchange for a body deprived of one of its members. He had lost his leg trying to reach England and this proof of his attachment, this sacrifice, should make it possible for him to cross the border. My perceptions seemed to him to be too solemn and official; perhaps I seemed to reiterate the official discourse. As I spoke, he seemed overcome by an immense anxiety. He was not a hero on a quest or even a man seeking a home. He was simply a victim; handicapped and alone with his wound. His life would no longer be the same and he was filled with guilt and shame. His path had taken him in a single direction and now his trauma was such that it was impossible to conceive of any other plans. He felt lost to himself and asked me aloud: "What should I do?" Should he wait? Ask for asylum in France? Heal and then attempt to board another train for England? Return to Afghanistan? Try to find a new country that would be easier to enter? Ali simply did not know.

In order to weigh and respond to these questions, it would have been necessary for him to be able to regain his mental composure, not to have to live in a ruined and exhausted body and to have the support of other people. If he were a part of a group, the others would help him to make decisions and evaluate his options. Ali did not know what to do because he felt unable to decide alone. Leaving home was the result of a *collective investment*, a veritable *collective enterprise*. Failure in this enterprise was dishonorable. But whatever the price, one must, according to this logic, uphold one's honor that is also the honor of the group. I heard this in phrases such as: "I want to die for my family," "I cannot return empty handed," "I cannot stop before I get there," and "I must keep on going until the end." Because failure is inconceivable, to think about it, or to speak of it, is a sign of weakness. To fail individually is ultimately to fail one's responsibility to the group. But alone in France the truth was no longer contingent on the principle of the group constituted by his family and his former travel companions.

All he could do was wait: waiting is always one of the clandestin's fundamental experiences. From the start of his journey he waits to get money, and a contact, he seeks out a "passer" to help him get out of the country. He awaits the right moment to leave, the right moment to pass. He lies in wait of being thrown out wherever he goes. This eternal wait is animated by a desire for liberty, in theory and in imagination. But reality never ceases to reduce the desire for freedom, or any desire, to the management of day-to-day existence, which becomes terribly complex. As one becomes involved in a life of bricolage, it becomes hard to imagine a life line that stretches from the present toward the future. A thousand and one options, possibilities, contingencies, paralyze any directed move ahead toward freedom. But to abandon everything to return home, discouraged and/or self-disgusted, is subjectively unthinkable and objectively impossible. Failure will never be attributed to the law, the state, to the problem of borders. It will be interpreted and perceived as a *personal failure*, attributable to a lack of virility and of desire to conquer (Mai, chapter 6). Like so many others, Ali's failure points to the inability of the state to welcome strangers. Or more precisely, it indicates that although there is a kind of "hospitality," the welcome is always temporary due to the unwillingness to truly speak with the uninvited guest and, thus, to identify him.

THE STRANGER AND STATE HOSPITALITY

Hospitality is one of humanity's universal laws. It is a natural right that should be inalienable and eternal (Derrida 1997). On the other hand, welcome (*accueil*), in the juridical and political sense, obeys the constraints of the state. The universal laws of hospitality often conflict with national laws that determine how foreigners are welcomed and for how long. In no case is a compromise possible between the reason of the state and the way of conceiving of belonging of someone like Ali. The state would not be the state if it failed to conform to the essential characteristics that found its organization and its raison d'être, if it did not seek to count, verify, control, and direct the circulation of persons and populations. To welcome is to permit the entrance of another in one's territory or home under certain conditions. It is with an accountancy of entrances, exits, births, deaths, naturalizations, and crimes, clandestines and applicants for the status of political refuges that the state is charged. The state accounts for who is who. It tries to keep track of people's movements. It accounts for what is normal and abnormal in terms of services and social relations related to basic health needs, family relations, or right to legal procedures.

The state has custody of floating people like those who were temporarily parked at Sangatte. They are under its sovereignty. But when faced with someone like Ali, the state dos not even know what to call him. Bureaucrats do not have a ready-made identity for him and so they cannot count him. Since the state's manner of reasoning is antithetical to his, communication, dialogue, and negotiation are impossible. As a guest, Ali is assimilated into a world of universals—a world of "man." This means he has a right to hospitality. But as a particular being, he challenges the state's project of maintaining not only territorial but social boundaries and the social body. How many of these floating people, these people who are from anywhere and nowhere, are there anyway? Why have they left their homes and what do they want? These are not the illegal aliens who fight together and with French citizens for their rights. Most of them do not seem to be refugees fleeing disasters or wars either. Could there be many political prisoners among them?

More and more people are, like Ali, living at the edge of the political world. They are pushed outside the confines of regulated, counted, insular societies. Deprived of a sense of social belonging and virtually nameless, they come to feel that they live outside of the world. The very idea that they have a stake in politics or society fades for them because they no longer envisage themselves as part of any collectivity. For them the world is no longer a shared concern. The very idea of a politics of liberation is destroyed because they cannot act in concert with others. What Ali's tragedy reveals is not simply a humanitarian problem; it indicates a political blind spot. Ali's story illustrates the crisis of the paradigm of the territorialization of rights. It leads us to question the limits of law based on citizenship and nationality.

NOTE

1. It has been estimated that migrants, refugees, and displaced persons in the world can be numbered at between 130 million and 170 million: about 2 to 2.5 percent of the world's population. Half of all refugees come from Somalis, Bosnia-Herzegovina, Sudan, Iraq, Burundi, and Afghanistan. One refugee in three lives in Iran or Pakistan (Autrement 2000).

REFERENCES

Agamben, Giorgio. 1997. *Homo Sacer, le pouvoir souverain et la vie nue.* Paris: le Seuil.
Autrement. 2000. *Les réfugiés dans le monde.* Paris: Autrement.
Derrida, Jacques. 1997. *Cosmopolites de tous les pays encore un effort!* Paris: Galilée.
Laacher, Smaïn. 2002. *Après Sangatte. Nouvelles immigrations. Nouveaux enjeu.* Paris: La Dispute.
———. 2004. L'indice comme abrégé du monde, revue Terrains et Travaux. *Ecole normale supérieure de Cachan.* No. 7, Octobre.
Mandelbaum, Jacques. 2003. Interview. *Le Monde.* October 29.
Tassin, Emmanuel. 2003. *Un monde commun.* Paris: le Seuil.

2

Zacarias Moussaoui

Moroccan Muslim? French Terrorist? Benighted Zealot?
War Criminal? Serial Migrant? All of the Above?

Susan J. Terrio

This chapter considers the curious case of Zacarias Moussaoui, an avowed conspirator in the Al Qaeda plots against the United States and a serial migrant from Morocco. Moussaoui's trajectory cannot be understood, in contrast to many accounts, as merely that of a menacing terrorist or a delusional zealot. Despite the intensive media exposure during the four-year trial that ended on May 3, 2006, in the federal court of the Eastern District of Virginia in Alexandria with a verdict of life with no possibility for release, his profile does not fit that of the "new martyrs" drawn from the ranks of marginalized and alienated French-Arab-Muslim immigrant youth deemed overly susceptible to indoctrination by radical Islamist imams (Khosrokhavar 2005). The motives for his conversion to fundamentalist doctrine, enlistment in Al Qaeda networks, travel to Chechnya, Indonesia, Malaysia, and Pakistan, training in Afghanistan, and subsequent move to the United States as part of a terrorist plan cannot be blamed exclusively on the incendiary teachings of the Brixton Mosque in London, which his mother insisted turned the "carefree, happy boy" she knew into someone utterly different.

Moussaoui's attraction to radical Islam and hatred of the West, despite being born and schooled first in France and later in England, must be situated within a complex migratory path beginning with his father's departure from Morocco and move north to France as a labor migrant and continuing with his decision to settle the family there permanently. This is also a chronicle of an arranged marriage, when his mother was fourteen years old, followed by years of horrific domestic violence at his father's hand. It is a story of divorce and his mother's hard-won independence as a working woman and single parent. His childhood was marked by her faith in French secularism, avoidance of Islam, and insistence that her four children dissociate from both Arab culture and youth in the housing projects, which they escaped for a middle-class neighborhood thanks to her civil service job. Nonetheless, their lives continued to be fraught with family conflict and psychological trauma. Moussaoui's later rediscovery of his Moroccan roots and turn to austere religious practice must also be linked to his progressive disillusionment with the French educational system, a postcolonial legacy of anti-immigrant discrimination, particularly in the south where he lived, and the deteriorating condition of working-class and second-generation immigrant youth who came of age in the 1980s.

This was a period characterized by the crisis of the Fordist model of sustained economic growth and full employment that had fulfilled the promise of economic opportunity for North African immigrants like Moussaoui's father a generation earlier. This was also a period when the topic of juvenile delinquency, and its association with immigrant youth, emerged as a charged public policy issue and urgent social problem. By the late 1990s it dominated opinion polls, shaped campaign rhetoric, influenced election outcomes, spawned new crime experts, and produced legislative reform of the penal code governing minors. Most significantly, sensationalist media coverage of increases in urban violence in the so-called "immigrant" suburbs, site of the French public housing projects, focused public attention on what was termed a new type of youth crime, "a delinquency of exclusion." This delinquency was associated with the children of underprivileged Muslim families of North and West African ancestry, most of whom are French citizens, and was depicted as threatening the very fabric of French civil society. The peculiar amalgam of immigration, Islam, and youth became a politicized topic of public debate in the early 1990s at a time when Moussaoui was finishing secondary school and weighing his options for higher education. This was a period in which public discourses and media coverage worked to ethnicize delinquency, to stigmatize cultural difference, and to produce consensus across the political spectrum regarding the figure of the immigrant delinquent as a newly threatening social category.[1] Coverage of the suburban projects centered on the Islamic veil, urban riots, arranged marriage, excision, polygamy, gang rape, and radical imams. The projects (*cités*) were explicitly compared to American ghettos with their surfeit of drugs, lawlessness, and guns (Mucchielli 2005, 100). They also came to be seen as the site where cultural backwardness, economic marginality, and religious fundamentalism combined to produce Islamic terrorists.

HUMANIZING A TERRORIST?

After the verdict of life imprisonment was announced, one of the federal public defenders, Gerald Zerkin, interviewed on *Nightline* by journalist Terry

Moran, said the defense team was gratified to be "able to humanize Moussaoui" (3 May 2006). Writing about avowed terrorists as serial migrants who exercise the agency and choice that mark them "as cultural chameleons and social actors" (Ossman, introduction, 1) poses thorny ethical and epistemological dilemmas. Is it possible or even desirable to humanize a man who is a fervent apostle of Osama Bin Laden and has repeatedly called for the destruction of the United States? Does it do a disservice to the 9/11 victims, survivors, and families to try to understand someone whose behavior and rhetoric has at best been deemed inappropriate and irrelevant, and at worst inflammatory and evil? Is there merit in attempting to penetrate the ubiquitous media caricature of an intense, scowling man—"the bearded, balding jihadi" (*Washington Post*, 26 July 2002)—who was transformed as the trial progressed from a menacing conspirator—a "war criminal" according to Sen. Joseph Lieberman (*Washington Post*, 13 December 2001)—into a French buffoon who nearly ended his trial shortly after winning the right to represent himself in 2002 by inadvertently pleading guilty (*Washington Post*, 19 July 2002)?[2]

In the effort to take the measure of an individual like Moussaoui, we must ask to what extent religious and political ideology trumps class, ethnic, or national affiliation? This, as Mark Danner argues, is particularly relevant since the 9/11 attacks and the global war on terror declared by the United States as Al Qaeda has become Al Qaedaism, "a worldwide political movement, with thousands of followers eager to adopt its methods and advance its aims" (Danner 2005, 46). Was Moussaoui's conversion to violent Islam rooted in the same sense of injustice many other children of the second generation experienced? Was it a search for identity or dignity? Given the importance of class position and social mobility emphasized by his mother was it in part an acknowledgment that he could find no secure place for himself in French society? Did his estrangement from his parent's homeland in Morocco and what his peers and teachers, both French and Maghrebi, reminded him were his true origins, serve as a catalyst in an attempt, however misguided, to return to his cultural roots?

Given a family history burdened with domestic violence and mental illness—two of Moussaoui's siblings and his father suffer from serious psychiatric disorders—can sociological explanations be as useful as psychological ones? We should note that the vast majority of suicide martyrs are not suicidal clinically or desperate people suffering from psychological problems (Lelyveld 2001, 51). The insistence of many media and intelligence pundits that the 9/11 attacks were manifestations of a primordial civilizational clash between Western rationalist modernity and Islamic irrational tradition make the omissions with regard to individual intention and mental health all the more telling in the Moussaoui trial. His irrational outbursts, hyperbolic claims, technical ineptitude in flight training, and nonviolent record stood in marked contrast to the personal discipline, meticulous planning, chilling operational rationality, and horrific violence of the nineteen 9/11 hijackers. It is telling that the psychiatric experts called to evaluate Moussaoui's mental health disagreed completely. A forensic psychiatric appointed by the court, Dr. Raymond Patterson, claimed that Moussaoui suffered from a personality disorder but insisted that his actions were motivated by adherence to a religious subculture, not by mental illness. He made this diagnosis after two five-hour examinations of Moussaoui and study of his letters and notes to Judge Brinkema. In contrast, two psychiatrists for the defense, clinicians engaged in research, Dr. Xavier Amador and Dr. William Stejskal, later joined by Dr. Michael First, made a diagnosis of schizophrenia on the basis of extensive interviews with family, friends, and examination of his writings as well as French social service records.[3] This diagnosis, rather than the rationale advanced by the prosecution regarding the presumed derangement of the Islamic terrorist mind, would better explain Moussaoui's abusive and erratic behavior and mental state during the seventeen months he was permitted to represent himself as well as his reactions during the sentencing phase of the trial in 2006. Only someone who is delusional could be certain that President George Bush would free him before the end of his term of office and attempt, as Moussaoui did on 8 May 2006, to withdraw his guilty plea after the judge imposed sentence.

It seems unlikely given Moussaoui's legal circumstances and mental condition that we will ever know why the young man who showed academic promise and developed cosmopolitan ambitions abruptly ended his university studies, severed ties with his family, and decided to become a warrior for Islam. Does a warrior for Islam deserve the same rights and protections under the law as other defendants in criminal courts? Does it matter that he denied involvement in the 9/11 plot while acknowledging participation in a different conspiracy to free Sheikh Omar Abdel Rahman from a Colorado prison and to unleash weapons of mass destruction against the American government (*Court Transcript*, 22 April 2005, 28)?[4] Important lessons are to be gleaned from examining the trial of a noncitizen designated as an international terrorist. The choice of an American civil court as opposed to a military tribunal was, as Sen. Edward Kennedy predicted in December 2001, "enormously significant" (*Washington Post*, 13 December 2001). The unfolding of the trial raised issues at the heart of American jurisprudence, namely the integrity of the adversarial process, the guarantee of due process provisions for all defendants such as the right to cross-examine key material witnesses, to gain access to the evidence, to hear all the charges, to a fair and speedy trial, to determine fairly the legal competency for those who, like Moussaoui, waive counsel and represent themselves in court, and to take the stand themselves in a capital case against the advice of counsel.

THE MAKING OF A JIHADI

Zacarias Moussaoui was part of a second generation of youth born in France of immigrant parents in the late 1960s and schooled at a time when educational reforms were enacted to democratize access to secondary and university education. These reforms collided with the post-Fordist era in which Moussaoui came of age when high rates of youth un- and under-employment became a chronic problem particularly for children of working class and immigrant background. In some areas unemployment among children from these groups who had few or no degrees reached 40–50 percent (Beaud and Masclet 2002). This was a period characterized by the de-industrialization of entire regions and a difficult job market demanding greater professional credentials and longer schooling. Similarly, the urban geography of French cities was substantially transformed. Greater access to individual home ownership widened the gap between the public housing projects with higher concentrations of poor, ethnic minority populations clustered outside French cities in contrast to proliferating middle class subdivisions. The segregation of marginal populations in the so-called immigrant projects associated with disorder, anomie, and crime fueled feelings of insecurity, support for right-wing candidates, and anti-immigrant, particularly anti-Arab, racism. The post 9/11 context in France has been marked by the election of a center-right government with a law and order agenda, crackdowns on illegal immigration, more recourse to detention and deportation, and increased anxiety about the political radicalization of a resident underclass of adolescent Muslims, seen as potential Islamist terrorists.

Moussaoui's personal and familial history is inextricably intertwined with the history of France's postwar immigration policies and the painful process of decolonization that began in the 1950s. His parents were of Moroccan ancestry and his father accepted work as a mason in France, leaving behind a wife and two small children. He was part of a huge influx of immigrant labor recruited from former French colonies in North Africa to work in industry, construction, and agriculture. It is conceivable that he, like other immigrants, intended to stay only temporarily before a permanent return home. Enduring economic disparities between the North and the South transformed him, like many others, into a permanent settler. He sent for his wife and children to join him in France where Moussaoui's mother bore two more children by the age of twenty-two. After suffering horrific physical abuse, she divorced her husband, obtained custody of her four children, moved her family from the Northeast to the southern city of Narbonne, and worked her way into a permanent civil-service position. The financial security she established provided the means to advance a singular social project for her children—a move into the French middle class through housing and education.

As a secular, nonpracticing Muslim she stressed the importance of education, the possibility of social mobility through integration, and, significantly, limited her own and her children's contacts with the working-class Arab Muslim families they left behind in the public housing projects with their move to a French housing subdivision. She encouraged middle-class pursuits and raised her children according to French values, allowing no double standards for her sons versus her daughters, and insisting that all her children share household chores (Dominus 2003). She was proud of her own social advancement and the lifestyle she was able to provide for her children, particularly her ability to use the French justice system to gain protection from domestic abuse and, later, custody for her children. At the same time, she maintained ties to Morocco and her family, sending her children there for summer vacations and opening her home for extended periods to Moroccan family members, one of whom was a fundamentalist Muslim. It is clear that Moussaoui's turn to radical Islam began in France, not in London, and must be explained by a number of factors confirming in some sense the 9/11 commission's conclusion regarding the hijackers as a mixture of "highly educated zealots who could not find suitable places in their home societies or were driven from them" (The 9/11 Commission Report, 340).

Moussaoui does not conform to received images of impoverished and disaffected Muslim youth from the "immigrant" housing projects outside French cities that became the new martyrs of Islam. These images make for excellent courtroom drama and were used adroitly by his defense team as one of the mitigating factors in the penalty phase of his federal trial. Rather, he resembles in some ways a much smaller number of young men who were apparently the well-integrated children of North African parents who stayed in school, were highly motivated, earned coveted places in academic tracks, went on to higher education, and seemed ready to take their place in the middle classes but suddenly quit school, discovered Islam, and became Jihadis. Indeed, since 2001 French public opinion has been shocked to discover that France has produced a number of Moussaouis (Beaud and Masclet 2002).[5]

Although much has been made of Moussaoui's scholastic achievement and numerous degrees, his school history reveals not only his personal difficulties but the social and psychological obstacles that students from working-class and immigrant backgrounds face in French schools. He was an average student with promise whose progress in school was halting and labored due to recurrent discipline problems (Beaud and Masclet 2002, 162). It also seems clear that he had unrealistic expectations and little understanding of a system whose gate-keeping functions for the most prestigious educational tracks are increasingly difficult to penetrate for children of the second generation. He misrecognized the power structures and was unnerved by the symbolic violence he encountered there from teachers and students alike. Rather than internalize his shortcomings and drop out early, he clung to education as the only avenue to a coveted white-collar position and nourished the hope of placement in the academic track of a French *lycée*. He may have seen this as a way to avoid a culturally devalued vocational education and to rise above the degraded class position of his father.

Given his uneven performance, Moussaoui was moved into the vocational track during the critical orientation period at the conclusion of the fourth and final year of middle school. This was a decision that he experienced as unfair and humiliating—perhaps the beginning of his sense of being a victim of injustice and fueling both moral outrage and explosive anger (Pharo 1992). His mother remembered the day when she was waiting to hear the school council's decision on her son's future and overheard his teachers discussing the case. She insisted that only after learning that his father was a manual worker, a mason, did they make their decision, judging that "vocational education will be good enough for him" (*Libération*, 20 September 2001). Despite his anger and disappointment, Moussaoui persisted in the vocational track, earning good results, apparently hoping to use the professional diplomas at both the secondary (*baccalauréat professionnel*) and university (*BTS*) levels as a bridge back into the academic track (*L'Indépendant*, 18 September 2001, quoted in Beaud and Masclet 2002, 162). In 1991 he enrolled at the Paul Valéry School at the University of Montpellier earning a diploma in social and economic action after one year. He then considered a second one-year graduate degree in applied foreign languages at the University of Perpignan but disappeared from campus in the fall of 1991 without any explanation and left for England. There he earned a masters degree in international business from the University of South Bank. He apparently hoped to enhance the technical degrees he had earned in France that largely qualified their holders as skilled workers or factory foremen and held no guarantee of employment. Once again, his expectations may have exceeded both his performance and his understanding of the market value as well as the job opportunities of the credentials he sought.

Meanwhile, in 1990, radical Islam had come into the Moussaoui home with the arrival of a Moroccan cousin, daughter of a military officer and student at the University Mohammed V in Rabat, who fled her home and lived with the family for a year. Her embrace of fundamentalist networks in Morocco had alienated her from her father. Once in the Moussaoui home she apparently lectured the brothers on proper Islamic behavior, "not doing dishes, not shaking the hand of French people, taking several wives." During the same period, the family experienced pressure from Arab friends who accused them of being too French and of betraying their roots, and urged a return to their community of origin. Perhaps during this period the gap between the rhetoric of Western meritocracy and the reality of unfulfilled promises may have been too glaring for Moussaoui given the discrimination he faced. In addition to the institutional racism at school, the family also experienced anti-Arab hatred. Arabs were denied entry to the neighborhood discothèque, one of the French families in their middle-class subdivision forbade their children to play with Arabs, and when Moussaoui dated a French girl, her parents denied him admittance to their home.[6] In the end, Moussaoui's limited choices may not have allowed him to risk alienation from fellow Moroccans and Maghrebis. Finally, he seems to have embraced his Moroccan origins, religious ideology, and to have rejected French republican individualism. He had become the Islamic terrorist—one step removed from the "immigrant" delinquent, not only a menace threatening public safety and French values but a global threat, a stateless jihadi, the serial migrant par excellence.

What struck French sociologists Stéphane Beaud and Olivier Masclet, who read the histories of young jihadis such as Moussaoui, Daoudi, Khaled Kelkal, and Mouloud Bouguelane, is the similarity of their lives (before enlistment in international terrorist networks) with those of numerous young men of immigrant ancestry whom they interviewed. It bears repeating that Moussaoui and the others are not "social monsters or sociological aberrations" but are in part the product of a collective history that took place over the past twenty years in France and North Africa and produced intense alienation as well as a lasting feeling of social injustice among many young people of Algerian and Moroccan ancestry (Beaud and Masclet 2002, 167). That these young people were intelligent, motivated, and in more than one case, well on the way to academic achievement, makes their decision to drop out and to embrace violent fundamentalism all the more tragic and urgent to understand.

Moussaoui's travels to Afghanistan, Chechnya, Malaysia, Pakistan, and finally to the United States in the service of Al Qaeda will not be dealt with here. What is germane to our discussion is what followed his arrest and led to his trial in federal court in Alexandria, Virginia, as a presumed conspirator in the 9/11 attacks. Could an international terrorist get a fair trial?

A FAIR TRIAL? GUILTY OR INNOCENT?

Any discussion of the Moussaoui trial must begin with a discussion of the condition of his detention. As the presumed twentieth man in the 9/11 attacks, he has been detained under extraordinary security conditions, held in solitary confinement under twenty-four hour surveillance, in a cell that is constantly lit, with no unmonitored visits, calls, or mail except from his attorneys (*Wash-*

ington Post, 17 January 2002). Moussaoui's fragile mental health and recurrent emotional meltdowns, the subject of much media coverage, were exacerbated by the well-documented cruelty of the sustained solitary confinement to which he has been subjected for four years (Wachtler 1997).

The presiding federal judge, Leonie Brinkema, ordered a psychiatric evaluation of Moussaoui following one such outburst in federal court on 22 April 2002 in which he denounced his court-appointed lawyers "as experienced in deception," railed against the U.S. justice system, and demanded that he be allowed to represent himself. To determine that his waiver of counsel was informed and voluntary, the judge appointed a psychiatrist, Dr. Raymond Patterson, to evaluate Moussaoui. After studying Moussaoui's notes and letters to the judge, Dr. Patterson concluded that the erratic behavior was the result of the "subculture" to which Moussaoui belonged, not to mental illness. Another team of experts hired by the defense (see above), who had the benefit of detailed interviews with his mother and access to extensive French records, rejected this conclusion arguing that further evaluation was necessary. In a ruling from the bench on 13 June 2002, without hearing further testimony, the judge decided that Moussaoui was competent to defend himself. The question of mental sanity did not address the issue of access to the government's evidence or of Moussaoui's legal competency and the level of his cultural or linguistic fluency. Court observers and Moussaoui's attorneys point out that his ability to represent himself was severely compromised at the outset. His very status as an accused terrorist meant that he did not have the security clearance necessary to study the government's classified evidence against him. Moreover, the court outbursts for which he would become infamous, including his stated allegiance to Al Qaeda and denigration of the court, were tolerated by federal prosecutors, the defense attorneys believed, because they substantially undermined his defense.

In late July 2002, his attorneys again wrote to the judge conveying the substance of a report prepared by the same psychiatric team hired by the defense. They feared his mental condition was rapidly deteriorating as a result of the severe conditions of his confinement. Throughout the summer, Moussaoui serving as his own counsel, filed a stream of motions that contained "glimpses of acute intelligence and awareness" (Hersh 2002, 74) but more often were characterized by angry paranoia, repetitive diatribes, racist slurs, and devastating legal missteps such as his attempts to plead guilty, refusal to accept exculpatory documents from his former attorneys, and his failure to forward to the judge a series of crucial pretrial motions. His attorneys requested permission to visit him and questioned his ability to defend himself given what they saw as his obvious mental instability and ignorance of federal criminal law. Judge Brinkema rejected their request citing a lack of evidence of his incompetence and in August 2002 ruled that Moussaoui could continue to represent himself but ordered the sealing of future pleadings "containing threats, racial slurs, calls to action, and other irrelevant material" (Hersh 2002, 76).

Despite, or perhaps because of, his psychological fragility, it is difficult to dismiss Moussaoui as a mere lunatic given the conditions of his detention, his refusal to be labeled as insane, his attempt to educate himself in American federal court procedures with only the most rudimentary materials at his disposal, and, given his paranoia regarding the integrity of the American justice system, to defend himself in a high-stakes game involving the death penalty and, thus, his life. Although it is horrifying to read his admission of complicity to commit aircraft piracy, to use weapons of mass destruction, and to murder U.S. employees (*Court Transcript*, 22 April 2005, 20), we must ask if the enormity of these charges and the epic global war on terror that the 9/11 attacks precipitated justify the suspension of some of the due process guarantees at the heart of the American legal system—even for admitted terrorists?

One of the many ironies of the government's case against Moussaoui was that it was weak. It relied entirely on circumstantial evidence and the presumed similarities among the nineteen hijackers and Moussaoui. Prosecutors could produce no proof of e-mails or meetings between the nineteen hijackers and him. Moussaoui was only too aware of this and, despite a lack of legal training, he deployed tactics that repeatedly stymied federal prosecutors and succeeded in delaying his trial for over two years. His handwritten 2003 motion to the court claiming that excessive secrecy was denying him a fair and open trial, and demand for access to the transcript of a secret court hearing in January 2003 when the Justice Department outlined its case, clearly put prosecutors on the defensive. They issued a response to the motion insisting that concerns over secrecy were unfounded and suggested that national security imperatives "should not breed skepticism about the propriety of prosecuting terrorists in a civilian court" (*Washington Post*, 15 April 2005). The same day Moussaoui's standby attorneys filed a motion challenging, along with media groups, the decision of the court to seal numerous filings (*Washington Post*, 15 April 2003; *New York Times*, 16 April 2003).

Moussaoui based his defense on a denial of involvement in the 9/11 attacks and demanded to exercise his right to interview captured Al Qaeda members as witnesses arguing that their testimony would exonerate him. Judge Brinkema ruled in a 30 January 2003 decision that he had the right to question Ramzi Bin Al-Shibh, the self-described coordinator of the World Trade Center attacks. She noted that "the legitimate government concern [over national security] must be balanced against the equally compelling right of the defendant in a capital prosecution to receive a fair trial to which he is entitled under the constitution and laws of the U.S." (*Washington Post*, 3 June 2003). Federal prosecutors refused to grant access to Bin Al-Shibh and defended their imperative to shield pretrial documents from the defense in the name of national security. Their appeal of the judge's ruling to the U.S. Court of Appeals for the Fourth Circuit precipitated a public clash between the government and the court. At issue were core constitutional matters such as the separation of powers between the executive and the judicial branches and the defendant's right to a fair, open, and speedy trial (*Washington Post*, 3 June 2003). Over this period the Justice Department sought broad new powers to prosecute terrorists. The legal confrontation continued through 2004 as the federal prosecutors maintained their defiance of the judge's order to allow Moussaoui access to two additional Al Qaeda witnesses. Prosecutors submitted statements from Ramzi Bin Al-Shibh as a substitute for Moussaoui's questioning of him; defense lawyers responded that the government had "mixed, matched, integrated, and chronologically reorganized" Al-Shibh's statements "into one seamless script, or story line" (*New York Times*, 5 June 2003). Judge Brinkema rejected the proposed government substitution and left intact her January order allowing the deposition of Al-Shibh. When the government continued to defy her order, the judge barred the death penalty and the 9/11 evidence from the case in a 2 October 2003 ruling. Ultimately on 22 April 2003, the U.S. Court of Appeals for the Fourth Circuit ruled in favor of the government, restoring both the death penalty and the evidence and denied Moussaoui the right to interview witnesses (*Washington Post*, 22 April 2005). On 22 April 2005, one month after the U.S. Supreme Court declined to hear his appeal, he pled guilty, ending his trial and marking the first conviction in a case stemming from 9/11.

After entering his guilty plea in federal court Moussaoui insisted that his defense team had ignored a legal loophole that would have preserved his right of appeal and accused them of serving the interests of the government, effectively guaranteeing that he received the death penalty. He continued, "The only reason I have the right to speak today is because I'm pleading guilty. Otherwise I will be silenced. And I will be silenced in a few seconds because you will say whatever you are going to say and you are going to shut my mouth, and you are going to run your, your show, okay? . . . Everybody know that I'm not 9/11 material" (*Court Transcript*, 22 April 2005, 32–33).

It is ironic that Zacarias Moussaoui should have earned respect from the judge who in late 2003 lost her patience with his "frivolous, scandalous, disrespectful or repetitive" filings (*New York Times*, 15 November 2003) and revoked his right to represent himself after seventeen months. On 22 April 2005, she declared, "Mr. Moussaoui is an extremely intelligent man. He has, actually, a better understanding of the legal system than some lawyers I've seen in court" (*Court Transcript*, 22 April 2005, 23). It should give us pause that a Muslim zealot and a sworn enemy of the West should have been the one, acting as his own counsel in a capital trial, to remind us, angrily and forcefully, of a defendant's rights to hear all the charges, to have access to the evidence against him, and to interview material witnesses. These rights are now at risk for us all because they were not extended to him. As one former federal prosecutor noted in 2002, it was a case in which the integrity of the adversarial process was breached—with "Goliath on one side and a slingless David on the other" (Hersh 2002, 76). It should come as no surprise that the same U.S. Court of Appeals for the Fourth Circuit ruled unanimously on 9 September 2005 that the government has the authority to detain as an enemy combatant, indefinitely and without criminal charge, an American citizen, José Paudilla, who fought U.S. forces in Afghanistan (*New York Times*, 10 September 2005). Should we be shocked that such enemy combatants, senior Al Qaeda operatives detained by the United States for years without charge, were used to provide written statements that served as evidence in the Moussaoui trial after being obtained, in the judge's words, "under circumstances designed to elicit truthful statements" (*Court Transcript*, 29 March 2006, 2831)? This statement is all the more menacing for its understatement given what we now know about the circumstances involving the interrogation of enemy combatants such as John Walker Lindt (Mayer 2003) and others from Abu Ghraib to Guantanamo.[7]

THE PENALTY PHASE: THE DEATH SENTENCE OR LIFE IN PRISON?

The prosecution envisioned the sentencing phase of the trial as the opportunity for a dramatic reenactment of the events of 9/11, poignant testimony to the pain suffered by the surviving victims and family members of those who died, and a strident call for vengeance in the form of the death penalty for Moussaoui, whom the federal prosecutor Robert Spencer described in his opening statement on 6 March 2006 as "one of the cold-blooded killers" (*Court Transcripts*, 23). Spencer described 9/11 as a day that began as utterly normal but became one of abject horror and a "defining moment of a generation" (*Court Transcripts*, March 6, 2006, 22). He included Moussaoui in the group of killers "who were among us, to cut our throats, hijack our planes, crash them into buildings, and burn us alive" (*Court Transcripts*, 6 March 22). The facts of the government case relied on establishing that, although Moussaoui had been in jail for twenty-five days when the attacks occurred and had never had any direct contact with any of the nineteen hijackers, his lies to federal agents on 16 and 17 August 2001 concerning the Al Qaeda conspiracy had directly caused the deaths of 2,972 people. Had Moussaoui told the truth, Spencer argued, "it would have all been different." The Federal Bureau of Investigation and the Federal Aviation Administration would have been alerted and taken the necessary steps to prevent the attacks. Although Spencer was careful to insist that government agencies were on all-out alert and knew about a terrorist threat in the months leading up to the attacks, they were convinced it would come from outside the United States (*Court Transcript*, 6 March 2006, 34). Because there was no reliable intelligence on the internal threat, government agencies took no proactive security measures.

Defense attorney Edward MacMahon rebutted that vision by casting the defense of Moussaoui as a national imperative driven by constitutional guarantees of due process protections such as the right to counsel and to a jury trial as a check "against the abuse of government power with roots in law as far back as the Magna Carta" (*Court Transcript*, 6 March 2006, 48). For the defense the central question was, "Can we judge fairly our sworn enemy"? The answer was an appeal to the democratic values that many saw as the very reason for the attack on 9/11 — "they hate us because of the value we place on freedom." MacMahon admonished the jurors to give Moussaoui a fair trial "because of who we are and what we stand for" (*Court Transcripts*, 6 March 2006, 50). The facts of the case showed no evidence of his involvement or knowledge of the attacks. Moussaoui had talked in grandiose terms of wanting to kill infidels but "never harmed a soul when he was free" (*Court Transcripts*, 6 March 2006, 52). When the 9/11 plan was activated, no one in Al Qaeda tried to find him or warned him to flee. The facts, MacMahon argued, were that a number of government agencies, including the National Security Agency, the Pentagon, and the Department of Defense, did not act the way we wish they would have. "No one," he concluded, "should be executed on such flimsy evidence" (*Court Transcripts*, 6 March 2006, 57).

The first phase of the trial to determine if Moussaoui was eligible for the death penalty was notable for a number of reasons. Egregious misconduct on the part of a government lawyer, Carla Martin, who improperly coached witnesses, angered the judge for breaching the defendant's constitutional rights, and nearly ended the trial by excluding some aviation witnesses for the government. In addition, one of the government's star witnesses, FBI special agent Harry Samit, revealed in testimony for the prosecution and in cross-examination by the defense, routine bureaucratic dysfunctions within a number of government agencies as well as a series of misjudgments and missed opportunities by government investigators following Moussaoui's arrest (*Court Transcript*, 9 and 10 March 2006). Finally in an act many predicted would ensure a death sentence, Moussaoui took the stand, against the advice of his attorneys, but with the encouragement of federal prosecutors, and repudiated his testimony of 2005. He insisted that he and Richard Reid were part of the original 9/11 plot and had intended to hijack a fifth plane to attack the White House (*Court Transcript*, 27 March 2006). It was left to the defense team to use the written testimony of senior Al Qaeda operatives in U.S. custody to refute Moussaoui's claims and to depict him as unreliable, unpredictable, "not right in the head," and never intended to be part of the 9/11 attacks (*Court Transcript*, 28 March 2006).

After the jury rendered a unanimous decision that the government had proved by a reasonable doubt that Moussaoui was eligible for the death penalty, the trial entered the second phase in which they were asked to weigh the aggravating factors of his crime against any mitigating elements in the determination of the penalty. The government prosecutors made a strong case for harsh retributive justice necessary to avenge the attack on the body of the nation in the context of a global war on terror. They urged the jury to reject the defense's suggestion of numerous mitigating factors including mental illness, childhood abuse, racial discrimination, and his wish for a martyr's death. They argued that his extremism did not result from racial discrimination or a tough upbringing but from his conscious decisions and his religion. He was a manipulative strategist driven by the dictates of violent jihad and had to be held responsible for the crimes he committed (*Court Transcript*, 24 April 2006, 4712). They urged the death penalty as a way to deny him a warrior's death because "he wanted to die in battle, like in a fight with prison guards."

In his closing statement, public defender Gerald Zerkin rejected the government's clash of civilization view and, in a blend of evocative religious and national imagery, told the jury that the trial "is about our history, the history we will write about how our justice system responded . . ." (*Court Transcript*, 24 April 2006, 4718). Noting the timing of judgment at Easter, Passover, the celebrations of the birth of the Prophet Mohammed, and Holocaust Remembrance Day, he quoted Robert Jackson, the head of the Nuremberg prosecution team, who had admonished the allies facing Nazi war criminals "to stay the hand of vengeance and voluntarily submit their captive enemies to the judgment of the law" (*Court Transcript*, 24 April 2006, 4719). Zerkin asked why the Herman Goerings or Adolph Eichmanns of Al Qaeda were not on trial? In contrast to the government's portrayal of the religious zealot whose every move was dictated by his group identity, Zerkin attempted to resurrect the idiosyncratic motives and individual psychology of Zacarias Moussaoui. Moussaoui was a pathetic Al Qaeda hanger-on, a mentally impaired exile, with little direction or will who was easily influenced by radical Islamic propaganda. "[He] couldn't shoot straight, was sent packing from Malaysia because his conduct was so inappropriate, could not learn to fly, and was thought by his Al Qaeda colleagues to be erratic and untrustworthy" (*Court Transcript*, 24 April 2006, 4720).

Just as the prosecutor evoked the gruesome images of victims burning alive, people jumping to their deaths, and passengers ripped to bits, Zerkin mimetically evoked the physical violence administered by Moussaoui's father who "literally crushed [his wife's] teeth in his hands" and broke a vase over his daughter's head as well as the neglect he suffered in the household headed by his divorced mother (*Court Transcript*, 24 April 2006, 4726). He mocked the forensic psychiatrist Dr. Patterson, who declared it reasonable, not delusional, that Moussaoui expected Bush to release him from prison (*Court Transcript*, 24 April 2006, 4728) and who dismissed Moussaoui's disjointed pleadings to the judge as Al Qaeda propaganda and not the products of a paranoid schizophrenic.

Like the prosecution, Zerkin ascribed strategic agency and choice to Moussaoui despite what his team insisted was his mental illness and lack of control. Moussaoui was a compulsive liar, who deliberately manipulated federal agents and the court when he said he was the intended pilot of a fifth plane on 9/11. In a logic that paralleled that of the prosecution, Zerkin urged the jury to deny Moussaoui the death of a jihadi. This could be accomplished not by killing him but by confining him "to a miserable existence until he dies . . . and [to give him] the long, slow death of a common criminal" (*Court Transcript*, 24 April 2006, 4723). Thus, Moussaoui's status as a pathological liar was used as evidence by both the prosecution and the defense in the pursuit of justice, the death penalty for the government and life in prison for his defenders.

The jury accepted two of the statutory aggravating factors, finding that Moussaoui had created a serious risk to others in addition to the victims and had committed the offense after planning and premeditation.[8] Nine jurors accepted the mitigating factors of Moussaoui's unstable childhood and his father's physical and emotional abuse of the family. Five found that his sentence of life in prison without the possibility of release was a powerful mitigating factor. Three believed that Moussaoui was subjected to racism during his childhood in France and would not pose a risk to prison officials or other inmates. None accepted the defense's argument that a sentence of life in prison would be a more severe punishment than death or that his execution would provide him with the rewards attendant to a martyr's death. No juror believed that he suffers from a psychotic disorder such as schizophrenia. Three jurors added a mitigating factor not mentioned by the defense, "Moussaoui had limited knowledge of the 9/11 attack plans" (Special Verdict Form from Phase II, 3 May 2006). In a vote that surprised everyone, particularly the defense, they rejected the death penalty.

CONCLUSION

The media coverage of the Moussaoui trial and of terrorism itself is reminiscent of what anthropologists Zuleika and Douglass term the terrorism discourse, a phenomenon which appeared in the West in the 1970s. Terrorism, they argue, in contrast to other forms of violence, is set apart in its capacity to garner public attention and to instill mass hysteria. Compared to the soldier, the mercenary, or even the murderer, who alone claims 25,000 lives in the United States yearly, the terrorist becomes the paradigm of inhuman bestiality, "the quintessential proscribed or tabooed figure of our times" (Zuleika and Douglass 1996, 6). Because the grip that terrorism holds on the collective imagination is inextricably linked to the power of threat and reinforced through resonant media images, it evokes intense fear. As a contemporary phenomenon terrorism relies on hyper real-media images and an army of terrorism experts as much as on the terrorists themselves. It not only blurs the line between fact and fiction but all terrorism discourse must conform to and borrow some form of fictionalization. The effect is one in which imagined events can be as real as factual ones and the latter, in their senseless horror, are often perceived as unreal (Zuleika and Douglass 1996, 4). The complicity between fact and fiction in terrorism discourse has "succeeded in imposing an apocalyptic frame in which suspension of disbelief appears to be the rational course and no commentary as to its discursive configuration seems relevant" (Zuleika and Douglass 1996, 30). Now that 9/11 has "thrust America through a portal in a strange and terrifying new world where the inconceivable, the unimaginable [has] become brutally possible" (Danner 2005, 46), the idiom of terror is even more dependent on images of cataclysm, irrationality, and evil. Still, brute facts and fictional portrayals combine to form the substance of terrorism discourse. Witness the proliferating literature on terrorism, particularly the recent novels centering on terrorists by Martin Amis (2006), John Updike (2006), and others. Or consider the recent forum on "America's Image in Fighting Terrorism, Fact, Fiction or Does it Matter?" organized by the conservative Heritage Foundation whose invited participants included national security scholars, the co-creators of Fox's counterterrorism show *24* and three of the actors who star in that series (*Washington Post*, 24 June 2006). The blurring of fact and fiction certainly seems relevant in the case of Zacarias Moussaoui. After reading hundreds of pages of court transcripts, I still have difficulty seeing the implacable Al Qaeda operative in the man who obviously suffers from a psychotic disorder, was legally and psychologically unprepared to represent himself in a U.S. federal court, and, as a result of his solitary confinement for four years, was substantially diminished in his psycho-social capacity.

The prosecution of a capital case that involved no direct evidence and a last minute confession from a defendant described by both sides as a pathological liar raises critical questions about the legal truth in the establishment of the facts. How are we to weigh the truth claims of one self-described jihadi over those of his Al Qaeda superiors now detained in secret prisons and subject to interrogations, in the words of Judge Brinkema, "designed to elicit truthful statements?" We know from Red Cross reports, Antonio M. Taguba's inquiry into the Abu Ghraib prison detentions, James Schleslinger's Pentagon-approved commission, and other investigations that after the 9/11 attacks some Americans began torturing prisoners and, as Mark Danner has argued, continued to do so (2004). How are we to evaluate the truth claims of the government prosecutors who built a death penalty case for "a cold-blooded killer" like Moussaoui even as the mastermind Khalid Sheikh Mohammed and the coordinator Ramzi Bin Al-Shibh of the 9/11 attacks were held in U.S. custody without charge? If the trial provided closure or engendered cries for vengeance from some victims and their families, to many others it was an emblem of the terrorism effect, a space of fictional reality defined by a fantastic enemy.

Compared to the nearly 5,000 foreigners who have been detained in the United States by the government since 9/11 in connection with antiterrorism measures, most of whom were initially held without charges, denied access to lawyers, judged in secret, and incarcerated for months without proof that they had committed crimes or posed a danger to national security, Zacarias Moussaoui is one of only a handful to be charged with a terror-related crime and prosecuted in a civil versus an immigration court. By comparison to other noncitizens and to the enemy combatants detained at Guantanamo, Moussaoui was fortunate to have had the benefit of a trial and legal representation by highly skilled public defenders. His final outburst after hearing the verdict that he had won and, "America, you lost" may be only partially delusional. Despite the public rhetoric on the trial verdict as courageous and the system as impartial, Moussaoui apparently missed a death penalty verdict by only one vote. Is a verdict of life imprisonment without the possibility of release in solitary confinement in the Colorado supermax facility a more humane alternative? Indeed the lurid depictions of that facility on *Nightline* (3 May 2006) following the announcement of the verdict reveal the aspects of spectacle and thrill that attend to the terrorism effect.

The Moussaoui trial was initiated by the Justice Department as an integral part of the global war on terror. Waging that war will continue to have many unforeseen results, not least will be to perpetuate a dynamic of mimetic violence that reproduces the very practices it seeks to eliminate and to close the space for constructive political engagements and true restorative justice (see Aretxaga 2001). As the prison doors close on Zacarias Moussaoui it is useful to remember that the global migration he began that ended in the United States was not to a place he journeyed to so much as it was a social territory sketched out by radical Islam. The extremist identity he embraced in France and in England provided him, and may provide him still, with a third space within which to retreat and to rehearse the resentments and hatred that set him on his migratory path at the outset.

NOTES

1. Mainstream political parties on the right and the left that dismissed the far-right National Front's racist assertion that Arabs were the main cause of crime in France just fifteen years ago now concur in imputing the blame for youth crime to youth in the projects, namely those of immigrant ancestry.

2. That was the first in a series of unorthodox courtroom antics that prompted reporters to depict the trial as "the Moussaoui circus," noting scornfully that "his accent flavors the courtroom like a ripe roquefort cheese . . . he seems quite theatrical, a born actor. But of course, of course. He is French" (*Washington Post*, 26 July 2002).

3. Dr. Amador apparently met once with Moussaoui, an event he described in court (*Court transcript*, 17 April 2006) and in press interviews (*Nightline*, 3 May 2006).

4. Moussaoui insisted on exercising his right to testify in the sentencing phase of the trial. On 27 March 2006 he reversed his story of the year before and advised the court that he was training to attack the White House on 9/11 in a fifth plane in the company of Richard Reid, the shoe bomber. Reid, a British citizen and convert to Islam, was arrested on 22 December 2001, while trying to detonate an explosive device in his shoe during a flight from Paris to Miami. There is no evidence of his involvement in 9/11 or in any other terrorist plots.

5. Some examples include Daoudi, the eldest son in an Algerian family who was an excellent student, earning a baccalaureat degree a year early from a highly selective Parisian *lycée* before enrolling in the preparatory classes for the elite Ecole Normale Supérieure of Cachan. Another case, Mouloud Bouguelane, also obtained an academic baccalaureat degree and went on to study at the University of Lille. Perhaps the most controversial case was that of Algerian born Khaled Kelkal who was an excellent student in primary and middle school and was admitted to the academic track of a good high school in central Lyon. All three encountered psychological and social obstacles that compromised their chances for social mobility. Kelkal felt out of place socially, resented the fact that his father had been laid off after twenty years of factory work, and began to get into trouble, graduating from petty theft to property destruction. During a term in juvenile prison, he converted to Islam and, after an early release and a trip to Algeria intended to set him straight, made contact with the Armed Islam Group (GIA) through a militant uncle. He was suspected of complicity in the 1995 terrorist attacks against the TGV and was the subject of a nationwide manhunt. When confronted by French parachutists at a bus stop outside Lyon he opened fire and was shot dead, an event caught live on film by a TV crew.

6. *New York Times* reporter Susan Dominus documented racist attitudes when she traveled to Narbonne in late 2002 to interview Moussaoui's mother and was told by a local shopkeeper, "That family is not worth one word of print. She (Madame Moussaoui) used to be one of those disgusting, dirty Arabs. . . . Now her son ends up in jail and she is sitting pretty" (Dominus 2003, 56).

7. The case brought by the U.S. government against the "American Taliban" fighter John Walker Lindt originally included a ten-count indictment centering on his activities, described by then attorney general John Ashcroft, as an "Al Qaeda-trained terrorist." In July 2002, several days before Lindt's lawyers planned to challenge the legitimacy of his FBI confession in court, "claiming that it had been coerced under shocking conditions," federal prosecutors offered a deal in which they dropped nine of the ten original counts in exchange for the acceptance of a guilty plea and a twenty-year sentence for Lindt (Mayer 2003, 59). See a description of the extraction of the confession of an "enemy combatant" such as Lindt by FBI agent Christopher Reimann under the so-called Ashcroft Doctrine. Federal prosecutors have argued that such combatants are not entitled to the ordinary protections of American civil jurisprudence and that Lindt was not covered by the Geneva Convention because he had fought for an illegal army (Mayer 2003).

8. There were three statutory aggravating factors that the jury had to find unanimously that the government had proved beyond a reasonable doubt. They rejected by one vote the third factor alleging that Moussaoui had committed the offense in an especially heinous, cruel, or depraved way in that it involved torture or serious physical abuse to the victim or victims.

REFERENCES

Amis, Martin. 2006. The Last Days of Mohammed Atta. *The New Yorker*, 24 April 153–63.

Aretxaga, Begona. 2001. Terror as Thrill. First Thoughts on the 'War on Terrorism.' *Anthropological Quarterly* 75 (1), 139–49.

Beaud, Stéphane. 2002. 80% au bac. *Et après? . . . Les enfants de la démocratisation scolaire*. Paris: La Découverte.

Beaud, Stéphane and Olivier Masclet. 2002. Un Passage à l'acte improbable? Notes de recherche sur la trajectoire sociale de Zacarias Moussaoui. *French Politics, Culture and Society* 20 (2), 159–70.

Court Transcript, United States District Court for the Eastern District of Virginia Alexandria Division, Criminal case 01-455-A, 22 April 2005; 6, 9, 10, 27, 28, 29, March 2006; 17, 24 April 2006.

Danner, Mark. 2005. Is he Winning? Taking Stock of the Forever War. *The New York Times Magazine*. 11 September.

———. 2004. *Torture and Truth, America, Abu Ghraib and the War on Terror.* New York: New York Review Books.

Dominus, Susan. 2003. Everybody Has a Mother. *The New York Times Magazine*, 9 February.

Hersh, Seymour M. 2002. The Twentieth Man. Has the Justice Department mishandled the case against Zacarias Moussaoui? *The New Yorker*, 30 September 56–76.

Khosrokhavar, Farhad. 2005. *Suicide Bombers. Allah's New Martyrs*. Trans. David Macey. Ann Arbor: University of Michigan.

Lelyveld, Joseph. 2001. All Suicide Bombers Are Not Alike. *The New York Times Magazine*, 28 October.

Mayer, Jane. 2003. Lost in the Jihad: Why did the government's case against John Walker Lindt collapse? *The New Yorker*, 10 March 50–59.

Mucchielli, Laurent. 2005. *Le Scandale des "Tournantes." Dérives médiatiques. Contre-enquête. Sociologique*. Paris: La Découverte.

9/11 Commission Report. New York: W. W. Norton & Company

Pharo, P. 1992. *Phénoménologie du lien civil. Sens et légitimité*. Paris: L'Harmattan.

Updike, John. 2006. *Terrorist*. New York: Knopf.

Wachtler, Sol. 1997. *After the Madness: A Judge's Own Prison Memoir*. New York: Random House.

Zuleika, Joseiba and William A. Douglass. 1996. *Terror and Taboo. The Follies, Fables, and Faces of Terrorism*. New York: Routledge.

3

From the Maghreb to the Mediterranean

Immigration and Transnational Locations

Nabiha Jerad

The assumption of a fit between a culture, a people, and a place has governed modern concepts of the nation and culture. Western projects of nation building and colonialism emerged from the association of these elements. So have conceptions of culture and society in the social sciences. Colonialism exported and strategically used this concept of a necessary territorial division between peoples to discipline regions where heterogeneous cultures coexisted. Although the examples of people like the Jews, Gypsies, or the Arab nomads teach us that it is possible for culture and identity to be formed through geographic displacement rather than a fixed space, anthropologists have been slow to critique "the notion that there is an immutable link between cultures, peoples or identities and specific places" (Lavie and Swedenbourg 1997, 1). National liberation movements in the colonies, social movements in the West, and migration from former colonies have put these preconceptions to the test. In spite of this, attempts to explain the dynamics of postcolonial relations have often gotten stuck in relationships of host to home, colonial to former colonial nation in ways that cannot take into account the true complexity and challenges to conceptions of fixed, static identities existing in the spaces that people actually live. In this chapter, I will explore how, out of the context of French colonialism and North African immigration to France, new categories of identity and new ways of talking, writing, and making music have emerged. I will show how spaces outside or beyond the nation and its territory took form, paying particular attention to the Maghreb and the Mediterranean.[1] By diverting and destabilizing the master codes assumed in territorialized concepts of culture, new linguistic practices, novels, and musical forms destabilize the centrality of national reference to create cultural spaces that transcend national boundaries. The complexities of the identities that emerge from these spaces defy the notion of hybrid identity or double belonging. They challenge the idea of a fixed identity to be related to the host country, to the country of origin, or the amalgamation of two elements in hybrid forms.

HISTORICAL BACKGROUND

In order to examine how language use and artistic expressions are challenging colonial constructs of space, a brief account of the history of Maghrebi immigrants in France is necessary. The border-zone of Maghreb/France is built on a long history of confrontations between political entities of unequal power. The *mission civilisatrice* that characterized French colonial policy was aimed at a careful separation of cultures ranked in a clear hierarchy. The subordination of other languages and cultures to French is even clearer in the case of immigrants to France, where it blurs the ethnic or national origins of migrants from North Africa. Already in the 1920s the term "North Africans" came to refer to immigrants to France from Algeria, Tunisia, and Morocco. The word "Maghrebin" has replaced it after independence and is still one of the terms used to designate people from these countries, as are the terms *étranger* (foreigner), *arabe* (Arab), and *immigré* (immigrant).

The first North African immigrants to arrive in France came from Algeria, where colonization began in 1830. But the first massive immigrations from the Maghreb to France took place in the 1960s, when unemployed men were recruited as workers to fill the needs of expanding industries. Those of this first generation of Maghrebi workers in France were almost all illiterate in French or any other language. Living as guest workers in segregated housing, their immigration was thought to be temporary, aiming simply to provide economic benefit to both the host and home country. Immigrants often had projects of *retour*, of going back home with their savings and setting up small businesses. In France they continued to count in dinars or dirhams and speak their native languages: dialectal Arabic, Kabyle, or Suissi Berber. It was not necessary for them to master much French since their work did not require communication. Unlike European immigrants to France they were generally not seen as candidates for assimilation because of their Islamic faith. As Abdelmalek Sayed noted, even in the 1970s, these men were a "line of connection to colonial history" (Sayad 1993, 158). The image of the "Arab migrant worker" conformed to that of the colonized. We should pay homage to Sayad for his perspicacity. His point is still true today. Eric Savernese shows the continuity between the image of the colonized and the immigrant in *Histoire coloniale et immigration*. He writes, "the perception of types of indigenous populations is part of what allows us to understand the categorization of immigrants and the kinds of fear that focalize around Maghrebis" (2000, 15).

The labor-migrant was seen merely as a working body, a being without history, culture, or professional qualifications. From the point of view of the country of origin, these emigrants were *muwatinina bil Kharij*, "our compatriots abroad." They were not highly regarded at home, yet they were a precious financial resource for governments and families. They were, as Sayad said, "present absents," from the perspective of their states of origin. They offered to their countries the opportunity to have thousands of "representatives" in France. They extended the territory of the home country through their bodies (Sayad 1999). None of the North African countries wanted emigrants to return home. They were simply pawns whose figures could be used in negotiations concerning bilateral relations by both host and home countries.

In 1974, France decided to curtail labor immigration and to allow the families of immigrant workers to live with them. As more and more families arrived, their children who moved to France when they were very young, or those born on French soil came to be called "young Maghrebi immigrants" or "second generation Maghrebis" or "offspring of Maghrebi immigration." This terminology indicated the attitude of the host country, which identified them in terms of their parents' country of origin. When it became clear that guest workers and their families were in France to stay, the French administration and society began to ask how these newcomers could be assimilated. Debates about cultural difference began to take form as the children of immigrants needed to be taught French and educated in French schools.

As we have seen, in France, "immigrant" and "Maghrebi" had become synonomous by this time. The designation of all North Africans as "Maghrebin" has become so normalized that it is used not only in the media and sociological discourse, but even in institutional documents as a category of nationality. However, from the perspective of socio-linguistics, the term is meaningless. It does not refer to a linguistic identification as in the case of other groups of immigrants: Portuguese, Polish, Italian or Spanish. It erases fundamental differences among speakers of different Berber languages and the different Arabic dialects of Tunisia, Algeria, and Morocco. France was constructed as a nation by eradicating linguistic minorities within its borders. Basque, Breton, Picard, and other tongues were eliminated and a standardized French language became a symbol of the unity of the French nation. Being a part of the nation meant mastering the dominant language. But in the case of North Africans, the ways in which this assimilation and integration into French identity might proceed were constructed on a dichotomy of Arabic to French, which did not correspond to the linguistic practices of those grouped together as "Maghrebins."

As more and more labor migrants raised families in France, the issue of how to address the linguistic and cultural differences between their children and those of the "French-French" became an issue at schools. The symbolic importance of schools in French history can hardly be overestimated; it has been seen as the pillar of Republican society. Schools are places where children were supposed to be turned into Frenchmen. It is the site where social integration and promotion are supposed to occur. But the ways in which schools were expected to promote assimilation and integration were paradoxical. On the one hand, concepts of culture and integration borrowed from American culturalist theses were very influential. In the mid-1970s the apparent crisis these children experienced due to their dual identities was addressed by a regulation helping children of immigrants to learn "their language and culture of origin" as a way to solve the perceived problems of uprootedness. Courses intended to teach children their "mother tongue" were organized outside the usual hours of school. Students were grouped according to their nationality and Algeria, Tunisia, and Morocco sent teachers to give instruction in classical Arabic. Clearly, this "mother tongue" had no meaning for people who spoke Berber at home. But for Arab children it was not the language they spoke at home either. As several other chapters in this book explain, the dialects of Arabic are very different, and learning the classical language might be likened to a French student studying Latin. Labor migrants were rarely versed in the erudite language of the Qur'an or classical poetry. Nor were they living in an environment that exposed them to the use of that language. Arabic teachers hired and paid by the states of the countries of origin and under the authority of their embassies rarely took this into consideration. The 1970s was, after all, a time when Arab nationalist sentiment ran high, when being an Arab nation implied repressing Kabyle and Berber tongues in Algeria and Morocco.

These policies placed the children of Maghrebi immigrants in a situation of cultural extra-territoriality. Speakers of Berber or Arabic experienced the double hegemony of the host country and the country of origin (Jerad 1988). The desire to understand the place of these children as located *between* two territories was confounded by the reality of their actual social and cultural location as exemplified in their actual linguistic practices. In fact, many of the children did experience difficulties mastering the standard French required at school and they were routed into nonacademic streams and technical schools. In addition to linguistic factors, the economic and social conditions of immigrant workers and their families also marginalized them. They tended to live with other immigrants on the periphery of major cities in the suburbs: "*les banlieues*."[2] Banlieues are border-zones, but not at all the positively connoted space of the "contact-zone" (Pratt 1992). They are zones of exclusion mapped by the same authorities who paradoxically argue for assimilation. Although the housing projects were not originally planned only for ethnic minorities and immigrants, people of French ancestry abandoned them as they were able to afford more salubrious and centrally located homes. So the process of acculturation is assumed to take place in an environment where there is little contact with people who are culturally identified as French. As Zahira, a young girl whose parents came from Algeria who lives in *La cité des 4000* outside of Paris, said: "Most are Arabs and Blacks, those four thousand are Arabs and Blacks" "More than French?" "Oh well, French people! If you remove all the Arabs and the Blacks, all the foreigners, you'll be left with three or four French households. There are almost no French people. The only French people you have are always of Spanish origin" (Khelil 1991, 67). This example shows that representations of French identity are indeed associated with place. There are places where the French are supposed to be: these are not the places where immigrants live. Even someone of immigrant origin who is born in France, has always lived in France, and who has French nationality is still a foreigner if they live in the projects. *Arab* and *Black* have become the ideal type of the foreigner, with the "Spanish-French" being exceptions to this categorization and therefore worthy of mention.

Today, the Maghrebi community constitutes the largest immigrant group in France with 574,208 Algerians, 522,504 Moroccans, and 201,561 Tunisians, according to the last census. Accounting of immigrants according to the country of origin is based on birthplace and nationality. We also need to add to this figure the thousands of people who obtain French nationality, and those who are in the country illegally. It is estimated that there are also 600,000 *harkis* (Algerians who fought on the side of France during the Algerian War) and their descendants living in France today. If we include the Jews and the people of European origin whose families came from Tunisia, Algeria, or Morocco, people of Maghrebi origin can be estimated at over 6 million people.[3] It is difficult to confirm these figures because, unlike in the United States, the nomenclatures of official population statistics do not contain any classification concerning ethnic, religious, or linguistic differences. Generally speaking, it is not considered proper to ask French citizens about their origins or religious or ethnic affiliations. Once someone is French, their other affiliations are said to disappear in the name of equality.

CULTURAL IDENTITY AND PLACE

Although most of the children of immigrants are indeed French, it is only too clear that they are not Frenchmen and women like any others. They are often portrayed as suffering from cultural uprooting and experiencing identity crises as a result of their double belonging. The children of the second generation are perceived as half Arab and half French. This reductive vision of identity places them in between two apparently irreconcilable cultures and deprives them of any positive identity. They are said to be in search of their identity, as though they were not French, as though they do not share in the Western legacy that ties identity to territory. Clearly, the notion of belonging to two cultures at the same time and therefore of having no real identity has to be revised. The assumption that identity is fixed and refers to a single language and a single space must be questioned (Schnapper 1991). Because of assumptions about the nature of culture drawn from old-fashioned anthropology, sociological studies on immigration tend to reproduce the idea of dual identities. Research is designed according to constrasts of clearly demarcated home and host countries. Thus, it always ends up highlighting the difficulty of assimilation. According to Nacira Guénif, this Manichean image of "double culture" is found throughout immigration literature. It is Eurocentric and it "has contributed to the collective amnesia in connection with the colonial past" (Guenif 2000, 44).

But if we observe actual linguistic and cultural practices, or look at literature and music, a very different account of what is happening emerges. The complexity and fluidity of the identities of those lumped together under the category of "Maghrebin," the deterritorialized places where they often live can lead to a critique of dualistic approaches. We reach toward a more sophisticated rendering of culture zones when we consider the language, literature, and music that the immigrant experience has produced.

Can we see these expressions as hybrid or the result of multiculturalism? The notion of hybridity does not quite work because it is based on an essentialist paradigm of cultures and of pure, clearly identifiable bodies. In this scheme, identity would be the result of melding two different cultures. References to hybridity underestimate individuals' ability to appropriate and use the codes of the dominant culture, because when they do so, they are said to be assimilated. Michel de Certeau writes, "We cannot reduce to assimilation the adaptability of a foreign body to the host country, an *anthropophagic* (man eating) phenomenon. This adaptability can be seen in a whole panoply of tactics to reuse parts of the culture for one's own purposes" (1985, 158) The tactical use of language in day-to-day encounters, literature and lyrics leads us to observe how immigrants' children engage with French.

PLAYING WITH WORDS

The generalized identity of the Maghrebin or Arab is toyed with and broken up by the ways in which people of the suburbs play on words. Not only do they speak of "Algerians" or "Kabyles," they also make up words like "tutu," which refers to Tunisians. Thus, they react to the general geographical identification of Maghrebins as too vague. Under certain circumstances, as Lepoutre notes, they do identify themselves as Arab. At the time of his research for *Coeur de banlieues, code, rites et langage*, he found many of those he spoke with in the suburbs expressed solidarity with Saddam Hussein (1997). In that work, he used a participatory approach to record conversations between youngsters about relationships to ethnicity and to each other. His analysis shows the extent to which their feelings of identity are dislocated from any particular place. Their speech involves many coexisting and shifting landscapes. Thus, they construct who they are in a variety of combinations. This can allow *beurs* to build bridges with other minorities. Lepoutre identifies Patrice as black and Jalal as Maghrebin: Patrice and Jalal: "*If les Reunois (noirs*: blacks in verlan) didn't fight the Whites, Jalal and me, we wouldn't be here in *jeans and Reeboks, we'd still be on cotton plantations at this time, right Jalel?*" "*Certainly.*"

Identity is thus based on a fluid, reconstructed sense of history and ethnicity. It is tinkered together from elements borrowed from the host country, but not usually identified as typically French. Fantasies about origins abound. Patrice echoes a vivid memory of slavery. In his reconstruction of this past, he forms an alliance with an Arab, another minority. In this process identity is fractured and invented as are ethnic differences. The shared reality of immigrants in the border-zones implodes divisions of time, space, and race. In another example of alliance, a young man from India indicated that he was Algerian on his registration form at school, confirming Abedelmalek Sayad's idea that Algerian immigration in France has become so symbolic that other immigrants identify themselves to it (Sayad 1993).

Verlan, the language of the suburbs, emerged from a variety of sources. The basic principle of this slang is that the sounds of words are reversed (*l'envers* becomes *verlan).* But syllabic inversion is not the only form of its encoding. As Bachman shows, other strategies of subversion of the standard French are also a part of verlan. Adding a new sound to a standard French word is common (Bachman 1996). Verlan can be applied to a proper name. Francis becomes *sifran* and by contamination Français becomes *sefran.* Borrowing Arab terms is also common; *Felfel* (red pepper) is used to refer to a policeman, and this term is then "frenchified" by translating it to an approximation of the French word for Red pepper, *piment.*

The use of verlan requires a good mastery of the French phonological system. It expresses a new space of identity that shows resistance to acculturation but also an awareness of the loss of any "mother tongue." The expression of a different voice is thus developed within the system of the dominant language (de Certeau 1985). Verlan not only expresses ethnic identity, it always gives ethnic identities new names. "Arab" first became *beur*. Now it has been replaced by *reubeux*, verlan of the verlan. This demonstrates the fluidity of the language.

Another way of acting upon the normative language is to use it in new kinds of expression. The *vannes*, or dozens, exemplifies this. Dozens or dirty dozens are exchanges of ritual insults. American linguists have studied this linguistic practice in the African American ghettos in cities in the United States (Labov 1972). They have shown that it is linked to African practices. In France, Lepoutre noted that teenagers in working-class milieu began to exchange dozens after the first wave of Maghrebin migration in the 1960s (Lepoutre 1997). This kind of linguistic performance requires a high degree of linguistic competence and creativity. It is the sign of a reappropriation of the master language within a ritual that did not originally belong to it. It is clearly an imported practice, but one whose origin is difficult to point to on a map.

BEUR LITERATURE: OUT OF BOUNDS

Literary critics and sociologists alike tend to assume that the beurs are defined by combination or confrontation of French and Arab cultures. The fact that the idea of double belonging is so widespread again reveals the power of definitions of culture in terms of territory and fixed identities. As Dominique Schnapper remarks, "The term of 'appartenance' (belonging) seems to imply that individuals belong to a culture that exists outside of themselves rather than seeing that culture is something that they themselves have constructed" (1991, 123). In fact, it seems to me that the space created by the literature of the second generation and now the third generation questions binary divisions and an assumption of a blending of already given cultures.

Like everyday language, beur literature has created a space in which assumptions about the diasporic Maghrebin identity are questioned. The novels of Azouz Begag, Leila Sebbar and Farida Belghoul, among others, suggest new ways of thinking about the spaces of identity. Their texts are not about a search for something lost: the language or the culture of origin. Rather, much of the work of the first generation of beur literature is marked by its autobiographical nature. Begag's *Le Gone du chaâba*, whose hero and narrator are both Azouz, narrates growing up in the slums, or *chaâba*. The main character only becomes interested in issues of identity in the supposedly neutral and secular space of school where his teacher continually tries to make the narrator feel like a foreigner and a non-French speaker:

"Isn't it scandalous that the only foreigner in the class should be the only one who can claim the honor of knowing our language," the teacher told the class. Azouz responded: "Actually, Sir, I am not quite a foreigner since I was born in Lyon like everyone else" (Begag 1986, 28).

In his other novel, *Béni ou le paradis privé (Blessed or Private Paradise)*, Begag mocks the question about origin that a teacher asks:

"What is your origin?"
"Human, I responded jokingly."
"No, really, be serious," she spoke with me as with an equal.
"Algerian."
"For a foreigner you speak French quite well. Congratulations."
"I was born in Lyon," I corrected her (Begag 1989, 38).

When we examine the critical studies of these first beur novels, it is notable that there is a tendency to interpret everything in terms of a tearing apart of the subject, as someone caught between two identities, two cultures, two universes that exclude each other. For instance, in writing about the main character of Farida Belghoul's *Gerogette!* one critic suggests that the many layers of personality and identity demonstrated by the main character can be reduced to a kind of "schizophrenia"(Bacholle 2000). But what is very important to notice is that *Georgette*, the title of Farida Belghoul's novel, is a French name, but it is *not* the name of the narrator. The narrator veils her real first name and introduces the virtual name "Georgette" through the voice of her father. The exclamation point in the title expresses the outrage her father would express if she did happen to have such a name, that is, if she had taken a name that was typically French. There is thus a deliberate playing on notions of identity. As Michel Laronde has written, "An explicit French identity hides another implicit identity, which remains unsaid" (1993, 58). By giving the main character such a fluid identity, she is conferred the kind of opacity that Glissant noted with respect to the rhizomic identity formulation first defined by Deleuze and Guattari.[4] Mireille Rosello has also pointed out the need to discard conceptions of identity based on a pull between two cultures. Texts like *Georgette* do not focus on the need to choose between Maghreb and France, nor do they express the lack of harmonious synthesis between the two cultures (Rosello 1993). Instead, through their structure and style, such texts displace the culturalist paradigm depicting beurs in France as trapped between two spaces. *Georgette!* inspired a host of critical studies because, it seems to me, it gave readers an opening for going down a new path to study questions of place and identity. The narrator confuses discourses and uses numerous voices to create a polyphonous text that allows the voice of the narrator to change as the character changes. This signals the opacity and complexity of a personality of a "youth born of immigration" living in France.

Other novelists like Ramdane Issad (1994) or Nina Bouraoui (1991, 1993), transport the reader beyond the borders of France and North Africa. In *"la Voyeuse interdite,"* Bouraoui uses fragments of stereotypes of Arab women and writes a story on human pain that transcends gender and space. Writers who began publishing in the 1990s, like Said Mohamed, Tassadit Imache, Ahmed Kalouaz, Mélina Ghazi, Soraya Nini, and Paul Smain, have written novels that have renewed the genre by diversifying style, structure, and themes. For instance, in *La honte sur nous* Said Mohamed situates his characters in psychological instead of cultural spaces. *A l'ombre de soi*, by Karim Sarroub, is very difficult to analyze from a culturalist perspective because the characters are not given identifying markers by which their ethnic or religious backgrounds can be discerned. These authors see themselves as participating in a universal literature. Their characters are decidedly not reducible to clear identity and narratives are not about the experience of migration.

Today, in light of the riots that raged in the French suburbs at the end of 2005, we might see the project of these writers as a failure. While they seek to move beyond identity, there is clearly a problem of negative identification and unequal national territories in France. Some French citizens are clearly not like the others.[5] A new wave of writings about life in the suburbs has emerged after the disturbances of last winter. Authors of the newspaper *Le Monde* called *"les enfants d'immigrés, fils de France"* (children of immigrants, sons of France) will certainly reintroduce issues of social difference and racism, if not immigration (*Le Monde* 2006).

RAÏ AND RAP: SYNCRETIC SPACES

While beur literature has tended to move out of the in-between of home and host societies, raï and rap have also promoted cultural spaces where diasporic identities find expression. Raï emerged as a musical genre during the colonial period. It originated in Wahran (Oran), a city in the West of Algeria that was created by the colonial authorities. It mirrored the evolution of the city as a kind of Mediterranean space where Arabic and Kabyle, Spanish and French mingled. From the start, it was marked by its subversive spirit (Schade-Poulsen 1999). Its lyrics spoke out against the dominant norms of Algerian society, in favor of mixing or *métissage*. This is apparent in the way that the genre incorporated several musical styles from the beginning. It drew on and influenced the music of Morocco and Tunisia as well as Algeria. It traveled to France with Algerian migrants. There, it developed a kind of Franco-Arab creole by drawing on musical influences including the pop music of the Americas, Europe, and Africa. Raï artists started performing with trumpets, electrical guitars, synthesizers, and drums. In France, raï has become synonymous with Arab identity. But it is not the result of acculturation, but of syncretism. This is why it has moved from being a local and popular form of music to occupy a place on the scene of world music. What started as a local popular musical genre to acquire international status and to become part of the mainstream because of the way it fashions a cultural space that resonated in the experience not only of Beurs, or of Algerians, but of a wide range of people. Raï appeal results from its creation of a musical and cultural space that transcends geography.

As a musical and linguistic genre, it illustrates the idea or the spirit of serial migration. Born in Oran, a city and a seaport with multiple ethnicities and traditions, it has created a new identity by borrowing and recycling the old songs of the Algerian masters and the language of the streets. Raï not only crosses the Mediterranean, but creates a Mediterranean space in a globalized world by working through a fusion of heritages. Its development parallels both colonial history and the history of migration.

In the early 1990s, rap became another important force in the lives of the youths living in the French suburbs. Unlike in the United States, French rap groups tend to be multiracial. Their main message is the unity between "Black, Blanc, Beur" (Black, white, Beur) (Aitsiselmi 2000). Beurs occupy a significant position in the rap movement even if its origins seem to be connected to black Americans or Sub-Saharan Africa. Rappers combine elements of Afro-Caribbean music with the specific concerns of the multi-ethnic people of the suburbs, linking the Mediterranean to the black Atlantic. Among the expressive cultural forms, popular music seems particularly amenable to syncretism and cross-fertilization because it is relatively unconstrained by the generic rules that fetter traditional elite genres. Thus the rock group *Carte de sejour* (Green Card) combines Arabic, French, and English, and musical styles ranging from rock to flamenco, raï to reggae. The process of reappropriation of the language as sociolinguistics would say is based on the need to express oneself within the dominant language. Raï and rap resulted from a dynamic whereby different cultural matrices impact each other reciprocally. They manage to be at once ethnic and transcultural. They both act as symbols of diasporic identities that transcend national boundaries. They show resistance and mark points of dislocation of identity, places to cross boundaries.

MEDITERRANEAN LIFE

This brings me to wonder what it means to inhabit the space of the Mediterranean. Although I live in Tunis, the capital of Tunisia, I am also an inhabitant of this cultural configuration, as well as my experience of living and working in France and the United States of America. Although I revolt against the dualisms of host and home, I grew up in a postcolonial environment marked by the linguistic, cultural, and political struggle between Arabic and French. I experienced a fight between two unequal imaginary worlds inside my own mind. It is perhaps not by chance that I became a linguist, given the way that each tongue warred with the other. And thus, I think of serial migration in linguistic terms as well. It was the English language and the time I have spent in American universities like Duke and Stanford that allowed me to relativize and resettle the place of Arabic and French, France and Tunisia. Bilingualism need not involve conflict, but the Arab-French world is not just about language. It is the result of the colonial history and the story of migration I recounted above. I have suggested that literature, rai, and rap are shaping a Mediterranean space of expression, that they are using different media to question dualistic conceptions of culture and find spaces where diverse systems of thought and imagination can be related to the experience of diaspora. But what of academic debates? What of the academic worlds I am a part of?

I have found that in research, we adopt ways of thinking and doing research that correspond to something in our lives. I was able to rethink that Mediterranean space as I knew it in my two native languages, thanks to becoming involved in the English-speaking academy. I moved from careful structuralist linguistic study to take on issues of broader social impact like immigration, because I felt authorized to do so in this new environment. Like a serial migrant who is suddenly able to get a new vision of his position as a "present-absent," becoming involved in a new linguistic realm led me to develop a new relationship not only with French and Arabic, but with the types of knowledge each language offered to me. The different way in which disciplines are configured in the American and French academy led me to relativize my conception of expertise. As I gained distance from my persona and intellectual duality, I changed. I became more adventurous, able to mix and match. In fact, I am writing this text in a mixture of my three languages, drawing on authors and concepts that might not be known to those of the "other" academies. The only problem I have is that my keyboard does not allow me to type in

Latin and Arabic letters at the same time. But in spite of this, all of my languages are on the horizon when I write. The space I inhabit is not geographic, and it slips and slides among various spaces, which themselves become less solid, more intertwined, as I think and write. A kind of creolization of the mind takes place, following Glissant's conception of the term (1990). There is a constant process of movement. Cognitive and symbolic references fluctuate. Sometimes, I find myself using fragments of a language that those I am speaking to do not understand. This kind of Freudian slip renders the process of creolization apparent to me and to others. It is as though I am unconsciously trying to make the processes apparent. Since a language is not simply a code for communication but a whole symbolic world, I am showing my involvement in this wider imaginative space.

In *Georgette!* Belghoul creates a third space by using the "double" of the narrator and the mixing of several narratives. Each time we try to anchor ourselves in an identified space, she pushes us beyond, out to a third space. This makes the prospect of identifying where one is at any point in time a very tenuous enterprise. She writes in French, but what she does with the language reflects my own experience of the necessity of getting past the conflict between two places, two languages, two cultures that enter into conflict because of history. Seeking to move out of the confined space between East/West, France/Maghreb, and Arabic/French is very much like trying to make ones way as a singular female subject in a world of couples. The third term questions apparent equilibriums. It brings in a space of possibilities and play. It opens up the possibility of further explorations and other languages on the horizon. As a postcolonial subject, born and educated in independent Tunisia, the lesson I learn from both my academic research about language and culture in a migratory space in the broadest sense and my personal experience of language is that someone living on "decolonized" soil is not exempt from the pushes and pulls of questions of identity symbolized and lived in the tension between Arabic and French. Obviously, there are many points of divergence between my experience and the experience of someone who lives as a "Maghrebin" in France. Still, on both sides of the Mediterranean, we are living in postcolonial times.[6]

CONCLUSION

As Hélé Béji writes, "The discourse of equivalence of cultures is an imposture" (1997, 45). The examples of cultural production and linguistic practices among Maghrebis in France that I have evoked show the conceptual limits of the "areas" of area studies and the poverty of continued analysis of migration and culture as a push and pull between sending and receiving societies. They also lead me to be wary of celebrating the hybrid as a miracle solution to all kinds of problems. If cultures are equivalent, we all become equally different. But we are not all equal. A Maghrebi immigrant to France will always have to deal with the social hierarchy of cultures that places the signs of French culture at the top of the scale. She will become a representative of Maghrebin culture or a generic Arab or Muslim. To join in the space of the Maghreb or the Mediterranean is not simply an exercise of entering into a shared geographic space, for while an imagination of a shared sea ties people together, the borders of Europe accentuate the differences between North and South.

Indeed, migration from former colonies is an opportunity to rethink the link between culture and space. The assumption of inseparability of identity from place based on the assumed homogeneity of the nation-state induces a necessary assimilation to the host country's culture as a marker of the persistance of the myth of its cultural homogeneity and superiority. In the case of former colonies like those of North Africa, the memory of cultural confrontations are still vivid. As Beji says of decolonization: "The civilizing project of the colonizer was confronted with the barrier of the culture of the colonized (1997, 45).

The study of "Maghrebins" in France requires developing units of analysis that enable us to understand the dynamics of transnational cultural relationships that multiethnic minorities live through. The subversive reappropriation of the dominant language signals resistance to assimilation through the use of the host country's language. Literary texts deny the notion of double belonging or hybrid identity dynamics and fracture territorial frontiers. The creolization of languages and syncretism of musical styles fracture binary opposition: dialect/standard language, Orient/Occident, north/south. Official state policies with regard to language as well as cultural expressions like raï migrate between the shores of the Mediterranean. They lap like waves against the many shores of this transnational space. This is not a region of hybridity or cultural syncretism, at least not as it is generally conceived in studies of diasporas and postmodern anthropology. When identity is perceived as hybrid, fragmented, multiple, this often leads the assumption that multiculturalism is just fine: *vive la différence*. But this discourse of cultural equivalence where everyone becomes "equally different" is just a new Western discourse of domination. After having set barriers between peoples and cultures, the civilized and the savage, anthropology has led us to glorify cultural difference and declare cultural equality. In our tour around the Mediterranean via the Maghreb, we have seen that this contact zone involves inequality among people and cultures. A Maghrebi immigrant in France will always have to deal with the social hierarchy of cultures that places the signs of the French culture at the top of the scale even in constructing the Mediterranean. He needs to display a mastery of the French culture codes and then he can engage in acts of resistance to assimilation, of negotiating a new identity that lives through the differences in the diasporic experience. This experience is a long history of confrontations between unequal cultures and forces in which the stronger partner struggles to draw strength from the subordinate partner.

What is it like to cross the Mediterranean from the other shore? People from the southern rim speak about crossing the sea as a *harq*, a "burning." How could someone burn water? This violent metaphor contradicts the natural image of the water that extinguishes fire. Usually we imagine seawater to be fluid, a natural connector between the two shores. But as the sea has become the rampart of the fortress of the new Europe, it becomes a solid barrier for people from the ex-colonies of the south. The northern rim of the Mediterranean is preoccupied with the security of its borders. It has closed its doors to immigrants. The Mediterranean has become the first border post of Europe. As Smaïn Laacher has noted, today, the "figure of the immigrant has exploded. Crossing the Mediterranean has become a hazardous adventure."[7] Every day people from the Maghreb and Sub-Saharan Africa try to break down the barriers of the Mediterranean and end up suffering a collective death. Those who succeed in getting past the barriers become clandestine wanderers whose future is uncertain.

In the era of globalization, there is a new remapping of territoriality. The displacement of population that created immigrant communities is no longer necessary for economic profit since they can hire cheap labor locally more cheaply. With the internationalization of financial markets and a global organization of production made possible by new technologies, multinationals can threaten states to relocate production centers if the conditions provided are not financially advantageous. Increasingly, ethnic and labor relations are in the hands of the global firms. This global remapping calls for new units of analysis to consider the new configurations of postcolonial hegemony. This new form of totalitarianism draws on older forms of domination. In India, English is the language of the call center. In North Africa, French is needed to participate in the national and global economy. Everywhere, not simply *intellectual* but *linguistic* labor comes to supplant the physical work of "the immigrant." In this situation, those English speakers or French speakers of the other shore are not asked to move anywhere. On the contrary, they are required to stay where they are. They are involved in transnational zones economically and linguistically, but they are unable to get visas to visit the other side. Clearly, we are far from the time when the Mediterranean for all of its tensions was a bridge among the different languages and people living along its shores.[8]

NOTES

1. The ideas in this paper were first presented at the International Conference *Crossings: Mediterraneanizing the Politics of Location, History, Knowledge*, held at Duke University in May 1999, then developed in a lecture given at Georgetown University in March 2004. I would like to thank Cristina Lombardi for her comments on an early version and Susan Ossman for her suggestions and assistance for the final text.

2. The French term *banlieue* refers to suburb areas surrounding large cities in France. These suburban areas, unlike American suburbs, are socially and economically poor. The wealthy population in France lives downtown where prices of real estate are the highest. The connotation of the word *banlieue* is pejorative (Ossman and Terrio 2006).

3. According to Benjamin Stora, for Algeria alone "no fewer than 6 million people—former soldiers, *pieds noirs* (French of Algerian origin), immigrants, *harkis* (Algerians who fought alongside the French during the Algerian war), *porteurs de valises*—have Algeria in their hearts" (*Le Monde* 31 October 2004). Other figures also show the dominance of immigrants from Africa among new immigrants: Of the 135,000 new arrivals in 2003, 90,000 were from the Maghreb and Africa (Source: Site INSSE, Insse,fr/FR/FFC :chifclé).

4. Glissant borrows the notion of the rhizome from Deleuze and Guattari in order to defend the thesis that identity is like a tree: a rhizome has several branches and nourishes itself at several sources that also nourish one another and communicate among themselves.

5. A report for the major administrative body charged with evaluation in France (the *cour des comptes*) published its very critical assessment of social policies with respect to immigration over the last thirty years in November 2004. The report indicates a crisis situation (*Le Monde* 23 November 20004).

6. In *Postcolonial Theory*, Leela Gandhi explains that the suffix "post" should not be taken to mean that we have gotten beyond colonialism. Rather, it suggests a present connection to the colonial period (Gandhi 1998). My research has shown this to be the case with respect to language policies in the contemporary Maghreb. I showed in what sense today's policies are still enmeshed in the socio-linguistic colonial symbolic order; how it is precisely a postcolonial policy (Jerad 2004, 525–45).

7. Smaïn Laacher, unpublished paper for the international conference on "L'étranger en philosophie et en droit" (Foreigners in Philosophy and Law), Université de Tunis, November 2004.

8. Perhaps the best example of this bridge between the two shores of the sea that modern Mediterranean history has to tell is about the "lingua franca," a language without borders, made up of a mix of roman languages with some Arabic and Turkish words. It was the linguistic witness of the connections of the people and cultures of both shores (Dakhlia 2004).

REFERENCES

Aitsiselmi, Farid (ed). 2000. Black, Blanc, Beur: Youth Language and Identity in France. *Interface: Bradford Studies in Language, Culture and Society*, Issue 5, Bradford.

Bachman, Christian and Basier, Luc. 1984. Le verlan: argot d'école ou langue des keums? *Mots* 8. 1984. 169–85

——. 1996. "Verlan 2000, Le Language des Cités et l'école." *Argos* no. 18 1996: 50–62.

Bacholle, Michèle. 2000. *Un passé contraignant. Double bind et transculturation.* Amsterdam/Atlanta: Rodopi.

Begag, Azouz. 1986. *Le gône du Chaâba*. Paris: Seuil.

——. 1989. *Béni ou le paradis privé*. Paris: Seuil.

Béji, Hélé. 1997. *L'imposture culturelle*. Paris: Stock.

Belghoul, Farida. 1986. *Georgette!* Paris: Barrault.

Bhaba, Homi. 1994. *The location of culture*. New York: Routledge.

Bouraoui, Nina. 1991. La *voyeuse interdite*. Paris: Gallimard.

——. 1993. *Poing mort*. Paris: Gallimard.

Certeau de, Michel. 1985. L'actif et le passif des appartenances. *Esprit*. June 1985. 155–71.

Dakhlia, Jocelyne. 2004. Trames de langues, usages et métissages linguistiques dans l'histoire du Maghreb. Paris: Institut de Recherches sur le Maghreb Contemporain et Maisonneuve et Larose Paris.

Gandhi, Leela. 1998. *Postcolonial Theory: A Critical Introduction*. New York: Columbia University Press.

Glissant, Edouard. 1990. *Poétique de la relation*. Paris: Gallimard.

Gross, J., Mcmurray, D. and Swedenburg, T. 1996. Arab Noise and Ramadan Nights: Raï, Rap, and Franco-Maghrebi Identities. *Displacement, Diaspora and Geographies of Identity*. Lavie, S. and Swedenburg, T. (ed). Durham: Duke University Press.

Guénif Souilamas, Nacira. 2000. Des "beurettes" aux descendantes d'immigrants nord-africains. Paris: Grasset/Le Monde.

Issad, Ramdane. 1990. Le vertige des abbesses. Paris: Denoel.

Jerad, N. 1988. L'arabe en France. Une langue, des langues. *France pays multilingue*. Boutet, J. and Vermes, G. (eds). Paris: L'harmattan.

——. 2004. La politique linguistique dans la Tunisie post-coloniale. *Trames de langues*. Dakhlia, J. (ed). Paris: Maisonneuve et Larose.

Khelil, Mohand. 1991. *L'intégration des Maghrebins en France*. Paris: PUF.

Labov, William. 1972. *Language in the Inner City: Studies in the Black English Vernacular*. Philadelphia:University of Pennsylvania Press.

Lavie, S. and Swedenburg, T. (eds). 1996. *Displacement, Diaspora and Geographies of Identity*. Durham: Duke University Press.

Laronde Michel. 1993. Autour du roman beur, immigration et identité. Paris: L'Harmattan. *Le Monde* 2006. Enfants d'immigres, fils de France. *Le Monde des Livres*. 14 April 2006.

Lepoutre, David. 1997. *Coeur de banlieue. Codes, rites et langages*. Paris: Odile Jacob.

Nini, Soyara. 2001. Ils disent que je suis une beurette. Paris: Fixot.

Ossman, Susan and Terrio, Susan. 2006. "The French Riots: Questioning Spaces of Surveillance and Sovereignty." *International Migration*. June 2006.

Pratt, Mary Louise. 1992. "Introduction: Criticism in the Contact Zone." *Imperial Eyes: Travel Writing and Transculturation* London: Routledge. 1–11.

Rosello, Mireille. 1993. *Georgette!* de Farida Belghoul: television et départenance. *L'esprit Créateur Post-colonial Womens Writing*. Vol. 33. 35–46.

Sebbar, Leila. 1985. Les carnets de Sherazade. Paris: Stock.

Savarese, Eric. 2000. *Histoire coloniale et immigration une invention de l'étranger*. Paris: Séguier.

Sayad, Abdelmalek. 1993. *L'immigration maghrébine en Europe et ses perspectives d'intégration*. Tunis: Publications du Centre de Documentation Tunisie-Maghreb.

———. 1999. *La double absence, des illusions de l'émigré aux souffrances de l'émigré*. Paris: le Seuil.

Schade-Poulsen, Marc. 1999. *Men and Popular Music in Algeria. The Social Significance of Raï*. Austin: University of Texas Press.

Schnapper, Dominique. 1991. *La France de l'intégration. Sociologie de la nation en 1990*. Paris: Gallimard.

4

Is It Possible to Be Both a Cosmopolitan and a Muslim?

Nadia Tazi

Claude Bernard once said, "Health is the silence of the organs." Identity can be thought of in the same way, when it is as silent, and mysteriously organic as the body. Identity poses a problem only when there is something wrong. And cosmopolitan identity is no different. Its plurality—which after all will be less and less noteworthy in a globalized world—emerges with the same naturalness, innocence, and quality of intimate well-being. Cosmopolitism should be examined only when there is a rupture, where there are problematic contiguities, discontinuities, and disparities that are too large to comprehend. It is when there is a crisis that identity reveals unthought hierarchies, sublimations, and denials, and exposes unconscious investments. On the contrary, when everything appears as if it is normal, one is just temporarily confronted by one becoming among many: there is a becoming-Indian just as there is a becoming-infant; a becoming-Arab just as there is a becoming-political. And these are nothing more than modalities of power.

Here I am intentionally using a Deleuzian vocabulary since Deleuze is the philosopher who really contested the idea of identity. I do not wish to speak about my unconscious or to engage in a reflexive exercise. Instead, I will tell you two stories concerning two events that opened up a breach in my own identity as a cosmopolitan. They show how my own cosmopolitism has failed me politically. I will thus focus on how politics confers depth and ethical substance to the cosmopolitan idea and puts it to the test.

RETURNING TO RUSHDIE

Satan, being thus confined to a vagabond, wandering, unsettled condition, is without any certain abode; for though he has in consequence of his angelic nature, a kind of empire in the liquid waste or air, yet he is . . . without any fixed place, or space, allowed him to rest the sole of his foot upon.

—Defoe, The History of the Devil (Rushdie 1988, prologue)

Like the main character in his novel *Shame*, Rushdie could be identified as the son of three mothers, as the child of the Indian, the Islamic, and the Western cultures. But in fact when you read him, he seems to rebel against all identities. It is as if he is hopelessly dissociated even from his own self. Indeed, it is certainly these tangled origins and the playful posture he assumes with respect to them that seduces me when I read Rushdie. In his writing I find myself. I too have bathed in the seas of mixed waters between Morocco, the country of my ancestors, and Spain, where I was born. I too shift between France, where I have chosen to live, and India, my elected homeland, where I have spent time each year for the last twenty years. If something solid subsists in Rushdie's writing, it is the need to leap beyond the logic of belonging. Unable to count on some ultimate signifier or on a unifying attribute, his cosmopolitism retains a certain incongruity and disorder as well as an enormous vitality. His cosmopolitism is overabundant, fluid, and metamorphic; it is not even quite baroque, it is unclassifiable. It is a movement that rushes toward expression in writing, toward a fiction that can translate this liberty. Writing becomes a move not to find one's roots but one's wings—even if one burns them in the process.

I have been inspired by *The Satanic Verses,* which I believe is his best book, to ignore the fatwa and honor Rushdie by writing this essay on his work.[1] *The Satanic Verses'* Felliniesque or Rabelaisian verve might deter some readers. Its Joycean ambition certainly discouraged others at a time when people had lost interest in formal literary experiments. Besides, its convocation of a stunning corpus of references is itself a challenge to any critic. Rushdie alludes to Bakhtine, Proust, Joyce, Borges, Garcia Marquez, Gunther Grass, Boulgakov, Cervantes, Dickens, and Andersen, as well as writers of Muslim traditions ranging from Tabari and the sira, the major Orientalists' works, the Indian *Mahabarata*, Penjabi and Kashmiri mythologies. In addition to these learned and literary references, the novel is intimately involved in popular mass media. It offers a razor sharp image of today's mediatized world.

The *Satanic Verses* is a charade: it should be appreciated as such, and it is a stimulating invitation to play with intertextuality, to enjoy its barely disguised codes and riddles. The novel leads you from the punks and gothic folklore during Thatcher's era to Bollywood and to Indian villages. It teaches you how to pinpoint stories in Indian newspapers and to appreciate their extravagant combination of fantasy and credulity. To use a Proustian metaphor, Rushdie is one of those rare writers who gives you a pair of glasses to see the world—a world as delirious and possessed as that of the *Satanic Verses*; a *leela* played by demons and laughing spirits. Rushdie's novel collects multiple voices that have been chosen for their hyperbolic quality. His is a contemporary choir with metropolitan hybrids, monstrous mutations, and very real bodies, not simulacrums and commodities. Once I realized that the movie producer Ismael Merchant had inspired the character of Sisodia in the book, or that the becoming-goat of one of the main characters, Farishta, mimicked some episodes of black magic that took place in British police stations during the 1980s; when I recognized in chapter 8, one of the *yatra* or sectarian pilgrimages that flourish in India today, I thought I should at least try to play the game, and to explore the subversive appeal and the multicultural challenge of the novel.

My curiosity was especially peaked by the theme of Iblis, the Koranic figure of the devil. He appears as a figure of rebellion, as in the Christian tradition as well as of one of division, of *fitna*, a concept that includes ideas of disorder, seduction, and sedition in Arabic. At first like many other readers, I noticed the strange coincidences between what happened to Rushdie himself after the book's publication and the apparent premonitions written into the text. For instance, on the very first page the quote from Defoe suggests that Satan is condemned to be a vagabond, a nomad without a home. (Rushdie 1999). Could he have imagined that a certain nomadic, creative cosmopolitanism would twist around into a perpetual condition of wandering similar to that of the fallen angels, the pariahs, the clandestine immigrants, and the persecuted of this world? Over time, I understood that the narrator 's voice in the novel—the voice that is not Rushdie's, but that sounds just like him—is the devil himself! And this realization led me to the heart of the matter: I had to explore the extraordinary montage that works the topic of deception and devilry into the text, disguised in several voices. We hear echoes of devilish voices between Iblis, the Prophet Muhammad, played by the actor Farishta, who becomes crazy, and in Rushdie himself, the demiurgic author of this carnival. The interwoven voices are not only numerous and plural, but schizoid and dissociated. They are perceived through a game of mirrors in which identifications lead to madness, possession, and self-denial.

I do not wish to deconstruct here this topic of devilry, which again is extremely sophisticated. I just want to mark the multidimensionality of the novel and the complexity of its structure. In regards to the Islamic strata, it is clear that under the mask of the grotesque and behind its apparent fantasy, it deals with a crucial issue: the historical rivalry that opposed the prophet and the poets of his time, the decisive struggle for the appropriation of discourse as a weapon as well as a source of enchantment (Who speaks? In the name of what? What status are words given? Toward what end?). In this way, it resembles the war Plato mounted against the deceptive powers of the poets, powers translated in *The Satanic Verses* not by the sublime but through farce, facetiousness, and irony. This fatal struggle concerning how to deal with the symbolic realm has long been impossible to discuss or even think about in the Islamic world. But we must remember that it was originally resolved by the putting to death of the poet by the Prophet: echoes of this event have reverberated ever since. This execution, unlike that of Socrates is not signaled in the Hegalian sense of *aufhebung*. Instead, the negation was overcome, foreclosed and consumed by hagiography. We need to recall this when we engage the idea of the Muslim community or submit it to any kind of reflection. Rushdie exposes this nonthought in his book, and he has paid the price for fighting against it. Here, we enter into an enigmatic realm: the karma as exception that is liberty and genius in every sense of the word. This karma and its genius are encircled by death. Evoking her friend Walter Benjamin, Hannah Arendt speaks of the little hunchback who is jinxed, as if under an evil spell. How can we but recall the most ancient myths when faced with this dizzying destiny that mixes reality and fiction and dances amongst the different epochs of history, perpetually brushed by the wings of the demon?

In the novel the stake appears under the guise of possession, a possession that oscillates among rapture, madness, and imposture and that is presented as a *mise en abîme*: therefore one can say that the devil is to the prophet what Rushdie is to his reader and what Mahound, the impostor, is to the actor Farishta when he becomes schizophrenic. Those very splits and doubles, this waltz that superimposes simulations, visionary raptures, and psychological troubles, does not cease to obscure at once the text itself and what is at stake, in other words, the truth, which is definitively lost. For the homologies I just mentioned put into a single perspective literature, prophecy and madness. This mélange gets even more vertiginous when you put the book aside and consider Rushdie's notion of literature as a demonic inspiration that positions him somewhere between the storyteller and the visionary, the chronicler and the avant-garde artist. We must keep in mind that the publication of *The Satanic Verses* led to extensive and excessive reactions, but it was never read by most of those who condemned it. No truth, no fiction, nothing—this made it as though the book simply it did not exist: its truth was thus occulted in the most perverse way. Here I will only note that a game of mirrors reflects fiction and reality in a way that makes the author and the book prisoners of one another. This situation is closed. The forclusion is redoubled: by hagiography and by the "Rushdie affair," by the political event that makes *The Satanic Verses* the object of a global terror, media spectacle, and diplomacy, opening a new chapter in the conflict between Islamism and political modernity.

In any case, there is no doubt that Rushdie's mingling of the spiritual and the political realms through writing draws both on his enormous erudition and his gift for prophecy. Rushdie invites us to rethink the zones of uncertainty that appear among the three regimes of truth: poetry and literature more generally, prophesy and religion, and politics and power. As I worked on this essay, I came to clearly perceive the trap in which Rushdie had found himself after the fatwa: he could not explain his book without recognizing its tremendous critical potential, a potential that exposed almost all the problematic points of the Prophet's life—the superb story of his doubts and fears, the episode of the copyist who changes the sentences Muhammad dictates, without Muhammad noticing it. Even *The Satanic Verses* themselves: the temptation to compromise and renounce monotheism in order to gain political consensus. It also describes his sexual appetites and some of his love stories, like the story of Aisha's necklace. Almost all the more famous episodes opposed by the internal and external enemies of Islam since its very inception are found in the novel. Rushdie, I realized, could not defend himself without handing out pebbles to those who would stone him. He had to remain silent about his intentions; the book had to speak for itself.

This made me realize that I could not defend him without encountering the same dilemma. I am not superstitious, but in this instance, I kept thinking of the saying that one should not tempt the devil. I decided not to write anything, but I was enraged to see that people like Milan Kundera and Bernard-Henri Lévy, while trying to support Rushdie, kept insisting that his book was *merely* a work of fiction! It was their only line of defense! None of them had any idea about what Rushdie was up to, since they knew nothing about Islam. Furthermore, none of these people seemed to notice his critique of Thatcherism. They just used him as a symbol. For years Rushdie became a ghost, the ghostly apparition that could be defended alongside other political causes like the defense of Sarajevo—another cosmopolitan victim. But for me, Rushdie's work opened up another question, a tragic and pressing question that was raised by the murders of Tahar Djaout and other Algerian intellectuals, by persecutions in Egypt, Sudan, Bangladesh, and elsewhere: it is the question of the abominable condition of the Muslim intellectual.

I do not want to leave *The Satanic Verses* behind before at least mentioning another critical line in the novel that simultaneously grounds its Islamic tropes and audaciously cuts across it. It is not possible to see in this extraordinary work a univocal political condemnation with respect to a single danger for the psyche faced with multiplicity. All of Rushdie's books before the fatwa deal with exile, exile as a traumatic experience that he himself lived twice (from India to Pakistan, then to England) before he became the hiding renegade, the fleeing nomad that he has been for years. On the one hand, we need to notice that Rushdie explores, interrogates, and puts to the test the foundation of Islam. In his text the actor Farishta loses his mind after having lost his faith and his profound rootedness. When God is lost everything becomes possible, Rushdie says, following Dostoyevsky. In *The Satanic Verses*, absolute deterritorialization is the death of God and it can result in obscurity and madness. A true cosmopolitan and what we might call a *cosmopolitique*, must face the trial of being torn apart and from this greatest loss, find his truth.

On the other hand, Rushdie develops the character of Chamcha in symmetry with Farishta. Chamcha is no less metaphorical than Farishta; he does not turn into an insect like in Kafka's metamorphosis, but instead, he becomes a billy goat. Chamcha is the face of hideous, mimetic zeal and self-loathing. He assimilates everything by his stiffness or excesses, in opposition of course to fundamentalism but also to the nomadic pluralism and jubilation of the cosmopolitan. What we might call the Chamcha syndrome is certainly a psychic stage for the immigrant. No one knows this better than Rushdie who takes mischievous delight in mocking the rules, good taste, seriousness, and stupidity that are exuded by the British establishment. Through his writing and the character of Chamcha he effects a critique of English society under Margaret Thatcher with its so-called good manners, its racism, and its drifts toward fascism. Seeking to be a cosmopolitan involves giving oneself the luxury of a crossed critique that does not simply denounce each side but denounces one through the other in a series of mediations and oblique movements. This always means one runs the risk of being attacked from every side, or worse of being misunderstood. One can only imagine Rushdie's solitude as he dialogues with his demons.

THE VEIL AND THE REPUBLIQUE

Recently France has shown to the world her lack of cosmopolitism. An enormous debate arose around the question of the *hijab* or the Islamic veil in public schools as opposed to *laïcité* or secularism. This debate is exceptional in its scope, length, the intellectual mobilization it has involved, and the divisions and reversals occurring among the feminists, the extreme left, or teachers. It is exceptional too in the content of these discussions. Nothing less than the foundations of the Republic seem to be at issue. The crises also have a symptomatic aspect: they express the malaise of French identity. I shall not recall the many veil crises and developments from the 1980s to the recent law forbidding the hijab at school, nor will I describe the very unusual alliances this debate has forged across the political spectrum in France. What I will focus on is how some of the arguments regarding the hijab upset my own cosmopolitism.

If one follows the logic of the opponents to the law, one finds a series of arguments based on principles, as well as tactics, and criticisms regarding the misunderstanding of the situation that eventually led to the imposition of the law. First, many opponents have noted the obvious contradiction between the supposed finality of the law and its possible consequences: if this law should fight Islamism and communautarism by forcing girls to remove the veil, why then are they banished from school—their only chance—if they refuse to do so? Why are they abandoned to the same danger that the law is supposed to avert: seclusion and presumed sexism with no alternatives other than Islamic schools and propaganda? There is more than inconsistency in punishing those who already are victims of racism and discrimination in a postcolonial society, and in such a troubled international context. The issue of the Islamic veil is veiling the real issues. As Emmanuel Terray remarked, we are dealing with a political hysteria (2004). French society has built up a dream image and been tempted by escapism as a way of confronting an enduring malaise. Instead of focusing on such a small number of cases of veiled girls (1,200 in 2003), one should consider the exclusion the children of immigrants face every day at school, when seeking housing and employment, for these encourage fundamentalist reactions. Rather than putting an end to the problem, the law sets up a series of dangerous dichotomies: French versus immigrants, the Republic versus Islam. A "shock of civilization" can then be assumed by extremists on all sides, by both the National Front and the Islamists.

The second issue at stake relates to schools and education. Education is in crisis throughout the world. In France, however, debates about schools often take a particularly bitter turn because the school has always been at the heart of the national Republican project. Education is seen as a particular problem in the poor *banlieues* (suburbs), where so many people of foreign ancestry live. Teachers complain that there is a crisis of authority in the classroom. Yet, the state and families demand that they fulfill their role of educating students. As they see their economic and social status decline and have to deal with more and more students and disciplinary problems, teachers can be tempted to inflate the importance of the hijab in their search for some kind of quick solution to the problems they face. The third issue concerns the decline of feminism in France in terms of economic and political matters as well as in social theory. Therefore, we have a breakdown in the assimilationist model (*une panne de l'intégration*), a crisis in education, and a problem with women. The story of the veil brings these together and distracts us from the fact that not so long ago the National Front's Le Pen came second in the presidential elections.

But of course one should not underestimate French political sophistication. Nor should one ignore the serious debates that the crisis has provoked: Etienne Balibar wrote an article on secularism, the historian Beaubérot postulated a difference between the *principle of secularity* (or separation between church and state and individual freedom of consciousness as guaranteed by the state) and "*the religion of secularity*," which has its roots in the nineteenth century, exemplified in the ideas of Auguste Comte. Following their ideas one might say that this law will render any public expression of Islam illegitimate. The distinction between religion and politics is really not so clear. Islam is not just a faith among many but the religion of the Other, a religion that challenges secularism (Balibar 2004; Beaubérot 2003).

Finally, there is a series of opinions that question the ability of the law itself to address a phenomenon concerning entrenched mentalities, customs, and manners, and requires education. School is there to help with this process and to reduce the gaps, the *dyschronies* I would say, in which the girls are caught, making them hostages of two opposite historical moments, and victims of both sexism and racism. Besides, one could point out that all the authoritarian laws during the twentieth century, be it to remove the veil (in Kemalist Turkey, during the Soviets in Caucasus and Central Asia) or to impose it (under Khomeinist Iran or the Taliban) have only raised hostility and provoked backlashes in the long run.

As I listen to and read about these different positions, I cannot help but find them extremely convincing. I notice that many of those involved in this critical debate have long shown a real solidarity with the Beurs in fighting racism. Yet, I cannot ascribe to such opinions. You might ask how I could fail to appreciate their ethical stand and their efforts to establish a common front against prejudice? But I must confess that I can only respond to this question by feeling uneasy, frustrated, and recognizing my inability to fully subscribe to "the cause." For me, as a rule, the fight against the discrimination against women in the Muslim world takes precedence over other struggles. As a European I agreed with many of these well-meaning, historically informed criticisms of the law. But as a Moroccan I supported the other side. In other words, I felt caught in between two. I was not *interested* (inter-esse as Arendt says), a situation my cosmopolitism usually leads to, but intersected, divided, trapped.

Cosmopolitism actually may seem to rhyme with opportunism—it is also related to universalism (or to some kind of syncretism), as if there was always the nostalgia of totality, the illusion of an exhaustion of meaning, the belief in a synoptical vision. As if it was possible to escape from the contingency and the limitations of the particular: this aspect is what makes it "charming" as Musil said in a rather deprecatory way, or restless, and intermittent. Cosmopolitans will support Europe with the Americans and vice-versa, the Jews with Arabs and vice-versa, the Muslim minority in India against the BJP, and Hindus with Pakistanis and so on. They will gladly argue for a Kantian cosmopolitanism and embrace globalizing utopias (pacifists, ecologists, *mondialists*) and yet not necessarily do so because they are genuinely idealistic, frivolous, or reluctant to engage in a cause. Rather, they permit themselves a certain distance that includes a kind of vanity or a perhaps naiveté, a belief that they are able to understand both sides. Or else, they imagine that they can lay hold of the real thing rather than the *symbolon*, the broken piece of truth in their hands. Cosmopolitans will naturally feel a great repugnance for Manichaeisms, or the brutal choices imposed by crises. When they find themselves in a double bind, they either go elsewhere, hopping from a dyschronic point to a consonant one, from a disparity to a comparity, or they must find their balance and mobility through an emotional and intellectual detachment that cuts them apart. They have to learn more in order to again find emotional and intellectual detachment.

This means that a cosmopolitan is someone for whom the development of globalization seems to correspond to his natural milieu. Yet, he is also the one who will suffer the most when crises take shape. He can find himself in a series of double binds. Since 9/11 there is a counterpoint to globalization. A devastating logic has been set in motion that leads us to ask what can be done with extremists in charge everywhere? Who determines the larger politics? How can one escape the pressure of the two poles that confront one another and work together to dictate the terms of debate, the stakes, the tactics, and the alliances that matter, whether these are the Islamists, on one hand, and the dictators, or proto-fascist groups or neoconservative leaders on the other hand? Can one fight on both sides at once? And how is it possible to oppose one without supporting the other? This dilemma is at the heart of the crisis of activist movements today. Many activists want to understand and explain everything with reference to the colonial question. But this sends us back not only to a series of contradictions but leads us into unnatural political affiliations while our natural allies, for instance those who champion the causes of the third world, end up in the other camp.

If the veil affair can escape being ridiculous, it is because it illustrates what has become a structural line of fracture. It superimposes a hyperbolic and disjunctive scheme onto the terrain of women and history. It moves and displaces itself to better strengthen its grip. Muslim cosmopolitans, democrats, modernists, feminists, and secularists have long suffered its violence, but they have not been able to move out of the schema, which is explained in great part by the silences, divisions, and paralyzing blockages it insinuates into the Islamic world. As for the hijab, on one side, history catches up with the French by a double dyschrony with respect to the colonial past and the European and global present that privileges the idea of multiculturalism rather than integration. On the other hand, as we all know, the crucial ideological problem that the Muslims meet today is the fact that they have not engaged yet in the massive work of theoretical historicization of their scriptures and religious references. They are still subjected to a theologico-political order. And not only do they tend to mystify their past, but they have extensively borrowed voluntarily or involuntarily major alien constructions and *épistémés*, as Foucault would say, as if they were simple commodities, hence the explosive dyschronies that intersect in their societies. Saudi Arabia has exported its form of the hijab all over the world. It has the most anticosmopolitan policies. It is the epitome of a dyschronic state, which is possible because of its oil wealth. But it is one state among many. Although almost all the Arab states have signed the universal declaration of human rights, they maintain family law codes that contradict them. As to the veiled beurettes they translate in a dyschronic way the knot between postcolonialism and Islamism—they are the unfortunate hybrids of two extremisms that silently and diffusely creep up in this society.

Let me quickly summarize the views of the veiled beurettes. Their main argument, which I find rather embarrassing, concerns their morals or their modesty. In removing the veil at school they feel naked and they betray their faith. This commonly held opinion gives a good idea of what Islam has become: a literalist and legalistic religion, which betrays its basic principle of interiorization of the law by using what, could be seen as an identity mark, a political sign or even a logo. Who could believe that they are seeking to be modest by not showing themselves? Nothing is showier today in France than a veil! It is not difficult to remind them that *shari'a* does not mean law but *path* or to remind them of one of the favorite authors of fundamentalists—Al Ghazali—who developed an ethic of intention (*niyya*) as opposed to a visible order where hypocrisy or conformism flourish. Or again to remind those wearing the hijab of one of the most seminal metaphysical couples of concepts that Islamic thought has produced: the *batin* (veiled, invisible) and the *zahir* (visible)

The real point is that the veil is clearly a reactive sign to a difficult situation. It is like a trick that the women play on French society and the state that has excluded them for so long. They say "you exclude us from the nation we are born to from the place we belong, and we include ourselves by using the principles that you keep claiming so proudly. Indeed, we are using them bet-

ter than you do to fight against you." It is a very old tactic. Actually it is a lesson of the harem. The veil has always been ambiguous and Muslim women
have used it for centuries to resist law, seduce, deceive, and establish their
power with the results we are familiar with. For the defenders of the veil to
support secularism is to support freedom of consciousness. Why talk about
Algeria, Iran, Afghanistan?

"We are French," they say. They are protected by the laws of the Republic:
no repudiation, polygamy, and so on. "The veil is not an instrument of op-
pression but of liberation," they continue. According to them, the hijab is an
instrument of integration, since it lets them be French without denying their
culture. They think they are paying a debt they owe to their colonized ancestors who were forced to remove the hijab in public during expiatory cere-
monies. "The veil is modern," they claim (an argument also used by the mul-
lah in Iran). They insist that it is imposed neither by atavism, nor by political
forces, and never in any case by men. It is a personal decision, a virtuous
choice as opposed to the loosening of morals symbolized by the string. It is
always the same dialectical and simplistic reversal that is used, a frivolous
and disgraceful treachery. We are not a minority, they say (to refute commu-
nitarism), Islam is in perfect conformity with human rights and with citizenship. We are learned and responsible, we just have to jump into the cloth of
the French Republic and the trick is done. The problem is that all those points
can be perfectly inverted; both the cloths of Islam and of the Republic are old
and shabby. The holes of one cannot be patched with the material of the other.
It does not work on dyschronic issues.

I shall conclude a bit abruptly by emphasizing that the feminist issue is the
touchstone of politics in the Muslim world. After all those years we know that
fundamentalisms have no political ideals worthy of the name, they just have
a puritan scheme of morality, of anticorruption and purification. They maintain a regressive hold following the worst patriarchal model, through which
they can oppose both the Western world and westernized groups in their societies, and the Muslim despots who domesticate politics. The shari'a has actually no real substance except its concern with private matters and more
specifically with women. The whole Islamic city is blocked by the Law of fathers and by domestic issues whose empowerment resonates from the top of
the state to the bottom of society. Political thought in this world has to find a
new lexicon and grammar to express and understand structural realities that
are different than in the West. This requires a new political anthropology.

The worst political failure of the Muslim world has been to give precedence to identity over liberty, in my opinion. But, following the cosmopolitan Edward Said, I cannot say such things without denouncing the other side,
without taking note of the marking also the massive responsibility of the

Western powers, in their direct or indirect support of fundamentalism and despotism, from colonialism to the war in Iraq and support of Ariel Sharon. For me the lesson to remember from Said and from Rushdie is to always take a distance with respect to each pole in order to better critique them both. This is a particularly difficult, courageous, and, I emphasize, *solitary* position. It generally corresponds to being politically anchored on the left, but for these two authors it also refers to their nomadism and their multiple origins. While they are very different, Rushdie and Said were both precursors in confronting the passionate triangulation among the Muslim world, cosmopolitanism, and subversion. I dedicate this article to them.

NOTE

1. I found the French translation of the book disappointing. It's style was too academic. It lacked the necessary neologisms, volatility, and insolence. At the time of its publication very few people in France fully appreciated the novel's avant-garde architectonic or its critical strength. In the Arab world, only Sadik Al Azmeh focused on the literary qualities of the novel.

REFERENCES

Baubérot, Jean. 2003. *Histoire de la laïcité en France*. Paris: PUF.
Balibar, Etienne. 2004. Dissonances dans la laïcité. *Le foulard islamique en question*. Charlotte Nordmann (ed.). Paris: editions Amsterdam.
Rushdie, Salman. 1983. *Shame*. New York: Knopf.
———. 1988. *The Satanic Verses: A Novel*. New York: Viking.
Terray, Emmanuel. 2004. *L'hystérie politique*: *Le foulard islamique en question*. Charlotte Nordmann (ed.). Paris: editions Amsterdam.

5

A New Take on the Wandering Jew

Shana Cohen

I was living in Morocco during the 1996 Israeli elections. Polls indicated that the contest between Shimon Peres and Benyamin Netanyahu was too close to call. I became obsessed with the results, as did a friend of mine, a French-Israeli man who had come to Morocco, like me, to conduct research for his dissertation. We called each other daily to recount the latest poll numbers, to examine any fresh piece of evidence that might indicate Peres would win. For both of us, loss for Peres meant the loss of the peace process. As I remember it, I became desperate during the final days before the election, as I suspected Peres would lose. My landlady told me to light candles in my bathroom for good luck. I accompanied a friend of mine to a *hilula,* or a pilgrimage to the tomb of a Jewish saint.

During the elections, Marc told me that the intensity of my interest in the election had earned me honorary Israeli citizenship. I thought my preoccupation suggested something more general, closer to a measure of my identity as a Jew. I was not involved with the Jewish community in Morocco beyond the acquaintance of a few people and occasional attendance at services, just as I was not especially involved with a community in the United States. However, I identified strongly enough as a Jew to become intimately involved with a critical election in Israel.

Similarly, when I have moved to a new country or a new place, I have always visited institutions or contacted members of the Jewish community within my first months of arriving. In Morocco, I went to synagogue during my first visit. In England and Washington, D.C., I started volunteering at Jewish organizations. Acting on my Jewish identity has seemed to provide continuity as I have migrated from place to place. This action has not led to incorporation into a larger population, perhaps because as an adult, I have been engaged in the flow of movement.

Drawing upon my own experience and that of two friends, I discuss in this chapter religious, specifically Jewish, identity within the context of contemporary serial migration. All three of us have lived in three or more countries and probably shall move again, for personal and professional reasons. I have lived in the United States, Morocco, and England, as well as Egypt and Israel. Marc has lived in France, Israel, and Morocco, and Emmanuel, the second friend, Morocco, England, and Israel.

In this chapter I focus on Jewish identity as a method of linking past, present, and future against the backdrop of movement. On a more profound level, Jewish identity offers an interpretative framework for subjective meaning in a life of singularity, or without belonging to a localized and present collectivity. This kind of analysis differs from debates on assimilation versus community-building or diaspora versus return (to Israel). Conceptually, within a process of multiple migrations, bipolar categorization of behavior/identity is impossible. Types of behavioral classification, from assimilation to conservatism to making *aliyah* (immigration to Israel), require settling in a particular place. More practically, integration into a diluted national culture without retaining Jewish self-identification or interpreting identity through juxtaposition of Israel and out of Israel become less important if not irrelevant in a life of movement.

I suggest instead that Jewish identity for such serial migrants provides existential meaning in that it lends the individual ethical and historical value where value can only come in limited fashion from social status, career, or family because of distance and nonlinearity. Theoretically, religious identity invested with such meaning has implications for how we associate globalization and religion. Participation in a religion for serial migrants has existential significance that sets it apart from questions of fundamentalism, laicism, or liberalism, which all, ultimately, refer to politics. More pointedly, the ethical position that emerges in religious identity is a positive sense of action in the world rather than a negative act of differentiation or the defense of a transcendent representation of "truth" or "good."

This position directly contradicts ethics as nihilism, the contemporary "reign of ethics" that Alain Badiou defines as a "symptom of a universe ruled by a distinctive [singulière] combination of resignation in the face of necessity together with a purely negative, if not destructive, will" (2001, 30). Rather, religious identity here incorporates what Badiou champions as the "immortality of man," a perseverance in being linked to a Truth, in this case the potential for humanity laid out in the basic principles of a civilization. The attachment to engaging in the potential for humanity comes from the structural experience of being a serial migrant, or a life of singularity in multiple environments. I suggest that this singularity, movement for personal reasons and not as part of a group (such as a religious organization), forces reflection upon and engagement with positive change since the inverse, defensive action dictated around a collectivity becomes impossible.

After listing caveats about writing on Jewish identity, I discuss what has been the dominant debate about Jewish migration, the meaning and significance of diaspora versus home or resettlement. The idea of diaspora, whether applied to Jewish or other identities, evokes questions about assimilation, conflict of values, and the intersection of religious and national identity. Differentiating the serial migrant from the bipolar contrast of diaspora/exile and home/return, I show how the attachment of serial migrants to religious identity both reflects their specific trajectory and transcends those debates that ultimately associate religion with place.

MIGRATION AND JEWISH IDENTITY

Any discussion of Jewish identity in reference to contemporary debates over cosmopolitanism, citizenship, and identity forcibly evokes the pejorative and often dangerous association of Jews with statelessness and, thus, the status of second-class citizen, pariah, or worse. Yet, a book on serial migration that revolves around living in Morocco must consider the experience of Jewish migration.

I hesitated to be the author of a chapter on Jewish identity for several reasons. First, I am an American Jew who lived in Morocco, not a Moroccan Jew who has migrated elsewhere. A number of Moroccan Jews have written about the experience of migration, although not necessarily about moving from place to place (Levy 2003). Second, I have not specialized in Jewish studies and am thus no expert in the literature of the field. Third, I know that I am writing about a subject that so many have discussed so well.

Having expressed all of these doubts, I will write about my personal experience as a Jew and serial migrant. I will refer to the experience of several Jewish friends who, like me, have led and continue to lead lives of wanderers. My friends and I have not only identified ourselves as Jews, we have also acted upon this identity wherever we go. It has underpinned in some ways our actions, our interests, our life commitments when we have certainly not committed to place. We have imparted this identity upon our children, and we have claimed our identity even when or because we are so clearly in the minority, whether in the Arab World or Europe.

THE SIGNIFICANCE OF DIASPORA

I asked Emmanuel, a Moroccan Jewish friend, at some point to compare his sense of being Jewish in the three countries where he had lived. He had spent his teenage and early adult years in England, studying at a yeshiva and working in various jobs. He responded that in England, Jews could practice the religion as they pleased but remained conscious of their marginality in terms of religious and ethnic status. In Morocco, a Jew had to be careful about appearing "Jewish" but only felt uncomfortable because of the political situation in the Middle East. Being a Jew in and of itself was not an issue.

> The difference is in the hatred. In England, I felt free to be a Jew, to wear a kippah and go to the *schul*, but not free with other people. When I was a kid in school—my school was next to a Christian school—we would get in fights. We could wear our kippahs to school but we could see in their soul the hatred. One kid told me that I wasn't put in the gas chamber because I didn't pay the bill. I didn't know anything about the Shoah before I went to school when I started seeing the pictures. In England, you could feel the hatred. You were free as a Jew, but the hatred means your neighbor hates you.
>
> In Morocco, we don't have the freedom to wear a kippah. You have to be more closed in your mind, when to say you are a Jew and where to say it. But they would never say "dirty Jew." You fear because it is an Arab country but you know that. You are free to go to schul and if you say you are Jewish depends on where you are. In Anfa, they know me, they know that I am Jewish and it makes no difference, Jew or non-Jew. In a *quartier populaire* (the working class quarters) like Hay Hassani, you don't make publicity about being a Jew. They think you are Israeli, a Zionist. You know Habib. When I go to Habib's parents to eat, I say that I am a vegetarian because I don't want to eat meat and chicken that are not kosher. But when he comes to my house, he eats meat. He didn't know what it means to be a Jew before he met me. For him, there is no difference, Jew or non-Jew. But the people, they watch al-Jazeera, and they hate Jews because of Zionism.

Emmanuel's distinction between being Jewish in England and being Jewish in Morocco falls outside of most contemporary debates on Jewish identity that focus on self-identity and assimilation (for example, Gitelman 1998; Hecht and Faulkner 2000), diaspora (Boyarin and Boyarin 1995; Golan et al. 1999), and "authentic" versus historically relative identity (see Whitfield 2002; Charme 2000; Benbassa and Attias 2004). Emmanuel moves as a Jew through strikingly different arenas, adjusting his behavior according to his perception of others but remaining indelibly a "Jew." It is his sense of being a Jew, or more precisely, how this sense helps to organize his life in movement, that I choose to explore here.

This identification with being Jewish in a life of movement contradicts correlations between geographic mobility and weak Jewish identity. In survey research in the United States, geographically stable (as well as less-educated and unmarried) Jews had greater tendency to participate in community organizations and practice the religion whereas more mobile (better educated and intermarried) Jews expressed less identification and showed less active participation (Goldstein and Goldstein 1996).

Serial migration also differs from conceptions of diaspora, whether theorized in relation to Zionism or assimilation. The term *diaspora* itself may not adequately describe a transnational migrant, someone moving from place to place with no fixed destination. James Clifford, elaborating upon a definition by William Safran (1994, 83–84), lists the multiple meanings of diaspora for his own explication of the term and its anthropological importance. Safran, and Clifford, first qualify diaspora as a community. This community originated in a "center" that extended to at least two "peripheries"; members of the community sustain a memory of the original homeland while simultaneously believing they are accepted fully by the host country. The goal of the community is to return to the homeland and its members orient contact with the homeland with this goal in mind.

Clifford questions Safran's definition by adding dimensions of nationalist or antinationalist sentiment but he maintains the notion that diaspora implies "dwelling, maintaining communities, having collective homes away from home (and in this it is different from exile, with its frequently individualistic focus)" (1994, 308). Although settling in a specific place, the diaspora community "shows selective accommodation with the political, cultural, commercial, and everyday life of 'host' communities" (1994, 308).

Aihwa Ong adds an economic dimension to the conceptualization of diaspora through her research into migrant Chinese communities (1998). She argues that Chinese businessmen manage migration as part of an entrepreneurial and financial strategy. Her work, as well as that of Johanna Waters, shows how gender figures into the construction of diasporic communities (Waters 2003). Husbands and fathers assume control of directing and growing the family business while women assume responsibility for migration. In Waters's research, husbands leave their wives and underage children in Vancouver, Canada, where they can attain citizenship through investment. The children, who Waters refers to as "satellite kids," remain in Vancouver for education and eventually, citizenship, while the wives either stay with the children or travel, sometimes for months at a time, back to Hong Kong or Taiwan.

Whereas Ong relates diaspora to the pursuit of economic interests and the evolution of a functionary position within late capitalism, Waters shows, through her interviews, how satellite kids and their mothers become acculturated to their Canadian surroundings and thus become more of a migrant community settling in a new place. They thus support the more conventional notion of a diasporic community in which ambivalence and engagement with the customs and values of the host country figure significantly into the community's self-identity.

Scholars of the modern Jewish diaspora reverse the questions posed by those studying relatively recent migrations. Israel, the "homeland," has emerged from the tragedies and prejudice caused by diaspora, the long history of marginalization and persecution in host countries. Israel represents today not only salvation from the bitter past but also restoration and continuation of an authentic Jewish identity not tainted by the secondary status of Jews in prewar Europe or the powerful assimilating influences of a country like the United States. The political implications of such a debate are obvious. To return to Israel, particularly for a European or American, implies supporting a cause, the settlement of the land, whereas the choice to remain in the diaspora suggests, for Zionists, a willingness to risk the loss of Jewish identity and, implicitly, the Jewish homeland.

Theoretically, conceptualizing the meaning and historical significance of diaspora translates into debating the influence of non-Jewish culture on the constitution and survival of Jewish identity. Some, writing for a popular audience, show how fractionalism both within Israel and diasporic communities has left Jewish identity with an uncertain future (Freedman 2000). More politicized and conservative writers (see Auerbach 2001; Hazony 2001) point to American cultural pressures, whether in the United States or Israel of the past fifteen years, as eroding the depth of what it means to be Jewish and the principles of Zionism. Academic writers have expressed concern as well for the loss of identification as a Jew. Voicing his anxiety over the contemporary fragmentation of Jewish identity into a multiplicity of disorienting identities and the erosion of identity ascription itself, Zvi Gitelman writes, "the crucial question for the future of Diaspora Jewishness is whether without substantive, manifest 'thick' cultural content it becomes merely 'symbolic ethnicity,' much like the ethnicity of most Polish-Americans or Swedish-Americans, or whether this type of culture is sufficiently substantive and sustainable to preserve a group's distinctiveness on more than a symbolic level" (1998, 113).

Challenging the notion that an autonomous Jewish identity can only emerge in Israel, Daniel and Jonathan Boyarin differentiate between a colonized Jewishness that led to Israel and a Jewish identity rooted in the tradition of Rabbinic thought and religious ritual. Their work, particularly that of Daniel Boyarin, attempts to counter what they depict as a nineteenth and twentieth century of adopting hegemonic European images of masculinity and strength, an appropriation that underpinned the Zionism movement. Daniel Boyarin writes, "The politics of my project to reclaim the eroticized Jewish male sissy has. . . two faces" (Boyarin 1997). He wants to challenge the traditional division of Jewish men and women into "sissies" devoted to Torah study and an insular world and "phallic monsters" engaged with the modern world. Ultimately, he wants "to reconstruct a rabbinic Judaism that will be quite different in some ways from the one we know" (1997, xxi). He writes, "Looking for a way of remaining Jewish, of preserving Jewish memory and being what I consider a politically moral human being, I (re)-construct moments and models in the Jewish past that seem to make this possible" (1997, 311). That said, he adds a critical caveat: "This is not intended as a fantasized restoration of an ideal or idealized Jewish past . . . but the critical deliverance of cultural materials and practices from that past and their resisting in a different modernity" (1997, 311–12).

Boyarin's intellectual project resembles that of Moroccan-Jewish scholars reconciling their identification to Morocco, the place of origin, to a life in "diaspora," in this sense from Morocco and not Israel. André Levy examines his own return to his place of birth as a scholar and Moroccan Jew. He notes that though most Moroccans left Morocco for Israel in the belief that they would find a safer environment there, they did not wish to abandon all contact with their former country. He writes, "Many are reluctant to endorse the (by now crumbling) Zionist endeavor to disavow specific Jewish pasts, to unwrite collective and personal memories of diaspora, and to erase cultural and emotional links to Morocco as part of becoming 'Israeli'" (Levy 2003, 389). On a personal level, he emphasizes that his connection to Morocco in Israel has influenced his professional choices, namely his research into the Jewish community still remaining in Morocco. For Levy, those Jews who remain in Morocco "stand in an intricate and oblique way as an alternative biography for me" (2003, 389). He perceives his return to Morocco as reflective of "longings," the manifestation of "an impossible desire to fill my own void" (2003, 389). He remarks that he, in turn, offers an alternative biography for the Jews that stayed.

Can we compare Levy, who migrated from Morocco to Israel, where he lives and works, to Emmanuel, who was born in Morocco, migrated to England, and then returned to Morocco to live and work? Emmanuel differs because he has not necessarily "settled" in a "homeland" and because, obviously, he has returned to Morocco. Where, in fact, would we situate him, if at all, among debates over the experience of diaspora? Specific to Jewish diaspora, could we point to one debate or another as relevant to his self-identification? I would suggest that the set of debates about diaspora in general ignores migration without community. The set of debates about Jewish identity in particular underplays ways of identifying with Judaism that are not grounded in particular places, community institutions and services, specific sects, cultural hegemony, or political position.

Emmanuel did tell me, "Of course, in Israel, I felt more free. I felt proud to be a Jew. You could do everything to be a proper Jew." Marc and his wife have retained an apartment in Tel Aviv to which they may one day return. Does this mean, however, that they regard themselves as Jews determined by connection to Israel, where Emmanuel can feel "free" or Marc can finally settle? What do we make of the fact that, as of now, neither has plans to move to Israel but rather to the United States or back to Europe?

I posit that we should look first at the substance of Emmanuel's practice as a Jew rather than the structure of connections he maintains to places or institutions in order to understand what he means by feeling Jewish. By practice, I mean not only his participation in Jewish customs or how he acts upon beliefs (for instance, keeping kosher or going to synagogue regularly). Rather, does being Jewish figure as an element in the constitution of meaning for Emmanuel? More specifically, how does this meaning sustain itself or translate from one location to another in the life of a serial migrant? I would suggest that existential meaning and movement reinforce themselves, that Emmanuel moves from one place to another as a Jew and that movement sustains his particular identity.

Before exploring the meaning of being Jewish for him, or myself, I should show how our choices distinguish us from other migrants and thus provide the possibility for our modes of self-identification.

THEORIZING (SERIAL) MIGRATION AND CONTEMPORARY JEWISH IDENTITY

The path of migration for Emmanuel, Marc, and me is distinctive from that of an emigrant moving to a particular location for work with the notion of returning home or an immigrant settling in a new home. Our migration, through multiple countries and without fixed destination, falls outside statistical or analytic categorization. For instance, the International Labor Organization states that most migrants enter a country through one of three channels. They can come for permanent migration, an option primarily available for highly skilled workers, family unification, or refugee resettlement. They can also come for temporary migration, which primarily pertains to guest workers filling persistent vacancies in professions such as nursing or teaching. Lastly, they can come as temporary migrants for seasonal employment or study (2004, 9).

The ILO report on global migrant workers goes on to say that most migrants from developing countries to wealthy countries fill low-skilled, low-wage positions while most migrants moving from one wealthy country to another stay in professional positions. Whereas wealthy countries—those in the Organisation for Economic Co-operation and Development (OECD)—debate the political risks of allowing large migrant populations from developing or the less wealthy countries of Eastern Europe to enter for work, governments welcome professionals, particularly from other OECD countries. According to the report, during the period 1995–2000, growth in the foreign labor force among OECD countries ranged from 3 to 4 percent a year whereas over the past five years, the number of highly educated migrants coming to the United Kingdom rose an average of 35 percent a year and for the United States, 14 percent a year.

Flying in the face of such statistics, Emmanuel, Marc, and I have all moved to a developing country, and, in my case, back again, from one wealthy country to another. Marc and I could certainly be regarded as "highly educated" and therefore capable of easy movement but our decisions about movement have not followed solely from professional or financial concerns. Marc wanted to live in North Africa, where his parents were born, and found a job teaching at a Jewish school in Casablanca in order to finance his studies. I wanted to return to the Arab world after living in Egypt and Israel because I felt drawn to the region culturally. Emmanuel left England almost purely for personal reasons.

We could also say that the choice of Morocco as a place to live reflects not only work opportunity, in the case of me and Marc, but also the long, long history of a Jewish population there. The population of Moroccan Jews totals hardly more than several thousand today, although Jews of Moroccan descent may number more than a million worldwide. Much of the larger population lives in France, Israel, and Canada. I could say that for Jews wanting to work or conduct research in the Arab world, Morocco, with its history of diversity, offers a more "comfortable" environment than other countries in the region. For the serial migrant not necessarily looking for a community of settlement, Morocco offers a connection to a Jewish civilization and thus a context for relating to a place.

Should, then, the ILO account for first, multiple migrations, second, migration for personal reasons other than family reunification, and third, from a developed to a developing country? The response may be that we represent too small a number to figure into data-collection efforts and calculations. However, multiple migrations may hint at population flows of the future and nontraditional migration paths may reflect the possibilities created by global market integration. For instance, Emmanuel works in tourism and tourism receipts in Morocco have nearly doubled over the last decade. I work with projects in international development and can look for possibilities in Morocco in order to return there. Morocco has seen dramatic growth in the number of community development organizations established since the beginning of the 1990s. Marc works in education and can market himself as a teacher for either Jewish or French schools.

JEWISH IDENTITY IN THE PATH OF GLOBAL MIGRATION

Religious Identity Through Practice

Associating continuity in Jewish identity with existential meaning for the individual in a life of movement does not mean that religious practice and, implicitly, participation in religious institutions and customs are not important. For example, Marc had each of his sons circumcised though he does not keep Kosher or attend services. In each of the places I have lived, I have attended services for High Holidays and occasionally during the year. I also had my son circumcised and joined a synagogue in Manchester, England, after he was born.

I asked Emmanuel if following the religion was important for being Jewish. He answered that certainly practice figured into the experience of being Jewish:

> Yes, that is one point. If you are a Jew, you don't have to be a crazy orthodox, but respect Jewish law. You don't have to be a fanatic, but respect Yom Kippur, Rosh Hashanah, you know the law. If you just say your name, but you do not respect the law, then you are saying you are a Jew like you are English. I have some clients [tourists] who come but they don't respect anything. But they are proud to be a Jew. Religion for them is a second or third category . . . For some Jews, to do Shabbat is not the first category. But for me, respect for the religion is first category. I am a Jew. I like to respect something because I want to feel it in my heart. I want to feel it in my heart that I am a Jew.

He went on to say that he has started to attend services more, asking rhetorically, "Why should I waste four hours in front of the television set? I can spend the four hours in schul."

Certainly, Jews settled in one place pick and choose the rituals they perform and the beliefs they follow. The difference between the serial migrant and someone living with more continuity is first, that for the migrant, these rituals alter between locations and places of worship and second, that the rituals may not involve in-depth or lasting social relations. For instance, Emmanuel, Marc, and I have all lived in countries where Ashkenazi Judaism predominates (England, France, and the United States) and where Sephardic

Judaism predominates (Morocco, mixed in Israel). When I asked him if place made a difference in his practice, Emmanuel commented that he studied Ashkenazi Judaism in England and maintained a more orthodox lifestyle.

> Well, before (in England), I was very religious. I changed when I came back to Morocco. I was brought up more Ashkenazi, with things Ashkenazi, than Sephardic. But no one told me I had to change. No one tells me, "It is so old-fashioned to do Yom Kippur—that was 2000 years ago." I will do Yom Kippur until the day I die.

In contrast, Moroccan Jews I knew who had spent most of their adult lives in Casablanca identified themselves solely with Sephardic practice and more specifically, attended one or two synagogues. They participated in *minyans* (minimum male attendance for a service or ritual) and hosted elaborate celebrations for Jewish holidays. North African Jews I have known who have settled in England or the United States have likewise focused their efforts on belonging to one synagogue and, implicitly, a community. They may feel ambivalent about members of the community or some of its institutions, but their efforts center on finding a place to belong.

Socially, Marc, Emmanuel, and I have all formed friendships among Jews, Muslims, and expatriates, taking advantage, I would suggest, of the status of migrant to disregard concerns for social status or accumulation of social capital. Emmanuel, because of his work, knows quite a few members of the Jewish community, but his position remains socially marginal. His contacts are not only social but also dependent upon his work, which makes him visible. He has taken advantage of being a Moroccan-English single man to form friendships with Muslim men and women. Marc, interested in developing an understanding of politics and history in Morocco, maintains friendships within the French community but also seeks the acquaintance of Moroccan-Muslim intellectuals. Like me, his friendships with Moroccan Jews relate to attending religious functions and becoming familiar, as a foreigner living in Morocco, with members of the local community.

Religious Identity as Existential Meaning

In their theorization of a diasporic Jewish identity, the Boyarins call for the "formulation of Jewish identity not as a proud resting place (hence not as a form of integrism or nativism) but as a perpetual, creative, diasporic tension" (1995, 326). They claim as their objective "a notion of Jewish identity that recuperates its genealogical moment—family, history, memory, and practice—while it problematizes claims to autochthony and indigenousness as the material base of Jewish identity" (1995, 326).

For the serial migrant, identity does contain the qualities of the "genealogical moment." Marc's identification with Judaism includes attachment to his ancestry in North Africa and his ongoing relationships with other Jews in Morocco, France, Israel, and the United States. When I asked Emmanuel about how he practices Judaism, he referred immediately to his parents and to tradition in Morocco, namely visiting a rabbi's tomb for counsel and aid:

> You know, you want to feel Jewish in your heart. I go to a rabbi's grave, a rabbi who has some power not because I think he can solve my problem. It is the faith you have in him, that can help. I go to the cemetery every Thursday to visit the graves of my mother and father. I feel very happy afterwards, I feel more relaxed. When I don't do it, I feel something very heavy on my shoulders. When I have the feeling, I have to go to the cemetery, not forced, but because I am a Jew. It comes to my mind that you have to respect the people who brought you up as a Jew.

Emmanuel's mother died several years after he returned to Morocco and his father passed away more recently. Almost all of his family has migrated to Europe, Israel, and the United States, although one brother remains in Casablanca.

Jewish identity means for the serial migrant, however, more than generational connection or perpetuation of tradition. It fills a gap in existential meaning created through migration and in particular, instability. Why Jew rather than Moroccan or English or French or Israeli? The existential meaning provided by Judaism arises out of the loss of connection to the nation-state and even to smaller ethnic-based communities. It also originates in the capacity of religion to provide, in an era where modern time is vanishing, contextualization within the vast time and space of history. As Emmanuel noted, "In Israel, you say I am an Israeli, not a Jew. Then you have some Jews who are proud to be a Jew and respect the laws. I am happy to respect the laws."

Respect for the laws or identification with a historical cultural system and body of knowledge more than a particular nation may seem to evoke, at its extreme, the core of religious fundamentalism. Certainly, leaders of Islamist movements like Abdessalam Yassine, the head of the Moroccan group Adl wal-ihsan, have glorified the "good" in following a global religion versus membership in a temporal, divisive, and ultimately corrosive nation-state. Yassine writes in *Winning the Modern World for Islam*, "Despite all the snares and difficulties, we have the capital—God's Promise—and we have the key to an Islamic future: faith and good works" (2000, 149). He goes further by claiming, "The mission of Islamists is to make hearts beat again with new faith, determine our cause and unite all wills to the work of reconstituting and reunifying. The desire is legitimate, the duty is sacred, the action is necessary for consolidating Muslim peoples in taking up the project of re-unification in order to surpass the prison-like narrowness of nation-states" (2000, 150).

If serial migrants relate to religion as a global arena surpassing the boundaries of the nation-state, they also act as supra-individuals, freer in decision-making about religion than even the citizens of a modern secular state. Social thinkers like Abdou Filali-Ansary interpret adherence to religion in a secular state as the 'interiorization" of basic principles like the Trinity or Immaculate Conception. In states like those of Europe, we now interpret the social and natural world through science and rational thought, leaving open the possibility to turn to religion for what Filali-Ansary reasons is its "true role," "that of orienting men to the meaning of their existence and to principles that should guide their action" (Filali-Ansary 2001, 111). In Morocco and other Muslim countries where poverty, inequality, and corruption throw into question the moral authority of current regimes, religion appears as a buttress for political opposition. Yet, Filali-Ansary insists, the choice to become an Islamist, or in lesser fashion, to pray five times a day or wear a veil, has become an individual choice in an increasingly modern society.

The symbols of religion have retreated from public space as modern political organization and cultural globalization have assumed control over popular images and media. For the serial migrant moving between different political systems and religious contexts, choice reflects the structure in a life of movement as much as education and culture within a Western state. Marc grew up in France and Emmanuel in England, but their own "interiorization" of Jewish principles comes as much from difficulty in identifying with a single nation-state, or a system exemplifying modern political thought and secularization, as it does from assuming modern compartmentalization of secular and religious. Therefore, both Yassine, the Islamist, and Filali-Ansari, the philosopher, can offer partial, but only partial, explanations of religious identity for a serial migrant. For someone like Emmanuel or Marc, multiple migrations diminish the lure of a nation and the strength of borders. Even identification with Israel returns to the issue of being a Jew rather than settlement.

Marc belonged to a Zionist movement in France and served in the Israeli army but he returned to France for his education and he dreams of continuing in the United States. Multiple migrations by nature relativize political systems, societies, and the integration of religion, minority cultures, and the state. Emmanuel indicated this relativization when he compared religious liberties and prejudice in England, Morocco, and Israel. Marc did the same when he compared living as a Jew in France, "a country that is still very Catholic," with living as a Jew in Israel or Morocco. "The Jews do well until they come to live together," he told me.

Jewish identity for Marc and Emmanuel has become the underpinning inspiration for action, the embodiment of freedom, because such an identity began at birth. It figures naturally into the singularity and the mobility of the migrant and into the amorphousness of the globe. Emmanuel explained to me, "Like the Arabs who do Ramadan because they were born Arab and have to, this is the same for me. If I don't do Kiddush on Shabbat, it will not be the end of the world. If I go to someone's house and the food is cooked (on Shabbat), then I will still eat it. I will not say you can't turn on the lights, and so on. I was in a Yeshiva, and I know you mustn't do that, you mustn't do that." Meaning does manifest itself through very temporal action upon the world, through the modern objective of overcoming mortality through "leaving a trace" upon the world (see Arendt 1998).

However, the migrant achieves "immortality" not through a modern act of adding to a body of knowledge or a schema of social progress, but rather from participation in "civilization," from demonstrating self-worth through a contribution to humanity in general and to the Jewish people in particular. The identification the migrant makes among existential meaning, action, and history reflects the undetermined space in which he or she lives, a space where fixed social order has diminished in weight. Inversely, positive action, demonstrated in choice of work and overt or understood personal goals, originates in the loss of symbolic order grounded in a place, and thus the loss of passivity in relation to an established order.

In theorizing the relationship between the social order and the subject, Zizek argues that "far from signaling any kind of closure which constrains the scope of the subject's intervention in advance, the bar of the Real is Lacan's way of asserting the terrifying abyss of the subject's ultimate and radical freedom, the freedom whose space is sustained by the Other's inconsistency and lack" (2000, 258). The inconsistency of the symbolic order, or the big Other, forces the subject into a process of alienation and separation: "this big Other is the name for the social Substance, for all that on account of which the subject never fully dominates the effects of his acts . . . alienation in the big Other is followed by the separation from the big Other" (253). Zizek then states, "Separation takes place when the subject realizes how the big Other is in itself inconsistent, purely virtual, 'barred,' deprived of the Thing—and fantasy is an attempt to fill out this lack of the Other, not of the subject: to (re)constitute the consistency of the big Other" (2000, 253).

We could say that the symbolic order fails the serial migrant, who not only must survive in new economic environments but also must adjust to new cultural, religious, and political hegemonies. I have lived in places where Islam, Judaism, Southern Baptism, and Anglicanism represent the majority religions; Marc, where Islam, Judaism, and Catholicism dominate. These places possess widely different political systems, from liberal market democracy to monarchy. Such differences, in religion, politics, and so on, negate the possibility of a single universality or hegemony while making contingency a function of everyday life. Consequently, social substance, the big Other, cannot determine identity in general or identification with Judaism. The absence of Determination provokes the fantasy of order, of belonging to a social world or, more specifically, what practices this belonging entails. As an example, returning to the Boyarins' project, we could compare the relationship between the social order and the subject within Zionism and multiple migrations. Contrary to the Zionist goal to "dominate" the subject through the restoration of a symbolic order actualized in political institutions, legal regulations, and settlement of land, the Jewish migrant fantasizes of a Judaism actualized through the actions of the subject. Emmanuel wants to feel in his heart he is a Jew, a desire he fulfils in part through religious rituals and in part through a mission, through existential purpose that he sees as inseparable from his religious identity.

A Talmudic saying dictates, "In the place where there is no leader, strive to become a leader" (Newman 1945, 249). Another states, "'And the man became a living soul.' This teaches us that we should make vital the soul, which God has given to us" (Newman 1945, 442). When Emmanuel moved to Morocco, he elected to shift careers as well as location. He had thought to become a kosher butcher in England but upon coming to Morocco, decided to work for the Jewish community. He now works both for a community institution and as a tour guide for Jewish sites. More personally, he has taken it upon himself to restore far-flung synagogues deteriorating from neglect. Working as a tour guide and, more explicitly, restoring decaying synagogues stem from a desire for belonging to Judaism and the Jewish people. In circular fashion, Emmanuel finds existential meaning as a Jew because he can take advantage of his unique position as an English-speaking tour guide to fill a void of leadership and human vitality. The ability to fill the void, or being a Moroccan Jew able to negotiate with American and European tourists to donate money to restoration efforts, reinforces its existential importance and thus the centrality of Jewishness for his identity. Emmanuel told me, "For me, respect for the religion is first category [primary concern]. I am a Jew. I like to respect something because I want to feel it in my heart. I want to feel it in my heart that I am a Jew."

How he "feels in his heart" I argue reflects the separation Zizek discusses, the subject who, in the absence of social reinforcement of the qualities of being Jewish, has made a fantasy of what manifests Jewishness the center of his emotional stability and personal fulfillment. More directly, the fantasy integrates temporal location and existence with transcendent fulfillment. This integration takes place in *makom*, the Hebrew word for place, or what Amir Eshel defines as "the exterior marker of an arbitrary 'anywhere'" that also "marks the sublime itself." Makom "signifies both the plain inhabitance of space and the urge to, the longing for, being in the ultimate sacred space, being one with God" (2003, 121).

Eshel interprets the writings of Edmond Jabès as an example of makom, where the book occupies a space between the script on a page and the beyond. "According to Jabès, for the Jew living out the Jewish condition, the book is the only place where he or she can find truth, can be. This place is indeed Israel, not the geographical locus but the Israel of Jewish history, the age-old dream of Israel, the idea of *makom*" (2003, 134). Wrenched from his place of birth, Egypt, by the Suez crisis and the inability to stay as a Jew, Jabès replicates his predicament in his writing in order to overcome it. "Like the Jew who lives between places, not in them, the text, the book, is located in between: between the cosmic void and the slant figures printed on the white page" (134). Jabès can find a home in the space between spaces that the book provides, a nonplace that connects the art of writing with spiritual grace, the beyond that gives meaning anywhere and everywhere. For Jabès, "the place of revelation is everywhere, that it can be folded like a notebook and carried anywhere, that *makom* exists first and foremost in the poetic idea, the hope, the constant striving to arrive at the unreachable while dwelling in the cosmos" (136).

Not "settled" in one place or another, I personally strive for location in the world and meaning for my existence through my work. My efforts lie not specifically in poetry but in carrying on the principles of social progress encouraged in modernity but diminished with the decline of the nation-state (Cohen 2004). However, like Jabès, I interpret my work for community development in the United States, Morocco, India, and England as linking my place, the place I have created for myself in the changes my work initiates, with spiritual purpose. Marc has spent years in Morocco as a student and teacher. Arguably, he invests his presence there with meaning by representing the Jew and Israeli in Morocco. He strives to present an argument for some Israeli actions while demonstrating that Jews/Israelis possess a range of political opinions. He has also attributed the same motivation to me, saying, "There is always a reason for choosing a place [meaning my reason for selecting Morocco as the site for dissertation research]." Acting for change in order to achieve existential meaning thus translates as well into presentation as a Jew for Others. Marc represents Jews in a Muslim-Arab-Berber country. Emmanuel is a Moroccan Jew who cares about his heritage for Jews from Europe and the United States.

Once, when I asked Emmanuel how he defines himself, he concentrated on distinguishing his behavior and beliefs from those of the members of his tour groups:

Cohen: You know some people define themselves as an American, a Jew, how do you define yourself?

Emmanuel: First, I tell him I am a Jew, then I was born here in Morocco. In our tradition here in Morocco, we have to respect Yom Kippur, Rosh Hashanah, and Sukkot. If I have clients over Hanukah—one time I did have clients—I still go to light the candles. Some of my clients, they say they are proud to be Jews, but to me, they are Jews in name only. They say we don't want to do anything religious. They follow the Christian rules more than the Jewish ones. They eat a turkey at Thanksgiving and they have a Christmas tree at Christmas. But when I ask about Hanukah, they say well, we don't do that.

When I asked him if this kind of negligence upsets him, he replied affirmatively. He mentioned a mutual friend of ours, saying that she had gone with her boyfriend to an event rather than eat Passover seder with him. He feared that she had eaten bread. "You know, you can go somewhere but just don't eat bread. She said that she did not eat bread. [She] is very reform, but even she did not eat bread. She asks on Shabbat about the laws—'I want to know what is this law, and this law'—but she will not follow the laws."

RELIGION AND COSMOPOLITICS

Relating the experience of the individual serial migrant to belief in religion has several potential implications for theory and policy. First, the perception of religion differs from those who settle in one area or another, raising the question if religious practice and, more significantly, the existential importance of religion will change with increased migration. Like migrants forming a community in a new home, serial migrants adhere to religion as a method of maintaining stability. However, the latter look to religion to invest individual action with purpose in a specific place while the former focus on giving a place meaning through participation in institutions, social networks, and rituals. The immigrants described by Ong and Waters engage in international social networks that span from Hong Kong or Taiwan to Canada and perceive migration as a legal process to secure political options and financial benefit. Likewise, immigrants to Israel may move there in pursuit of the benefits of citizenship, the desire to support the state of Israel, or the fulfillment of more radical religious-based ideology, all of which materialize into practice through well-established, centralized operations.

The serial migrant, on the other hand, moves as an individual or as a nuclear family, in the case of the people mentioned here, for a combination of personal and professional reasons. Movement reflects motivation to leave a particular place, where perhaps relationships or work have been disappointing, and search for new opportunities, often in unlikely places (such as Jewish tourism in Morocco or a lectureship in Northern England).

Interpreting the subjective position of such a migrant may help us to negotiate debates about the political implications of globalization and the position of religion in relation to the decline of the nation-state. Theorists of globalization like David Held argue for the creation of global institutions that can regulate truly international issues, such as the environment or human rights. His philosophy relies on the precept that "It would be wholly fallacious to conclude . . . that the politics of local communities or national democratic communities will be (or should be) wholly eclipsed by the new forces of political globalization. To assume this would be to misunderstand the very complex, variable and uneven impact of regional and global processes on political life. Of course, certain problems and policies will properly remain the responsibility of local governments and national states; but others will be recognized as appropriate for specific regions, and still others—such as elements of the environment, global security concerns, world health questions and economic regulation—will be seen to need new institutional arrangements to address them." (Held 2000, 407).

Held, like others who discuss the relationship between cosmopolitanism and democracy or progressive politics (Wilson 1998, 351–60), remains abstract and overarching in his vision. He analyzes institutional arrangements through different layers of social order, international, national, local; similarly, Etienne Balibar describes Europe as "overlapping sheets or layers, and that is specificity in this overlapping itself: to be precise, an East, a West, and a South" (Balibar 1998, 225).

Yet, in these visions of political structures based on overlapping interests and fading boundaries, where would we situate someone like Emmanuel, who expresses identity in religious terms and does not participate in political life? Marc, Emmanuel, and I all feel attachment to our country of birth as well as several other countries and we all sympathize with progressive causes, from gay rights to a just peace agreement in the Middle East. Would we then be regarded as potential participants in the global, progressive institutions that Held supports? If I view expressing Jewish identity as fundamental to my own sense of existential purpose in the cosmos, as an underlying justification for my commitment to social service, then am I a likely candidate for a cosmopolitan democrat? Inversely, if I translate my religious origin into individual existential meaning and thus location in the world, then do I prove or disprove the relevance of organized religion today? Emmanuel told me, "You have to have faith in the religion, or you are not a Jew. To feel like I am a Jew, I have to respect some of the religion." I have some faith, like Emmanuel, at least enough to respect some of the customs and basic principles as well as the rich history of the Jewish people.

I suggest that we think first about the existential meaning and subjective position of populations in different relations to migration and settlement before we continue with abstract discussions of cosmopolitanism. I believe it is unclear whether or not Emmanuel, Marc, and I would lead the movement toward cosmopolitan democracy based on our mobility and changing attachments. Our contributions have remained individual, even if they contribute to larger efforts, from the restoration of Jewish monuments in fading communities to living as a Jew in the Arab world. My own work in social theory and social development has concentrated on autonomy from state structures and organized movements. I would argue that a progressive politics considering the potential of migration, communication, and cultural flows for civic engagement must first consider how individuals, constituted as they are within these trends, find meaning. We can develop a politics from there, and not the other way around.

REFERENCES

Arendt, Hannah. 1998. *The Human Condition*. Chicago: University of Chicago Press.
Auerbach, Jerold S. 2001. *Are We One? Jewish Identity in the United States and Israel*. New Brunswick, N.J.: Rutgers University Press.
Badiou, Alain. 2001. *Ethics: An Essay on the Understanding of Evil*. Trans. Peter Hallward. London: Verso.
Benbassa, Esther and Attias, Jean-Christophe. 2004. *Jews and Their Future: A Conversation on Judaism and Jewish Identities*. London: Zed Books.
Boyarin, Daniel. 1997. *Unheroic Conduct: The Rise of Heterosexuality and the Invention of the Jewish Man*. Berkeley: University of California Press.
Boyarin, Daniel and Boyarin, Jonathan. 1995. Diaspora: Generation and the Ground of Jewish Identity. *Identities*. Kwame Anthony Appiah and Henry Louis Gates, Jr. (eds.). Chicago: University of Chicago Press.
Butler, Judith et al. 2000. *Contingency, Hegemony, Universality: Contemporary Dialogues on the Left*. London: Verso.
Charme, Stuart Z. 2000. Varieties of Authenticity in Contemporary Jewish Identity. *Jewish Social Studies* vol. 6, no. 2, 133.
Clifford, James. 1994. Diasporas. *Cultural Anthropology* vol. 9, no. 3, 302–38.
Cohen, Shana. 2004. *Searching for a Different Future*. Durham: Duke University Press.

Eshel, Amir. 2003. Between Cosmos and Makom: Inhabiting the World and Searching for the Sacred Space in Jewish Literature. *Jewish Social Studies* vol. 9, no. 3, 121–38.

Filali-Ansary, Abdou. 2001. *Par Souci de Clarte*. Casablanca: Editions Le Fennec.

Freedman, Samuel. 2000. *Jew vs. Jew*. New York: Simon & Schuster.

Gitelman, Zvi. 1998. The Decline of the Diaspora Jewish Nation: Boundaries, Content, and Jewish Identity. *Jewish Social Studies* vol. 4, no. 2, 112.

Golan, Daphna et al. 1999. The Jewish Diaspora, Israel, and Jewish Identities: A Dialogue. *The South Atlantic Quarterly* vol. 98, no. 1/2 (Winter).

Goldstein, Sidney and Goldstein, Alice. 1996. *Jews on the Move: Implications for Jewish Identity*. New York: SUNY Press.

Hazony, Yoram. 2001. *A History of Zionism and Post-Zionism*. New York: Basic Books.

Hecht, Michael L. and Faulkner, Sandra L. 2000. Sometimes Jewish, Sometimes Not: The Closeting of Jewish American Identity. *Communication Studies* vol. 51, no. 4 (Winter), 372–87.

Held, David. 2000. Regulating Globalization: The Reinvention of Politics. *International Sociology*. June, vol. 15, no. 2, 394–408.

International Labor Office. 2004. Report VI: Toward a Fair Deal forMigrant Workers in the Global Economy. From International Labor Conference 92nd Session. Geneva: ILO.

Levy, Andre. 2003. Notes from Jewish-Muslim Relationships: Revisiting the Vanishing Moroccan Jewish Community. *Cultural Anthropology*, vol. 18, no. 3, 365–397.

Newman, Louis I. 1945. *The Talmudic Anthology: Tales & Teachings of the Rabbis*. New York: Behrman House Publishers.

Ong, Aihwa. 1998. Flexible Citizenship among Chinese Cosmopolitans. *Cosmopolitics: Thinking and Feeling Beyond the Nation*. Cheah, Pheng and Robbins, Bruce (eds.). Minneapolis: University of Minnesota Press.

Waters, Johanna. 2003. Flexible Citizens? Transnationalism and citizenship amongst economic immigrants in Vancouver. *The Canadian Geographer* vol. 47, no. 3, 219–34.

Whitfield, Stephen J. 2002. Enigmas of Modern Jewish Identity. *Jewish Social Studies* vol. 2, no. 2/3 (Winter).

Wilson, Rob. 1998. A New Cosmopolitanism Is in the Air: Some Dialectical Twists and Turns. *Cosmopolitics*. Cheah, Pheng and Robbins, Bruce (eds.). Minneapolis: University of Minnesota Press.

Yassine, Abdessalam. 2000. *Winning the Modern World for Islam*. Iowa City, Iowa: Justice & Spirituality Publishing.

Zizek, Slavoj. 2000. Di Capo Senza Fine. *Contingency, Hegemony, Universality*. Butler, Judith (ed.). London: Verso.

6

Errance, Migration, and Male Sex Work

On the Socio-cultural Sustainability of a Third Space

Nick Mai

N: Why are so many young people leaving Morocco to come here?

A: There are people who came for money, people who came for freedom, people who came for both. I came for freedom.

N: Why freedom? Is there no freedom over there?

A: No, there is no freedom there . . . the police, people, no work . . . nothing . . . the family . . . no accommodation . . .

N: When did you leave home?

A: I was thirteen to fourteen years old . . . alone . . . I went to Spain . . . from Marrakech . . . I went first to Tangier . . . three months . . . waiting for *la suerte* (luck) to come . . .

N: What did you do in Tangier to survive? How many times did you try and go to Spain?

A: Fourteen times . . .

N: Did they always repatriate you?

A: Yes, each time . . . and each time I returned to Spain . . . I should have tried to go somewhere else . . . because Spain has a bastard government . . . I have spent five years here now and have no papers, no passport, nothing . . . this is not a government . . . this is shit. They are all racist . . .

N: But why didn't you try to go through the centers for minors, they say that they have ways to give documents . . .

A: That is not true . . . and also if I have to stay in a center, I could have well stayed at home, no? I told you in the beginning, I left home to be free . . . in a center there is no freedom . . . you have to sleep at 11 o'clock with the chickens . . .

N: How are you going to fix your papers?

A: Leave the papers . . . they are never going to be fixed . . . I spent five years looking for the papers . . . the papers . . . the papers . . . all the time. . . . I can't anymore. If papers come . . . they have to come alone . . . all the way to my wallet . . . if they don't come, fuck them . . . . If Spain gives me the papers . . . right now . . . I call my family . . . and stuff . . . but if not . . . well . . . someday I'll kill a son of a bitch and spend the rest of my days in jail. What can I do, keep running after them . . . I can't . . . anymore . . .

N: And when were you in Amsterdam and Paris . . .

A: I was twice, last spring and when I was fifteen.

N: And how did you find it?

A: De puta Madre. Amsterdam is better than this puta de España. . . . It is very good . . .

N: Were you in Paris as well?

A: Yes, I was in Paris, Marseille . . .

N: And why did you leave Amsterdam?

A: I did not have anywhere to stay . . . it was cold . . .

N: And why did you go?

A: Because I was tired . . . tired of this country . . .

N: In what way is it good in Amsterdam?

A: If I had a house where to stay I would not return, I swear . . . I would not return here . . . Hombre, if I had papers I would go and live there . . . I liked shops there . . . what you can buy . . . If I had the money I would buy these thing in Holland . . . a Mercedes . . . a beautiful home . . . a blond girlfriend . . . and fuck the rest . . . If I can have just one week like that . . . then people can kill me . . . I don't care . . . a beautiful blonde . . . with nice little tits . . . I swear . . . that makes me hot. . . . And now we are at the bridge . . . there is no house, no blonde, nothing . . . no tenemos suerte hermano . . . (I'm not lucky brother) But it must happen . . . if Spain does not give me any money . . . I will send somebody to the cemetery . . . I will cut somebody's fat barriga coño . . .

N: You are very aggressive . . . why are you so angry?

A: Coño . . . what am I going to do . . . return home empty-handed? I can't, primo . . .

N: Why can't you go back . . .

A: Tiengo mi cara . . . hombre, no soy sin verguenza . . . It's five years since I left . . . for nothing . . .

N: Why, what do you have to do? What do you care about what people think? Do you have to have a Mercedes to go back?

A: This is the problem, this explains everything . . . I don't care about people . . . I am talking about my family . . . coño . . . I return there after I have not called or anything . . . Where have you been? I have been to Spain . . . mama . . . And why didn't you stay at home with us? Why did you go to Spain? What will I say, eh primo? With nothing in my hands to come back with . . .

—A., twenty, from Morocco (interviewed in Seville, Spain)

THE PERSONAL GENEALOGY OF RESEARCH

There is a direct connection between my own life and the topics I've decided to study in my research. My experience of migration is as central to my academic life as it is to who I am as a person. Here, I will explore this by first writing about myself and then writing this self into the emotional and cognitive texture of my research experience. Then, I will write myself out of that texture to further analyze how my trajectory is not equivalent to my research, which involves people whose trajectories are not similar to my own. I will start this self-reflexive practice by attempting to reconstruct *a posteriori* the genealogy of my own migratory project as it emerged during my adolescent years in Northern Italy. By "migratory project" I mean not so much the actual physical and geographical displacement but the wider discursive processes and practices of cultural consumption through which prospective young migrants imagine themselves with reference to supervening social needs at home. In order to understand the complexity of the condition of young migrants one has to acknowledge their subjection to different, competing, and contradictory regimes of subjectification (Rose 1996, 128–50). These originate from the increasingly fragmented and contradictory social and cultural contexts of origin, which in the last twenty years have been increasingly open to the cultural products from different countries through electronic media, in particular television. The encounter between these different narratives of subjectification fosters deep dynamics of social change. The phenomenon of youth migration is a manifestation of these dynamics.

In my research, I address the interconnection between youth identity formation, media consumption, and migration. I have studied how people construct their identities in terms of new cultural formations and identified a "migratory cultural formation" emerging out of connections between media consumption and migration (Grossberg 1992, 70–71). I found that by entering into a "migratory cultural formation" young people seek alternatives to the kinds of subjectivities available to them in the places they grew up (2001, 95–109).

My own experience of migration highlights the importance of media in terms of this kind of cultural formation. Media lead people to project themselves into alternative cultural spheres and then to migrate to places associated with media narratives and images. During my own adolescence, the cinema opened up new worlds to me. Films provided me with a refuge from things in my life I was unable to deal with. I spent entire afternoons at the local repertoire cinema. As I watched "Queen Christina" (1933), starring Greta Garbo, I remember feeling deeply moved when she said, "Sometimes one can miss a place one has never been to . . ." I could relate to that longing for a place of freedom, peace. I also felt that longing. In my diary I wrote:

> None of my friends can understand why I like so much to stay under water when we go to the swimming pool. They don't have to go back to where I go when they emerge. That is why. When I swim through the blue water, over the blue tiles and below the surface, I feel far from everything . . . My sight is blurred, but I can see things better. I can only hear my breath. I wish I never had to go back there, to those compromises, those expectations, those rules, that noise, I feel free and safe here, swimming in between, in the company of my own hopes and dreams. From here, these dreams seem solid and the reality liquid, would not that be better if it was like that?

I was fourteen, just starting to come to terms with my homosexuality and coping with a difficult family environment. One evening I asked my mother and father to go and see a "gay" movie that had been advertised on television: *Another Country* (1984), starring Rupert Everett. Based on a play by Julian Mitchell, the film explores the effects of public school life on Guy Bennet (Rupert Everett) in the 1930s. The film follows how Bennet's identity as a homosexual and his unwillingness to "play the game" led him to reject his own country for another, Soviet Russia. This story mirrored my own. I too wanted to find a country where I could be the person I felt I was. I began to locate this dream space in London.

At an age where being gay led me to think that gay was all I was, I found confirmation that England was the place for me in British films, pop music, and novels. I read Italian newspapers to seek out news about the UK, always on the lookout for more information about Boy George, Jimmy Somerville, or Marc Almond. I was indifferent to Italian politics, but passionate about the political struggles in the UK during the Thatcher years. I felt that I had been born in the wrong country. I felt English inside. I was certain that English people would understand me better than Italians. Only by moving to the UK could I be free to be myself. I saw things in terms of a choice: I could be either Italian and straight or English and gay. I envisaged no possibility of a third space beyond this binary gridlock.

As I was growing up, I befriended English teachers living in my town. I found myself saying to myself and to other people in English things that I could not even think about in Italian. In English I felt that I could finally understand myself. So I went to London to study English every summer. In London, I envisaged a path of total assimilation. I tried to do away with my Italian accent. I tried to pass as English. Indeed, I had decided that I *was* English. It was only when I lived in England for a year that I started to see that "being gay" was only a part of "being me." Only once I moved to England could I start to accept that I was actually born in Italy and that I was Italian. I went home to visit my grandmother over the holidays. It was Sunday lunch and she was serving steaming *tortellini in brodo*. As I sat in her kitchen watching steam condense on the windows, I enjoyed a glass of red wine. I was vaguely aware of the hypnotic hum of the television in the background. My grandmother, my mother, and I all started quarrelling about something unimportant, but after a couple of seconds we all broke into laughter. I noticed how unified we were in the rhythm of our emotions. I thought, "I get angry the way they do, I reason in the way they do, I even breathe the way they do." I remember this moment because it signaled the start of a slow process of repositioning of London and Englishness in my mental landscape. I still wanted to live in the UK, but gradually this came to be because I was able to carry out my research there. Little by little, England didn't have to be a place of utopian perfection. Instead, it became a place that offered me specific opportunities for self-development. It became a place on Earth instead of an abstract, dreamed-up "elsewhere." As I started breaking out of the world of binary opposition, I ventured into the world of heterogeneity and complexity introduced by the conjunction "and." It was possible to be Italian *and* gay *and* English *and* . . . all of the other things at the same time? Wouldn't it be better? Isn't it the way it is anyway?

In 1997, I settled in London to work on a Ph.D. in media and cultural studies. In my dissertation I examined the role of Italian television in attracting Albanian young migrants to Italy. The choice of the topic was obviously subliminally linked to my own experience. By asking Albanian young people about their own imagined trajectories, I could relate to my own experience of voluntary mental displacement onto an alternative cultural landscape. Moreover, their experience of repression and denial of desire was echoing many important passages of my own history. I could engage with this topic, because it explained parts of me to me. Italy had been for Albanians what London had been for me, a utopian world where "being you" was attainable. While I did my research in Albania, I reconciled myself with Italy. Confronting the Albanian scenario made me relativize my perception of having been subject to a crippling renunciation to desire. The relatively emancipatory role of Italian popular culture in the emergence of alternative understandings of youth and mobility in Albania made me question my own representation of myself as a victim of conservative populism and repression.

Apart from the banal relief brought about by witnessing worse experiences of repression and suffering than my own, what I call the "trip to India" syndrome, other considerations brought me out of the double bind of host and home countries. In Albania, I became the director of four youth centers for a development program promoted by the Italian government. By working with Italian colleagues, I experienced a version of Italian identity that could include me. I met Italians critical of Italy's conservatism who did not subscribe to a predigested, essentialist canon of Italianness. I could share my perspectives with these people without being seen as something exotic or "special." This led me to see that I could be myself in Italy too. As I started feeling increasingly comfortable within Italianness, my relationship to the UK changed. The adolescent drive to assimilate started losing its grip on me. My Italian accent resurfaced when I spoke English. I accepted that, far from having been born in "another country," I was actually born in a particular place and time and my feeling of being different was related to questions of political as well as sexual dissidence. I started to see that I was simply a leftist Italian migrant working in the UK. Oh, *and* gay too, by the way.

In my research I have continued to explore the interconnection among media consumption, the emergence of social mobility, and migration. I have also been studying how bodies and gendered identities are negotiated by marginal migrant groups in terms of survival strategies (sex work, stealing, and drug smuggling). In Albania, Italy was associated with a utopian understanding of the West in terms of a universe of freedom and easy-to-attain material plenty. The aspects of Western popular culture that have the most appeal for prospective young migrants are those referring to an individualized and hedonistic lifestyle, which implicitly challenges the patriarchal, authoritarian and conservative morals of their society. Whereas their parents seem to accept the renunciation to individual pleasure if they contradict existing social norms, most young people want to enjoy a plurality of lifestyles. They want to engage in sex, leisure, and education like their peers in Western Europe. In this respect, foreign television-watching is very important within the Albanian socio-cultural landscape. Europe provides the narrative and visual scripts according to which alternative models of personhood, lifestyles, and regimes of everyday life are imagined with reference to the local context. This prepares for migration, if migration is understood as a condition of subjective deterritorialization, as an uprooting of subjectivity from the narrative and visual scripts that have previously shaped it. The search for new articulations of personal identity is ambivalently embedded in Albanian young people's migratory project. For many, migrating to Italy has been a way of mediating between their "late modern" desire to experience new aspects of their selves (freedom), and their socially more established and hardship-bound roles as loyal sons and daughters, sacrificing their lives for the survival of the family unit (money). During the 1990s, the utopian sensibility structuring the migratory cultural formation evolved into a more pragmatic one. This was consistent with a more realistic cultural construction of the Western social and cultural context and of the actual possibilities it offered to migrants.

In another project I carried out from 2002 to 2004, I explored Albanian and Romanian cultural constructions of masculinity, sex work, and the risk of HIV/AIDS diffusion both at home and among migrants. The research showed that for both gay and straight Albanian and Romanian young men, sex work is a way to reconcile their economic priorities and needs with their understandings of the relation between their gendered selves and their involvement in sexual practices. While for young straight men selling sex to other men can be coherent with their own performative construction of masculinity in penetrative and active terms (i.e. according to the "I am only active in the sexual intercourse, therefore I am still a man" discourse), for the few interviewees who recognize themselves privately as gay, sex work is a possibility to earn money as well as to experience previously unknown aspects of, and relations to, their selves. However, the emancipation from the stigma attached to homosexuality and sex work was never complete as all interviewees still had to present themselves to their families—and often to themselves too—as straight honorable men for fear of being rejected and in order not to jeopardize their family's reputation within the wider community (Mai 2004, 45–58). The following two excerpts, from twenty- and eighteen-year-old Romanian men living in Rome, illustrate the problems encountered by young men involved in selling sex and maintaining a masculine identity.

N: Did you ever feel scared to become a queer . . . by fucking all of these men . . . perhaps sometimes you think about men when you masturbate?

A: No, never . . . I like women too much . . . but I know Romanian men who changed . . . who became gay . . . by doing this . . . they were living with a queer . . . little by little they gave in . . . "come on it is just a kiss . . . I give you more money if you let me fuck you" . . . then they tried many times . . . the first time for money . . . and then . . . because they liked it . . . that is how it happens . . .

N: Is this the difference between a queer and a man . . . that you get it up your arse and kiss?

A: I know what you mean, I think, many people say that if your cock goes up you must a bit queer as well . . .

N: Who says this?

A: Older men . . . that is what they say . . . a man is a man, if your cock goes up . . . you must be a bit queer as well . . .

N: And what do you think about that?

A: Well . . . what do I think about that . . . I think maybe I am a bit . . .

N: Really?

A: Yes, really . . . I thought about it . . . I mean, it is true that my cock is always up . . . it is enough for me to look at a girl . . . and it goes up . . . but it is also true that it goes up with men . . .

N: But are there customers with whom it is a bit easier to go? Nicer than other?

A: Yes, there are . . .

N: And do they pay the same or less . . .

A: No, they pay the same . . . sometimes they pay more because they are nicer people and more generous . . . many people want just the company . . . they take you out, to talk . . . There is an Italian older guy who takes me out for entire weekends, he says he wants to stay in the company of a nice young man . . . I think he likes me because I talk to him a lot . . . I like talking to him because he is older and he knows life more . . .

N: And what do you talk about . . .

A: Well, things you can talk about . . . those you can't talk about you just can't . . .

N: And what can't you talk about?

A: Well, for example, what other guys do and not do . . . we don't even tell each other, between Romanians . . . like "this one makes this and that . . . the other one makes this and that . . ." These are things even we Romanians don't know about ourselves . . . I would never tell another guy that I was passive with a customer . . . I am too ashamed . . . I would never tell another Romanian . . . but I have no problem at all talking to an Italian about it . . .

N: So, you are telling me that you are passive as well, sometimes?

(He looks at me a bit nervous . . . frightened.)

A: No . . .

N: Ah, ok, so it was only an example . . .

A: Mmmmhh . . . I know many Italian people here and they are passive as well, they give blow jobs . . . we Romanians are different . . .

This the beginning of the second interview excerpt.

N: Did anything change in the way you see life . . .

B: Yes . . . to be honest I think differently about queers now . . . I also think that maybe we are a bit queer too . . . no really . . . we always go with them . . . I am a bit afraid . . . Sometimes after I go with one of them . . . if I did not come . . . I jerk myself off and I convince myself that it is disgusting . . . I want to get it into my head that it is only disgusting . . . that I did not like it at all . . . I am afraid that by thinking about it I end up by liking it . . . Sometimes I can not even masturbate . . . because those faces . . . those images of customers come out . . . You are jerking off and you are thinking about fucking a woman and suddenly these other things come about you fucking a man . . . that's when you have to stop . . . other wise by doing it you become queer . . .

N: Or maybe it is the opposite? That you end up fucking queers because you like it a little bit?

B: It is possible . . . I think that a gay is born gay . . . maybe you can discover being gay after thirty years . . . At some stage I started worrying that I became gay . . . I stopped fucking gay people . . . It's happened to me with a trans . . . I started thinking a lot about fucking him and I used to come thinking about him . . . Some of them are very beautiful . . .

N: So this scared you . . .

B: Yes, a lot . . . for me it is a very bad thing being gay . . . I don't want to become gay . . . I mean if you are gay you are gay, if you are not you are not . . .

N: So you should not worry, according to what you say . . .

B: But I want to marry, I do not want to become like those old men paying us for sex . . .

N: But not every old gay man pays for sex . . .

B: But how do they do?

N: I mean look at normal men . . . they do not all pay young women . . . What do I know . . . they masturbate . . . they try and go with women of their age . . . sometimes they pay for younger women . . .

B: But I would accept paying a young woman but not paying a young man . . .

N: It depends on what you like . . . I think you need to have the courage to look into what you like in life . . . and go for it, no?

B: Yes . . . well, maybe I do not have that courage . . . I do not even want to think about this . . . I don't want to talk about this anymore . . .

The very same ambivalence in challenging (hetero)normativity is mirrored in the hegemony of survivalist and familistic narratives over narratives of hedonistic fulfillment and individual realization. When asked to explain in some detail their own reasons for migrating or to get involved in sex work, the majority of interviewees referred almost exclusively to the necessity to survive economically (i.e., according to the "I am only doing it for the money" discourse) and the desire to conform to a "normal" living standard: to have the money to build a new house at home, to marry, get a "proper" job, and have a car. However, in semistructured interviews, life histories, and ethnographic observation, a much more complex and ambivalent situation is revealed, as this excerpt from a twenty-four-year-old Romanian man living in Rome illustrates.

N: Why are there so many Romanians in Europe? I mean young Romanian men?

B: Yes, everywhere you go, you find one, I have been to Belgium, to Germany, to France, and it was full of them everywhere! Well, I think it is because you cannot enjoy yourself in Romania. You work as a dog for 60, 80, 100 Euro maximum . . . they are enough just to pay the bills and the rent . . . not even for the food. And then what you do . . . My life here is different . . . I spend up to 2 000 Euro each month in drinks, disco, women . . . Especially in the beginning . . . I used to pay everybody a drink . . . my Romanian friends . . .

N: Do you send some money home to your family?

B: Well, I send 200 Euro each month . . . it is quite a lot for her . . . She can have a better life . . . Now she has a better life . . . she does not have to worry too much about the money . . .

N: Does this make you feel better about yourself?

A: Of course man . . . that is the reason why I am here . . . (His voice becomes deeper and his face sadder.)

N: But you said that you came here to have fun . . .

A: But that was more in the beginning . . . now it is a bit more complicated . . . when I feel nostalgic about my mother and about Romania I go to the disco and drink . . . And then I phone them . . . it hurts man, it hurts . . . I haven't seen them for a long time . . . almost three years . . .

N: Why did you wait all of this time . . . the documents?

B: No, no, now I can go when I want . . . it is just that with the money I spend to go home I can help my mother for two or three months . . .

N: But you spend 2 000 Euro per month on drinks, come on now . . . and then you don't have the money to go home . . . there is something a bit contradictory here, no?

B: (He smiles.) But I cannot stay here without food . . . or drinks . . . or going out at night, no?

N: Well, it seems like you are not really depriving yourself of these things . . . come on . . .

B: You know how it is . . . I have to eat out as I can't cook . . . the mobile . . . the clothes . . . and then I have to go to the disco . . . if you meet a girl you have to show her you have the money, no? Especially if she is Italian, they are very racist and for them to go out with you is like going out with a beggar . . .

B: When I called my Romanian friends living in Italy they said, come, there is everything, freedom, girls, money . . . then I arrived here in Rome and all of their mobiles were off . . . I slept in the park and there you go. . . . They change the fucking sim card or even the city . . . And before then they say things like "tell me what woman do you want to fuck . . . Black, Chinese, white? What do you want to eat?" And then nobody is there . . . You sleep in the park, walk around the station, and eat nothing until you fuck the first queer . . . you understand?

N: And why do they say that?

B: Well, because they want to tell you that they are good, that they are rich, that they have a luxury apartment . . . everybody admires them in Romania, but then they live in the same shit places we end up living and they are ashamed to tell . . . they don't want people at home to know . . . we do the same . . . when I phone home I don't tell them I did not eat or I am lonely . . . I tell them I am fine, I am happy, I work, and I have a house . . . Now things are changing . . . people start knowing a little what happens.

It was during this second project that I became interested in the relation between the intrapsychic and the physical mobility of errant young male migrants. I saw how for many young people the impossibility to reconcile their ambivalence vis-à-vis their sexual orientation with their affiliation to their country of origin into a coherent and morally acceptable life trajectory was consistent with an "errant" mobility pattern. This was how I became interested in *errance*, or wandering, of young people from the Balkans and North Africa into the European Union and the strategies of survival, prostitution in particular, this is consistent with.

Since June 2004, I have been the main research for a project on "Male Prostitution: Strategies of Survival and Risk Behavior of Errant Young People." Although the initial idea was to focus on young Moroccan migrants, after a first series of reconnaissance missions in Belgium, France, Greece, Germany, Morocco, the Netherlands, Spain, Tunisia, and Turkey, it became evident that the places and practices of errant mobility were shared by many different migrant groups. Romanians, Algerians, Kurds, Moroccans, and Tunisians were the main groups involved in this form of mobility and in these strategies of survival. We broadened the scope of the research to look at the migration experience of unaccompanied minors and errant young people from the Balkans (Romania and Albania), North Africa (Algeria, Morocco, and Tunisia), and Turkey into the European Union (Belgium, France, Germany, Italy, the Netherlands, and Spain). Prostitution is one of the main strategies of survival for these young people. We are trying to look at the cultural, social, economic, and psycho-social determinants of errance, which means both "drifting" from normativity and "wandering" in search of adventure. Errance is a social practice involving multiple levels of social, cultural, and affective deterritorialization and social exclusion. It involves either the impossibility of settling or an unwillingness to reterritorialize.

ERRANCE

Errant young people are a potentially vulnerable social group in three main respects. When they smuggle themselves from one country to another they become easy prey for the criminal networks that provide illegal transportation services, especially when they are minors. These networks often force them to beg, sell sex and drugs, or work in sweatshops. Their lack of life experience and inability to understand Western capitalist societies makes them extremely marginal. It also leads many of them to develop an extremely utopian conception of what migration to the West will involve. They idealize the West as a place where everything is possible. Once confronted with reality, many of these young migrants experience strong feelings of disappointment and as a result continue to engage in sex work, theft, and drug smuggling as the only viable ways to sustain their utopian life trajectories.

The condition of potential vulnerability characterizing errant youth is exacerbated by the contrast between different cultural constructions of adolescence in relation to different socio-economic and cultural backgrounds. Whereas European social services address these youths mainly as vulnerable victims in need of protection, the subjects, even when they are minors, see themselves as young adults who have to provide the means of subsistence for their families left at home and for themselves. In fact, they feel victimized by the very instruments of protection that prevent them from working. As a result, many leave the programs intended to help them and decide to live in the street because it seems to offer more of a chance to realize their utopian expectations.

> I: After I got to Seville I managed to find my uncle. Once I got there everything was fine, he gave me a lot of food, I slept well, and after a couple of days he took me to the institute.
>
> N: Why?

I: So that I could study and for a better future.

N: Could not you stay in his place? Wouldn't you have preferred it?

I: Well, of course I did not like the idea to go to an institute, but I kept my mind on my papers . . . although I was very young then . . . I had a very mature head . . . It was my uncle who said I would have stood better chances to get my papers by staying there . . . I was there for six months . . . studying . . . the school program . . . I was a professor in math!

N: And then?

I: Eh . . . I wanted to get money . . . I wanted to study only in order to get the papers . . . that was my idea in the very beginning . . . this is a very difficult country to live in . . . you need a lot of cojones . . . solo the dejan fojar maricones . . . si no hay trabaho tienes a fojar . . . comprendes . . . sin papeles . . .

N: Why didn't you go back to your uncle?

I: Because I wanted to be free, not to be told what to do all the time like at home . . .

Thus, the mobility patterns of errant young people are caught in a contradiction between a utopian cultural construction of Western modernity as a world where upward social mobility can be attained easily and the lived experience of exclusion and social marginality.

Young migrants seem unable to accept the failure of the utopian migratory project in whose name they have left home in search of better opportunities. The fear of losing face by returning home empty-handed explains why they do not want to return home even after their imagined life of utopian emancipation collapses. Their migratory project is inextricably embedded into their own self-image and its projection into the future. So instead of returning home when they fail they simply follows the same project into other places; they end up traveling from country to country. They even rank countries among themselves according to the perceived modernity of each: from Italy, Greece, and Spain they try to move on to France and Germany, ultimately reaching the UK and the Netherlands. Sometimes however, this hierarchical order is subverted and young people simply choose to reproduce their migratory dream in a more distant and unknown setting, as this excerpt from R, a twenty-one-year-old Romanian man living in Amsterdam, shows.

N: So, why do you want to go to Spain now?

R: I want to go to Spain because I hope to find something else from here, something better. I don't want to go again into the life with queers or sleeping on the street. I want to find one job. This is the priority for me. Because if you have a job, you also have some money. And I want to live normal. I don't want again to go with queers and I want to make some money because I'm young and I want to send money to Romania and to go back there to make my life. One wife, my house, my car, some money, one-two children. This is my dream.

N: But did you have the same dream when you left Europe?

R: Yes.

N: What makes you think that Spain is going to be better then here?

R: I don't think it's easy in Spain because nowhere it's easy, but I think it's another life, maybe, I don't know, but I want to go try.

N: I was in Spain and I know many Romanian people in Spain . . . many sleep rough, they fuck queers, steal here and there . . .

R: Portugal?

N: I am afraid it is pretty much the same . . . I am sorry to tell you, but I have to. I went to the center of Seville, Madrid. Everywhere there are Romanian young men in the streets.

R: I know there are many Romanians in Europe . . . but I thought at least in Portugal . . . things could be different . . .

N: But how could they be different . . . just because it is far away from Romania? It's the same! If you don't have papers it's the same.

R: Oh, well, if things go wrong over there I will come back here then . . .

Many errant young people end up returning to the country through which they first entered the European space. For Romanians and Albanians this is usually Italy. Greece is the entry point for many Kurds, and Spain is the point of reference for Moroccans. The fear of "losing themselves" during the migratory process seems to bring them back to their first point of contact with Europe. These places may also attract them because they are perceived as places whose moral and social worlds are perceived as closer to those of their countries of origin. There are two main spatial and social scales according to which one can trace the passage from aspired vertical and linear socio-economic emancipation to a regressive and spiral circularity. At a macro level, this passage is manifested in young migrants' resignation to a life of deviancy in the country representing the first experience of Western modernity. At the micro level, this passage is shown by the way in which they adjust to the relative stabilization offered by deviancy with each move to a new place. The encounter between a utopian migratory project and the social exclusion young migrants face makes deviant behavior seem an attractive alternative to the levels of exploitation they experience in other sectors. In any case, it is often the only possible option. Excluded from the work, educational, and recreational opportunities available to the citizens of host societies or having been pathologized and infantilized by social intervention, many migrant young people find that only drifting allows them to perceive themselves as relatively successful. This excerpt from A, a twenty-one-year-old Albanian man living in Rome, illustrates the way deviant behavior can be experienced in terms of agency and control over one's life.

> A: Look, this is how it is . . . I don't want to work as a builder for €35 a day . . . look at my hands . . . they have to stay like this . . . they are not builder's hands . . . here in Rome I have to spend €600 in rent every month . . . what can I do . . . back at home I have already built the second floor . . . for myself, when I go back . . . I need money also for my friends and neighbors . . . you know, when I go home I pretend . . . I mean I tell my friends that I am a boss here . . . they don't know anything . . . they see I have money . . . I have been living here since the age of thirteen . . . got here with my cousins and started selling drugs on their behalf . . . dope . . . pills, coke . . . sometimes . . . Then they were arrested and I had to run up here in Rome . . .
>
> N: So how do you find the money now?
>
> A: Can't you see what I am wearing? It is all good stuff, Armani, look, look, how the hell do I find the money for this, eh? Not working as a builder . . . You know, when you live in the street you have to make a bit of everything . . . sometimes rich people come here and bring you home . . . sometimes you do what they want, sometimes you go there and empty their apartment . . . what can you do . . . they have so much money and we have nothing . . .

In this respect, sex work is just one of many strategies of survival, alongside theft and drug smuggling. Within this constellation, however, it occupies the lowest position in terms of masculine respectability. Unlike stealing and drug smuggling it jeopardizes the credibility of the male subject. The pusher, the gangster, and the thief and can be seen as potentially sustaining a sense of superior and omnipotent masculine self. It is exactly because of its lower moral status that prostitution is perhaps the best prism through which to understand the moral ambivalences shaping the errant mobility pattern of young migrants. The hierarchical positioning of different strategies of survival according to the perceived level of masculine respectability is illustrated by the following excerpt by an eighteen-year-old Albanian man living in Rome, who occasionally sells sex.

> N: So, what do you do for a living . . .
>
> E: Well, I steal . . . I do things . . .
>
> N: Like what?

Nick Mai

E: Well, I usually pickpocket . . . at the station . . . at night . . . I steal things in houses . . .

N: Alone?

E: Well, sometimes alone, sometimes in group . . . sometimes it goes well, sometimes not . . . I even ended up in jail . . .

N: And what about this place here . . . I mean fucking queers . . .

E: Eh, I do it . . . everybody does it . . . I started doing like all others . . . for money . . . it is not the kind of life that I would like doing . . . but it is the life I was given and I try and live it as much as I can . . .

N: What do you do more often, steal or sell sex?

E I would rather steal and I do it more often . . . I think it is better . . . if you sell sex you are over, you are not a man anymore . . . it is better to go to jail than to become a queer . . .

N: What does it mean for you to become a queer?

E: It is different from here . . . in my country it is the greatest shame not only for me . . . I mean if I become a queer than all of my family loses its honor . . . if I sell sex . . . as it happened to many people here . . . you begin by being a man and then you end up like them . . . one week you have no money, somebody offers you a lot of money to fuck you . . . what can you do . . . then you do it again and again and then you end up liking it . . . this is why I decided to steal . . . it is better, I sell sex only when I have to . . . and as a man . . .

N: What does it mean for you to be a man . . .

E: It means staying the way you were born . . . not to be fucked like a woman . . . to fuck like a man . . . Better to go to jail . . .

Can we interpret the search for normality among people coming from countries as different as Albania, Morocco, and Romania in the same way? I found that lifestyles, models of personhood, and canons of success and failure are all measured in the same way regardless of migrants' national origins. They mirror the socio-cultural and economic order of the contemporary world, characterized by the hegemony of neoliberal modernity. On the one hand, globalization has heightened the contact points between different cultural systems and introduced the possibility of an infinite array of experiments with different lifestyles, practices, and relations to the self. On the other hand, translating across different and often contradictory systems of knowledge and moral worlds can be a deeply unsettling process. The socio-cultural environments most errant young people come from are characterized by a very gradual waning of collective values. Individual differentiation is still generally stigmatized and repressed. By framing their attempt to look for a different and alternative life through migration in terms of the search for economic betterment they accomplish several things at once. They are able to break away from the group. They obtain social legitimization of their project by minimizing the way it can be perceived as disruptive to existing social norms. Finally, they allow themselves space to move between models of personhood still socially acceptable at home and the ones they actually prefer, those they first learned about by watching foreign television.

Migration can thus be experienced as an informal ritual of passage. Moving into a cultural formation that allows mediation between established and alternative models of personhood allows young people to address the contradictory set of priorities and roles they need to negotiate as adults-in-the-making. Imagining and then enacting migration becomes a new liminal practice. It mediates between the established family-based models of personhood addressing young people as subjects of sacrifice, authority, and discipline and the scripts of entitlement to individual self-fulfillment disseminated by the media. Imagined and lived migration is a way to respond to the globalization of Western canons of adolescent experimentation and passage to adulthood. This migratory cultural formation can thus be seen as the context in which the search for new rituals accommodating the passage between new articulations of adolescence and adulthood takes place. The desire to migrate emerges from the aspiration to models of personhood that are not hegemonic in the milieu or country of origin. This means that postliminal reinsertion into sending societies can be very difficult. An Albanian, Moroccan, or Romanian young man is unlikely to be acknowledged as successful if he returns as a single young men with an openly metrosexual or even an individualized and hedonistic lifestyle. In order to be fully reintegrated into an established enhanced status he would probably have to conform to the "successful married man with children and car" model of the immigrant.

The late modern lifestyles that errant young people aspire to are consistent with introspective relations with the self and ultimately with moral worlds that are very distant from the social and cultural environment they come from. Individualized lifestyles and fashions can easily be deployed strategically and mimetically rather than assimilated in their emancipatory potential. This means that, ultimately, the subject is not able to face the moral and social implications of his aspirations and desires. In other words, errant young people cannot assimilate and accept the moral implications of the hedonistic lifestyles they want to enjoy. They remain suspended in the interstices of the different moral worlds between which they articulate their migratory projects. This impossibility of reconciliation between the aspirations to individualized late modern lifestyles and established canons of subject formation and relations to the self is a key factor differentiating *errance* from other forms of mobility. In other words, what characterizes *errance* is the lack of agency and awareness enjoyed by the subject in relation to his aspiration to deterritorialize him/herself. This depends on whether the migrant has the necessary introspective tools and the cultural capital to accept the moral and social implications of his desire to migrate.

Unsurprisingly, the migratory project of most errant young people encompasses a dream of return to a regime of normality and discipline, an imagined and complete reterritorialization into the socially established and morally accepted canons of successful masculine adulthood, as these two excerpts from A and B, two twenty-one-year-old Romanian young men living in Amsterdam, illustrate.

A: I would like to go back to Italy . . . maybe because it is more similar to Romania . . . I don't know, I think it's the single country in which I would settle down . . . I want to go in two months, and work legally.

N: Why?

A: Because I want to have a regular job, my house, to own things . . .

N: But you already own things, look at you, what you are wearing, the mobile . . .

A: No, you don't understand, I want to work for my own things, to be able to say ok, nobody gave me this. Because it's something, there's a saying that says nothing is for free. OK, maybe they give us but it comes a time when they ask for something back. I want to give. I want to go to Italy, meet a girl, have a family. It's time.

N: It's time?!!? You are only twenty-one!

A: I'm twenty-three but I think about this. Future, family, kids, home. You think about this. I want to have two kids, a beautiful wife, a nice car, money, a nice job, to have a life, not like this.

N: Is this your dream?

A: It's everybody's dream. Nothing special. Everybody wants this sometime. Most people.

N: And what about the life that you live here?

A: I close it like a book.

N: Do you like anything about this life?

A: Well, you know, I'm a clubber. All my life I've been a clubber. Everywhere, starting from Romania. Clubs, girls, party . . .

B: I am saving money, you know, I have an account in Romania and I am saving money to buy a house . . . a car . . . to have a better life . . .

N: Where are you going to do that?

A: In Romania, you know, it is my country after all, you know how it is . . . you go, but where you were born is always special.

N: But you have just told me that it is so backward there and that there is nothing . . .

B: Yes, that is why I am not planning to go right now, but in ten to twelve years, when things will have developed there . . . I need to get together enough money to open an economic activity . . . Also, not all the money goes to me, at least half of it I give it to my relatives, who are very poor, my cousin, in particular . . . You know, I don't want to have this life, with queers and stuff, in the future. I want to marry, have a kid . . .

N: So that is your dream, to marry and have a kid . . . in Romania . . .

B: In Romania or elsewhere, but the project is that . . . you know what I want to do? I want to enroll in the foreign legion, for five years, and when I finish I go straight to Romania and never get out again . . . I want to close with this life forever.

N: I see a contradiction here, don't you? On the one hand, you left Romania because you were bored there and you wanted to have new experiences. And now you are here, a lifestyle of experimentations and transgressions, as you put it . . . then a minute after you tell me that you want to enroll in the foreign legion and to marry and have kids . . . At the age of thirty-five, after all of this excitement, you close the door and settle down in the very same boring village you dreamt of leaving behind for years . . . Aren't you going to be bored? What makes you think you are going to be able to stand it?

B: Yes, because it is my country, it is my home, my friends . . .

N: But you chose to leave all that behind . . . I live in London and I got used to London. Each time I go back to Italy I like it for a while, but then I get really bored . . . I remember all of the reasons why I wanted to leave and start counting the days . . .

B: Maybe if stay here in the West another ten years I will get used to this even more. It is true that Romania will change, but so will it here, so maybe I will not want to come back after all . . . I am not sure about this, maybe I will marry here, maybe in France, maybe in Germany, but the fact stays, I am going to marry and have children, a car, and a house, the project does not change.

These Augustinian accounts of redemption after the excesses of youth, show how for many errant young people the moral and geographical deterritorialization from established boundaries is psychologically sustainable only if they can imagine a complete reterritorialization into a socially established adult world. What they show most of all, is the impossibility for errant young men to integrate the new experiences gathered during the phase of liminal exploration into an adult third space where all of the different components of one's subjectivity coexist. Paradoxically, by relegating undesirable aspects of themselves into a past to be left behind, errant young people are relegated to a perpetual liminality, because it is only in this space that they can accept the complexity of their desires, hopes, and ambitions.

REDEFINING ERRANCE

Although the term "errance" is commonly used in the European continental world of psycho-social intervention projects, the references to this term in the sociological literature are few and scattered. The most important reference is the work on nomadology carried out by Deleuze and Guattari in *Mille Plateaux* (2002). They elaborate two main concepts. First, that of the "code-territory," which they use to indicate the relation between a specific social and moral order and the space it is inscribed into and that is defined by it. Second, deterritorialization/reterritorialization, by which they capture the constant movements between subjects and different codes-territories. They claim that the nomad and the migrant are distinguished by a different relation to the territory, rather than by their different mobility patterns. They argue that whereas the nomad never leaves his own territory, "the migrant leaves behind a milieu that has become amorphous or hostile" in order to subsequently reterritorialize. In their concern with the nomad it is deterritorializaton that constitutes the relation to the code-territory to such a degree that the nomad reterritorializes on deterritorialization (Deleuze and Guattari 2002, 380–81). What of errance? What kind of mobility does this concept describe? The absence of clearly defined point of return? This is not enough of an explanation. Many migrants lead their lives postponing their return to their homeland in the name of the so-called myth of return. Is errance the constant movement between established code-territories? Then in what way would it be different from transnationalism? Does the errant youth give up on reterritorialization or set up circular movements between known code-territories?

Whereas the nomad can be seen as somebody who accepts and chooses deterritorialization as a constitutive dimension of his/her relation to a code-territory, the errant can be seen as a deterritorialized migrant who errs just because s/he is not able to articulate his reterritorialization and for whom this prolonged uprootedness is not sustainable socially, psychologically, or economically. Errance refers to a dimension of suspended liminality that is experienced as dis-emancipatory and transitional by the migrant himself. The impossibility and incapacity to fully deterritorialize and reterritorialize is the defining dimension of errance. Errance can thus be seen as a particular route within the adolescent search for psychological autonomy and individual fulfillment and one that is characterized by these four interrelated main factors:

1. an irreconcilable tension between models of personhood belonging to different socio-economic and cultural contexts,
2. the endurance of a utopian understanding of Western modernity in the elaboration of the migratory project,
3. a condition of unresolved uprooting from home as the locus of both identification, morality, and emotional attachment,
4. the subjection to multiple forms of social exclusion.

Most of all, errance is marked by an inability to take responsibility for one's deterritorializing ambitions and desires. As a consequence one can spend his life pretending to be a migrant, while subconsciously aspiring to becoming a cosmopolitan. Many errant young people can not see the reasons why they choose to lead the lives they do because they cannot accept their moral implications. This prevents them from locating any opportunity for a psychologically and socio-economically sustainable reterritorialization. These dynamics are particularly evident in the relation between errant young people's attitude to their sexual orientation and their form of subjective and physical mobility. For many, engaging in sex work "because of the money" is the only way to express the ambivalence of their sexual orientation in a way that is morally sustainable. In a parallel fashion, errance becomes the only place allowing them to express their contradictory aspirations to a late modern lifestyle of fun and self-realization, their detachment from models of personhood and canons of morality established at home (freedom) and the necessity to provide for themselves and their families (money).

THE PRIVILEGE OF INTROSPECTION
AND THE SUSTAINABILITY OF A THIRD SPACE

I would like to conclude this chapter by returning to the self-reflexive practice I introduced in the beginning. Throughout my research on errance, I asked myself about the differences and similarities between my migratory trajectory and those of the young people I interviewed, befriended, and observed. On the one hand, errant young people's utopian and imagined migratory projects were very similar to the one I had when I was their age. Their dreaming of Europe mirrored my vision of London as the only place where I could find myself, a place where everything was possible. Their experiences of repression and dreams of escape reflected my adolescent desire to deterritorialize, to escape in search of a better place. Their reluctance in accepting the ambivalent nature of their sexual orientation reminded me of my first adolescent years, of my mimetic holding on to heterosexuality, which then gradually gave in to the acceptance of my homosexuality. On the other hand, there was a substantial difference between their way and my way of dealing with all of these issues: although it took me a while, I could now name the game, they could not.

An incident that dates back to April 2002 illustrates this. I was having a pizza in Rome with one of my best informants, who was also a friend. While we were eating, a colleague of mine from the university stopped at the table to talk about a work-related issue. We went on for about ten minutes and when she left, my informant gave me an angry look. "You never told me!" he said. I started reviewing what I had just said to my colleague trying to figure out what could have been so offensive. He went on, "You never told me that you could speak like that, son of a bitch, like a professor, like people on television, when you are with me you speak like me, like a guy from the street and all that and now I see you are one of them, you speak like them as well . . . look at the way he speaks this faggot, like a fucking news program!" We started laughing, but his eyes were filled with rancor and envy. I realized there and then that the main difference between us was that I was able to translate myself across different social and cultural settings, while he was stuck where he was, linguistically, discursively, and socially.

Throughout my research, one of the most interesting moments comes when I observe errant young migrants' reactions when I tell them I am gay. I do not always bring it up, but sometimes it is strategically important to signal to them that they can talk about "it" if they like. Most of them do. Many young men ask questions about the way I came to accept my homosexuality, how my parents and the people surrounding me reacted, and how I felt about "it." They wanted to know about my family, my parents' divorce, whether they remarried, how I felt about them now. Sometimes it was very painful. Some of the questions were extremely personal and forced me to reflect again on aspects of myself I thought I had dealt with once and for all. I was wrong, some things will never be dealt with completely, and it hurts each time we tamper with them. But it was fair. It made me understand how being asked painful question feels like. I like to believe that my interviewing improved as a consequence of that experience, that it became more respectful, more tactful, less intrusive. But most of all I remember the difference between the way they were forced to talk about other people's experiences as a way to talk about their own (i.e., according to the "a friend of mine told me . . ." strategy) and the way I was free to talk about myself, directly.

In this article and throughout my research, I have used the issue of homosexuality as a point of departure from which to explore the issue of difference and the way this is dealt with in different socio-cultural environments. What these two examples show is what I call the privilege of introspection, by which I mean the socially, economically, and culturally determined privilege to access the discourses and information, which make the imagination of a third space beyond binarism cognitively and morally sustainable. The main difference between me and the subjects of my research on errance was this privilege, which allowed me and prevented them from acknowledging that I could be an Italian researcher and gay and (a bit) English, that they could be Romanian and Moroccan and not want to have a family/car/children lifestyle, that they could be Albanian and want to have a good time in Rome more than sending money home. Whenever I named these possibilities, I encountered amazement and fear. As if I had been speaking too loud and exposed something meant to be buried away from consciousness. I saw that the problem was that the people I was talking to had no language to talk about their desires in ways that would make them morally acceptable, they also had no lived experiences of those possibilities. They had only seen them on television and that was evidently not enough to metabolize them. All of these desires and dreams were unspeakable and therefore invisible to consciousness. They were silenced within and without by a thick layer of guilt and shame. How can we look into ourselves if we do not know how to deal with the information we might retrieve? How can we accept difference and integrate it into sameness if we do not have the tools to understand it? How can we escape feelings of guilt and shame for not being the woman and man society wants us to be if we cannot access discourses that legitimize our difference socially? And finally, how can we take responsibility for our desires and dreams and of the life trajectories they elicit if we do not accept them?

REFERENCES

Deleuze, Gilles and Guattari, Felix. 2002. *A Thousand Plateaus: Capitalism and Schizophrenia*. London & New York: Continuum.
Grossberg, L. 1992. *We Gotta Get Out of This Place*. London: Routledge.

Mai, Nick. 2004. Albanian Masculinites, Sex Work and Migration: Homosexuality, AIDS and other Moral Threats. *National Health: Gender, Sexuality and Health in Cross-cultural Context.* Worton, M. and Wilson-Tagoe, N. (eds). London: UCL Press.

———. 2001. "Italy is Beautiful": The role of Italian television in the Albanian migratory flow to Italy. *Media and Migration: Constructions of Mobility and Difference.* King, R. and Wood, N. (eds). London: Routledge.

Rose, Nikolas. 1996. Identity, Genealogy, History. *Questions of Cultural Identity.* Hall, S. and Du Gay, P. (eds.). London: Sage.

7

Moving into Morocco

A Cosmopolitan Turn in the Médina

Justin McGuinness

Bab Menara, Tunis; Marx Dormoy, Paris; Bab el Guissa, Fès, all areas on the edge of historic cities, edgy areas—and places where I feel at home. They are all neighborhoods in flux, places where numerous migrants have settled in recent decades. Thus, when I started thinking about the experience of migrant Moroccans, I felt I had plenty of ways into the theme of moving out of Morocco. There were friends in Tanger and Tripoli, also a contact in my *quartier* in Paris: Ali, in his late twenties, who had traveled (migrated?) illegally, to the Canary Islands three times to work. Once he'd been flown back to Morocco by the Spanish authorities and once he'd got a boat back to Laâyoune because he was homesick and wanted see his family. For his final departure, he'd taken a plane to Madrid and then on to Paris where he had a student friend. Illiterate in French, Ali has adapted well to Parisian life—and even took a break back in Morocco, traveling on a friend's passport.

However, the rationale for my participation in a project on serial migration through Morocco arises somewhat paradoxically, since for me North Africa has become home, my reference point—along, I add, with France— or should I say Paris. (The details belong in a lengthy footnote.) In the late 1990s, after completing my Ph.D., I began working on guidebooks on the "visitable" North African countries. I knew Tunisia well, having settled there after my first degree in the mid-1980s, ostensibly to learn the Arabic I was never taught in my first degree. I stayed, "for personal reasons," as they say. Morocco, I'd come to know since working as an interpreter for a company in Rabat in the early 1990s, had always been a country that attracted me. I suppose if I ever write a book on Fès, it'll be prefaced with something like "I've been working on this book since the age of seven, the age at which I saw a television documentary about Morocco that fired my imagination." Perhaps I was destined to have a multisited life from that point on, especially growing up in an English medical family in the 1970s when emigration for better positions was always a subject of conversation.

At the end of the 1990s, the work on the guidebooks took me all over Morocco. In summer 2003, I did yet another stint in the country. Part of my intention had been to gather material for the present chapter. Marrakech was humming, having recovered from a momentary dip in tourism after the start of the Anglo-American occupation of Iraq. The city was busier than I had remembered. Every evening, the Rue Bab Agnaou, the busy pedestrian street leading into Jemaâ el Fna, was crowded with Marrakchis and Moroccan *zmagriya* (migrants) back from abroad. Half the population of the *neuf-trois*, or "ninety-threes" as the *département* of Seine-Saint-Denis is called by the locals because of its postal code, seemed to be in town. So thinking about the research, which eventually became the present article, I thought I'd have no problem meeting those "serial migrants."

But the research-work took another turn. The migrants turned out to be living between Sidi Kacem and Granada, or Zaouiat Ben Cheikh and Torino. There were no triple-country migrants. However, during a particularly hot and sweaty week in Fès, gathering information for the guidebook, I explored decaying houses and came across a cosmopolitan bunch of people who had opted to make the beautiful—if rather provincial—Fès el Bali their home. Moroccans, both town and country folk, have often come under scrutiny from anglophone social scientists. However, since the late 1990s when I had begun writing books which package Morocco for the visitor, I'd come across a new category of person. This highly educated individual, mobile in professional and geographical terms, opted to spend part of their career outside Europe, devoting time and energy to restoring historic property with a view to letting rooms to other foreigners. (Writing this, I feel that language has escaped my control, I've fallen almost automatically into the jargon of human resource management. How many of the people of Fès would describe themselves in these terms?)

This chapter is based on a series of interviews I carried out with a selection of the new Fassia from July 2003 to March 2004. All those interviewed were recent migrants to Morocco. (The longest-established resident had been in the city for eight years.) While much material was drawn from formal interviews, I also make use of my own experience and material drawn from the print media. My thinking about the issues of migration and settlement, on writing at the interface between cultures has been shaped by my readings of works by Buck-Morss (1987), Faubion (1995), Florida (2002), and Bruner (2004).

While I had a certain number of issues I tried to explore in the interviews, as a whole I allowed the discussions to take their course. I wanted to allow the serial migrant's experience to emerge naturally, to see what forms an *identité bricolée* might take as a cosmopolitan settled and adapted to what is after all a rather quiet, provincial city. During both my stays in Fès I was also functioning as a participant observer, as I was looking for a small house to buy. So the whys and wherefores of different areas of the city, the advantages of one house over another, relationships with the locals, inevitably came into the discussions. As I tramped up and down the narrow streets, clambered up the steep and narrow staircases of *misriya-s* (annex, often upstairs) and crumbling riads, I was constantly called upon to stretch my Arabic to get the most out of each interaction, realizing the areas where my language resources were inadequate, observing how my local guides—estate agents of various kinds, engineers specializing in conservation—interacted with residents. I was developing a feel for the preparatory phase of becoming a new Fassi—of the rather rare kind who has a polymigratory background.

ON FÈS AND THE RIAD PHENOMENON

The old quarters of Fès have largely been abandoned by their original population, drawn to Casablanca in the early years of the French Protectorate. Enormous courtyard houses were left in the hands of poorer family members, or else divided and rented out on a room-by-room basis. The phenomenon, classic in older neighborhoods in expanding urban areas, continues until the fall in value of the decaying property is such that substantial value increase can be realized by outright purchase and restoration. The fall of an old elite and massive in-migration from the countryside or periphery of an empire tend to feature in the decline phase. The renewal of the built environment tends to be spearheaded by migrants or new settlers with considerable cultural capital (see Florida 2002) and is reinforced by government investment in infrastructure and major cultural projects.

The garden-courtyard houses of Morocco's cities or riads came to the attention of the French public in the mid-1990s. *Capital*, a popular television program focusing on brands and entrepreneurs on the trendy M6 channel, ran a feature on the handful of young French people who had restored Marrakech houses as up-scale restaurants and romantic retreats. Within weeks—the urban legend goes—planefuls of Parisians were seeking property to renovate in the médina of Marrakech and the outlying *palmeraie*. There was an immediate impact on property values. In the early 2000s, the phenomenon was further amplified by the new thirty-five-hour working week in France, the availability of direct cheap flights from France to Marrakech, and, so the rumor went, by the need to put "under-the-mattress" savings out of various European tax authorities' reach before the introduction of the new single currency in January 2002. Essaouira, a picturesque Atlantic port two hours' drive from Marrakech, popular with surfers, was touched by the wave of gentrification, too. Despite reports of unseemly behavior by new residents—or rather their visitors—on the whole native Marrakchis (people from Marrakech) were delighted by the phenomenon. Modest families in multioccupancy dwellings were able to move out to apartments in the city's spreading suburbs. By 2001, rumor in the Red City ran that there were over seventy restored properties being operated as guesthouses, in one form or another, in the old city. By 2005, a new phase was beginning. Riads with full property deeds were now on their second or third European owners, the original buyer-restorers having moved out of the médina to the countryside outside Marrakech, up the Ourika road toward the Atlas mountains. A sign of the times, Marrakech now has an American school, situated in a large compound outside town.

The phenomenon of European in-migration has reached Fès as well. In summer 2003, there were at least nine restored properties operational as guesthouses, mostly serving the upper end of Morocco's tourist market. (Visitor accommodation in Fès-Médina is a very accurate reflection of the wider country's social divide, there being little between the cheap back-packer hotels near Bab Boujeloud and the palatial accommodation offered by the riads, mainly in the Batha, Douh, and Ziat neighbourhoods.) In spring 2004, three neighborhoods, all in Fès el Bali (the Left Bank), had significant numbers of foreign-owned properties: the Oued Rachacha area, Aïn Zliten, and Batha/Douh. Smaller foreign-owned and restored properties were rented out on an annual basis to students. However, for the moment, the momentum for building is not as feverish as in Marrakech. Factors including the greater difficulty of restoring property in Fès (due in part to the physical nature of the city, with its steep narrow streets, inaccessible to motor vehicles) and fewer flights limit the city's attractiveness. Far fewer entertainments have kept the harder-nosed profit-seeking investors away. Here again, urban rumor in 2004 went that a major Swiss investment company was looking to acquire large numbers of houses in the médina. For the moment, however, the adjective generally applied to the old town "el Bali" continues to fit rather well.

THE RIAD IN MEDIA DISCOURSE

Images of properties restored and transformed by foreigners feature in lifestyle magazines, both international and Moroccan. Barefoot luxury and

BCBG-basics revisited are the staples of the upscale French decoration magazine *Côté Sud*. The plush hotels and riads of Morocco feature frequently, alongside similar ventures in Mediterranean, Indian Ocean, and the Antilles. Since the mid-1990s, Morocco has had its own aspirational home-elegance magazine, the successful *Maisons du Maroc*, which regularly profiles restorations of historic homes.

The riad phenomenon has given writers for such publications a new take on an old trope: *luxe, calme et volupté* for the privileged few in an exotic location, accessible nevertheless with a minimum of initiative (and cash).[1] In the case of Fès, they had another city with a timeless past, deep roots, unsullied by modernity, all ripe for framing by middle-class visitors with cultural acumen. In April 1999, *Côté Sud*, often the first to spot a potential destination, ran a feature in its "green number" titled, "Fès, fugue en verts". The city, wrote Alix de Dives, was beginning a "une renaissance timide" and "certain private palaces, deserted by their owners, are changing into guesthouses." This transformation of old houses into tourist accommodation featured in an article in *Architecture du Maroc* in 2001. The travel journalists soon woke up to the phenomenon and pieces hailing the as-yet-undiscovered charms of Fès began to appear in the early 2000s. Alongside the usual backpackers and the coach tourists, discerning individuals were called upon to enjoy the urbane qualities of Fès: "Why stay in a characterless hotel when you can live like one of the locals?" asked Caroline Roux as she relaxed for *The Guardian* "amid oriental exoticism"; in "A Fez of the Heart", a piece in a consumer magazine produced by a major British supermarket chain, two London chefs went shopping with Koko, resident cook of a leading riad, and discovered the food markets of a "daunting" médina. Such articles draw heavily on the images of Moroccan cities that have been the stock in trade of jobbing writers since the country began to attract tourists: stinking tanneries and the time warp, narrow streets, hordes of people, and courtyard sanctuaries where water trickles in a wall fountain.

Anglophone lifestyle television, too, has explored the possibilities of residing in Morocco. In October 2003, *Design 360*, a documentary program screened by CNN, profiled riad life in both Marrakech and Fès. In early summer 2005, the BBC program *Uncharted Territory*, one of the raft of makeover programs popular in the early 2000s, featuring ordinary Britons in search of radical changes in their lives, ran a Morocco story. Presenter Juliet Morris and home-buying expert Nigel Leck lent "a hand to adventurous property hunter Yvonne and her son Daniel" who were "looking to be the first British house buyers in one of Morocco's best kept secrets—the medieval city of Fez." The city was now on par with undiscovered locations in countries and regions on western Europe's eastern and southern edges: Tunisia and Sicily, Poland, Slovakia, and Hungary, Slovenia, and Turkey.

THE NEW FASSIA

The power of lifestyle journalism, both print and audio-visual, to put a city on the aspirational tourists mental map is a moot point—and clearly an interesting cultural interface for media researchers. Whether or not they were sold an unbelievable mediaeval city by the media, the new foreign inhabitants of old Fès in the early 2000s fall roughly into four categories. The most temporary are the Arabic students and teachers, most of whom come for just a year or two and live in rented houses or with Moroccan families. Almost all are from the anglophone world. Then come the "sensitive gentrifiers" (my label) who buy and restore fairly small properties as part of much longer life plans. Most are in their late twenties/early thirties and already have experience living in a variety of cultural settings. Larger restoration schemes are undertaken by older "settlers," many of whom, but by no means all, are Moroccan and returning to the médina, often after careers outside their home country. Finally, there is a more nebulous category—from the outsider's point of view—that of the fundamentalist Christians. Contacts in Fès suggested that this group proceed discretely, operating by example in the hope of winning converts. By the very nature of their activity in a country whose authorities have strongly resisted all forms of non-Muslim proselytism, they are the least visible group to the outsider. Their activities have not escaped the notice of the sharper end of the Moroccan press, with articles featuring in critical publications like *Tel Quel* and *Al-Ahdath al-Maghribiya*.

The group with the most self-reflexive take on their residence in Fès are the gentrifiers. They are also those with the most to lose, putting considerable time and personal effort into their projects in the city. While the students of Arabic and TEFL teachers move on to other things, the gentrifers are ready to spend a significant part of their adult lives, possibly the most formative years, in a city where they will have to struggle with a largely unfamiliar language and a very different set of social mores. The twenty or so people interviewed for the present project can by categorized in terms of age and language. There are the married-with-kids and those on the cusp of their thirties; there are the anglophones, generally American, often with a smattering of Arabic, and the francophones, more likely to have one or more languages other than French. The older foreign residents often have full careers behind them, so the stakes are lower and, possibly, the desire to achieve something through the move is not as pressing. Despite their young age, even the most youthful North Atlantic residents all have atypical backgrounds. As one resident put it: "Most of us here are serial migrants."

SOMETHING OF THAT OLD ORIENTALIST THING

But without the desire to convert Moroccans to Christianity, what makes an educated, well-traveled European or North American settle in Fès? Involved in a large-scale restoration project, one American migrant mentioned that "there is definitely something of that old Orientalist thing." With more than a trace of irony, the same informant mentioned *The Sheltering Sky*, a Bertolucci film adaptation of the Paul Bowles novel *Tea in the Sahara* as a formative influence. She found "the possibility of running off with a Touareg fascinating." F., a Spanish woman in her late thirties, stressed the authenticity of Fès, "la seule ville au monde que je connaisse qui pourrait me ramener à moi-même" (The only city in the world that can bring me back to myself):

> A Fès je me sens très libre. Je venais ici en tant que touriste. Je sentais l'odeur du bois, je ramenais des choses juste pour l'odeur . . . je savais ici que je pouvais commencer mon chemin en tant que femme . . .
>
> (In Fès I feel very free. I used to come here as a tourist. I could smell the scent of the wood, I would take things home just for the smell . . . I knew that here I could begin my road as a woman . . .) Interview March 2003.

Said another informant:

> In London I had all this stuff, here you have much less, you really have to define what you need . . . All of us have come to make money, but that's not the primary goal. Most of us are looking for a way of life. . . . the relaxed, stripped down life that you don't get in the West. (Discussion December 2004)

In different ways, the interviewees also cited the importance of the city as spiritual resource. Working with the *Festival de Fès des Musiques Sacrées*, a yearly festival of sacred music, had enabled one convert to Islam with a strong mystic bent to live in the city, restoring a house in the process. Though the word "escape" was never used, the desire to live in a less consumerist environment was frequently mentioned. A young Franco-American with several years of activity in NGOs behind him, described how the year before coming to settle, he'd been off for a journey to the deep south of Morocco, the desert trip had marked him, the empty, clear space, the return to the essence of things. He added that:

> C'est des attirances. Le Maroc c'était mon premier pays arabe—je connaissais déjà la Turquie. Je suis très sensible à l'ascetisme théologique de l'Islam.

(It's a matter of attraction. Morocco was my first Arab country—I already knew Turkey. I'm very sensitive to Islam's theological asceticism.) (Interview March 2003)

In contrast to this, the human life of the city held a lot of fascination for certain respondents. This was particularly stressed by the younger interviewees, less solely obsessed by the aesthetic qualities of the buildings:

> If only I could characterize my neighbors like Steinbeck in Cannery Row . . . I'm amazed by the life around me when I walk out of the door. Then I'm amazed if the novelty seems to have worn off . . . I suffer culture shock when I return to the States. In the local natural food store, I handle and smell the produce. My Dad says, "Stop fondling things, it's like you just got out of communist Russia."(Interview March 2003)

Another resident, a teacher in the city for a year away from the north-west of the United States and resident on busy Talaâ Kbira, stressed the human contrasts:

> I leave my house in the morning, out of the alley and you're on the Talaâ, and there are all these people, and I think to myself, who are they all, I know nothing about them, where are they all going. I've no way into that flow. (Discussion December 2004)

A CITY OF OPPORTUNITY—AND OPPORTUNISTS

Fès also offers people a chance to do something new, an opportunity to succeed, both for retirees opening riad businesses and younger migrants with greater ambitions. Particularly lucid, a thirty-year-old American woman who had moved to the medina from London discussed her new business in Fès:

> A desire to be my own boss was primordial. That's impossible in London. High capital is necessary. However, Marrakech as a market is saturated, it's far more expensive to get started and the chances of success are lower. There are 700 guest houses—and that's official. It's not Morocco any more. I saw houses with zero charm and prices were around the $300,000 mark. (Interview March 2003)

For other migrants, although they had not originally had any intention to settle in either Morocco or Fès, and had moved on a permanent basis following a spouse, the city had given them the chance to make a new start—in art photography, arts administration, or the craft restoration of old buildings.

As I interviewed and observed, it became increasingly apparent that although my serial migrants had much in common, they were all unique in their ways of crossing boundaries into Moroccan society—or perhaps I should say, into the different social worlds of Fès, in establishing places and roles for themselves in the city. For some, children were central to establishing ties: one couple had adolescents in the French school, another had a daughter married to a Moroccan. An intellectual Frenchman had converted to Islam and become part of one of the larger mystic brotherhoods. Two examples stood out: a fortyish American who had built himself a strong career position in Fès as manager-director of the city's English and Arabic language teaching institute, and a Middle Eastern architect who had developed a deep knowledge of Fassi building techniques.

Respected by people across the city, the American aesthete was one of the first to settle in Fès el Bali. By early 2004, he had restored three properties and was contemplating the long-haul process of restoring houses four and five. His role was almost that of an evangelist for potential new settlers in the city—no religious overtones intended here. With a rare single-mindedness, he invested considerable energy in a website providing information on the process of buying a house to English-speaking neophytes. Such devotion to the cause of old Fès—and time spent showing prospective buyers around— was not without risks for his reputation in the city. Once more urban rumor (a key feature of small-town life anywhere?) reared its head: locals thought the American was really a *simsar*, an estate agent, who was buying up the city. However, in a city where *bazaristes*, often members of the long-established families, have traditionally played the role of intermediaries between the local and the prosperous incomer, a new form of cultural translator was bound to be seen with some jealousy.

At a stage further on in the immigration process, another form of cultural mediator becomes essential: the building expert. The first neo-Fassis at the end of the 1990s worked with *maâlemine* (master builders). However, for complex buildings to be brought up to Western norms requires more than the experience of the *maâlem*. In a totally uncalculating sort of way, the Middle Eastern architect had found another window of opportunity: assistance and advice to restorers. After completing the lengthy process of restoring a fine house in one of the oldest parts of the city, Sebaâ Louyet, (the street of the seven bends), A. had acquired an in-depth knowledge of the restoration methods. His professional training and language skills gave him a plus over the *maâlemine* and soon he found himself contacted by incomers for help with refurbishment projects. The initially vague project of "restoring the house and running it as a place where people who are interested in the Islamic city can hang out" began to move (to drift?) toward the creation of a professional practice specializing in the restoration of houses for a demanding migrant clientele.

Previous experience—in the art market in the case of the American buyer-aesthete, in the professional architectural milieu in Scandinavia in the case of the Middle Eastern restoration specialist—had obviously prepared these particular settlers to find themselves roles from the opportunities opening up in Fès. Others benefited from the general lack of regulations and the cheapness of property, labor, and materials to launch grandiose refurbishment schemes. On a summer's day in 2005, a building technician from the ADER, the urban regeneration agency in Fès, took me round several such projects:

> Up near the Institut culturel français in Batha. Good-sized house being restored by an Italian. Rooms are color coded: yellow tadelakt, green tadelakt. Says B., pointing to a crack in the back wall of the big salon downstairs: "But you know, he should have had that done first. You have to open up the wall and see what's going on, what's happening on the neighbor's side. But he's coming back to Fès next week, and he'll want to move a window in a bathroom. Or he'll have all a partition changed, even though we're doing the finishing touches. Money's not an object for him." (Fieldnotes July 2005)

Sometimes the opportunism was on the other foot. In a discussion with a builder and his son, an experienced carpenter, I learnt more about the view of the incomers—and their exploitation by opportunistic locals—from the Fassi side. The son was working on a huge house owned by a Frenchman on Talaâ Sghira. Work was advancing apace—but at a price:

> So F. comes in from France to supervise the works . . . But it's B. [a Fassi with a university background abroad and something of a reputation for restoring houses] who's the one responsible. He's loopy, he says "do this, do that" but he doesn't understand. The structural engineer said he couldn't approve the work. So he's doing this big kitchen . . . and then they're building a pool where the storeroom was. The other day the trench collapsed and a workman was hurt, but B. just said carry on. (Fieldnotes, Bilan August 2005)

FROM CULTURAL TRANSLATORS TO COMMUNITY

In such a climate, incomers with their hearts set on creating an "at-home" in the médina need to rapidly develop a help network. (The same need for network is probably true for migrants everywhere.) In Fès, in the early 2000s, such support tended to get set up initialy through the *simsar* (property agent) or through chance meeting with local foreign resident. Some incomers found that the level of attention being paid to their affairs was invasive, to the point that they referred to the home owners with a touch of irony as "the house-club."

Given that the process of buying property is largely unwritten—or at least in a form immediately available to the incoming non-Arabic speaking people, incomers share information about experiences with simsar-s, *adoul*-s (traditional notaries), and banks. The network is most important of all when it comes to choosing contractors for work. Here the development of a real community of interest can be felt—and certainly emerges during discussions of the successes and catastrophes of the home refurbishment process. Neo-Fassis who had had minor disasters in their homes with plausible foremen or dodgy electricians had plenty of information for others. Not all advice was helpful, however. A simsar who had negotiated several purchases for one buyer could leave another purchaser losing a potential property and a 50,000 dirham (5,000 euro) deposit along with it.

Once a house has been purchased and works are underway, a further cultural translator comes into play: the *homme de confiance*. The employment (or underemployment) context in Morocco in the early 2000s was such that any casual reference to a *projet touristique*, or indeed any commercial project at all, would immediately have potential candidates for a job, many with good language skills. All those interviewed had helpers. Though their job descriptions would be hard to define in a European context, they make the lives of the neo-Fassi migrants much easier. Typically, such men, in their twenties or early thirties, start by working on the restoration, in one capacity or another. They then move from (say) wood cleaning to conciergelike responsibilities, or from house seeking right through to supervising work. The brightest and most ambitious prove hard to keep, however, and like many Moroccans with a good level of secondary education, connections, and poor prospects at home, will be working on a project to get themselves to Europe or eventually North America, via employment contracts or marriage.

AFFIRMING DIFFERENCE, GAINING ACCEPTANCE

The interface with local people can be problematic, however. At some stage during a visit to Morocco, any non-Muslim visitor will be asked whether they are Muslim, whether they've thought about converting. These conversations can be quite short—or can lead to lengthy philosophical discussions round campfires or café tables. Although the neo-Fassia were keenly interested in their adoptive city, almost none had gone so far as to convert to Islam, even when they had Muslim partners. Said one young cadre, married to a Moroccan woman with a high professional profile in publishing:

> It's a great frustration not to be able to go into the mosques . . . but for on religious things, people don't bother me too much. The important thing for me is to have an exchange. Sometimes I want to have conversations on the big issues . . . However, I always make it a point of honor to say I'm Christian . . . I couldn't stand in front of an adoul (notary) and lie to him (about my religious beliefs). For me that would be a total lack of respect. Some people can do that however. (Interview March 2004)

The new Fassia often find themselves crossing internal Moroccan as well as international identity boundaries. Médina resident K. T. wore an elegant djellaba to her French class in the ville nouvelle, the only person to do so in a class of Moroccans. People in the class, all professionals in their late twenties/thirties, questioned her on her choice of the médina, of her house restoration project:

> I do the wood restoration myself. I tell people I'm a menuisier (carpenter). It doesn't compute for most of them. Also I don't have a maid—why should someone clean my house for me? The kids used to pester me to carry my shopping. I resisted for a long time. "No, no," they said, "you shouldn't have to carry them." In the end, I had to give in. I still get asked when I'm getting married. There's a social pressure, when are you going to become a Muslim. Ultimately, I don't think you can ever become a Fassi—but L. (a Middle Eastern incomer), says you can. Even the Moroccans say that of rural migrants who've been in the city for thirty years. (Interview March 2004)

Sometimes locals take the incoming resident under their wing and explain the whys and wherefores of managing their relationship with the new human environment. There is a well-established etiquette in dealing with neighbors, in walking through one's *quartier*. Who do you say hello to? Who do you ignore? The new European resident is immediately targeted by the local adolescents, the *drari*, as a potential source of cash. The phrase *daouir ma'ya* (very rough translation: "Got any small change, guv?" accompanied by a sharp movement of the cupped palm is one of the communicative moments the incomer comes across most frequently. After all, the médina neighborhoods have a high concentration of poverty. Small children can be a source of constant pestering. Said a friend after I'd moved in to Zkak Rommène, "Ignore the *drari (kids)*—they'll give up after a while. And don't ask anyone into the house."

There is an etiquette to walking and looking, greeting or acknowledging others in the city. Somewhere along the line, the incomer begins to walk around with the air of a local; one's persona is known well enough to go without comment. Said one new resident:

> You don't say *salam alaykum* to street kids. You fend off the persisent "give me a dirham" kid with a "give me five dirhams" or make a joke of it and walk on. When you're in the street, in the middle of a big discussion with the builder, you multitask; you smile hello and do that right-hand tapping on the heart gesture to say hello, too. Your face has to be mobile—a wax mask Parisian metro-face is no use in Fès (Interview summer 2005).

When the neo-Fassi has been observed enough, then contacts begin to take shape through the incidents of everyday life. A neighbor asks for an opinion on the work he's having done and takes the incomer on a tour of his house. The man from the residents' association asks you to get involved. You have your favourite *épicier*—and know that he can't read the list of things you've written out laboriously in Arabic.

Migrants willingness and ability to understand the mindset of Fès is often severely tested, however. ("Putting it bluntly, you either learn the way they do things or you get out," said one neo-Fassi.) In the older parts of the city, few people speak French or English beyond a few basics. Migrants often found themselves in situations where their adaptive potential was heavily stretched. Situations ranged from the hilarious to the serious. K. T. described her puzzlement when the required *safra* (donkey loads of sand) failed to be delivered one day:

> So Abd el Ali finally showed up and said, "Someone stole my donkeys." Work was already behind so I was a bit angry. In the end I understood. There are only two *ramla* (sand) suppliers for the neighbourhood, and their profit margins are thin—a sack costs 5dh to deliver. So the only way to nobble a rival is to deal with their donkeys. Word was that the competitor had stolen them. Eventually Abd el Ali found the donkeys wandering in the hills. No one wanted to go to the police of course. You know, you really have to have a healthy dose of "oh fuck it" when you live here (Interview March 2003).

Slow delivery times are just part of the network of problems incomers have to face when coming to Fès, be they working on a home-restoration project or not. As a researcher for a guidebook, I had come across numerous cases of new residents being "taken to the cleaners" to various degrees by unscrupulous local contractors. Dealing with seemingly sincere local craftsmen requires time, effort, and a healthy helping of scepticism. The ability to predict and forestall major dishonesty seems to be a requirement for the successful new resident. In addition to developing a new relationship with time (It'll be done when it's done), the North Atlantic migrant has to be prepared to learn the real capacities of contractors and service providers. Coming from a world where such things are clearly regulated, where there is no language barrier, the constant evaluation of others' intentions and abilities in face-to-face situations was often mentioned as central. Said one respondent:

> People try to exploit all the loopholes: it's astonishing. It's exhausting to deal with. You have to fight for everything (Interview March 2003).

A European couple who have a small guesthouse business had many an anecdote of dealing with local bureaucracy—and alluded to the importance of understanding the local hierarchies:

> We didn't realize in the beginning the extent to which this city is sewn up (. . . à quel point cette ville est bouclée . . .). If you're not ready to pay *bakchich* . . . Clients would arrive at the rail station and ask to be taken to our riad, and the taxi driver would say, "No, it doesn't exist" or "It's closed" . . . And the client is completely lost, because they'd made the whole reservation by Internet (Discussion August 2005).

Situations sometimes reach surreal proportions: a young American with limited funds took on the restoration of a small house locked away in the network of streets up on Aqbat Bensoual. Works progressed well until a neighbor complained of drainage problems. Excavating the patio floor to replace a pipe released a flood of backed-up sewage into the courtyard. Part of the problem was due to the inadequate collector pipe for the street. Said the man from the city agency called round to look at the problem: "Well, you can just wash the courtyard down once a day."

In such situations, the temptation is to lose one's temper. But on becoming homeowners the neo-Fassis quickly realize that temper loss is almost the worst reaction to the frustration. In the end, the real adaptors take on something of the character of *ahl Fas*: a measured circumspection in daily business. And for this they are accepted into the complex social fabric of the city.

A HOME IN THE MÉDINA?
THE TRANSFORMATION OF DOMESTIC SPACE

In the course of my visits, several informants mentioned a Paul Bowles novel set in Fès, *The Spider's House*. In 2004, I finally got round to reading the book. The first sections, in which Bowles seems to enter the mind of young Fassi apprentice Amar and describes the city as seen by American novelist, rang particularly true. The writer often visits a Fassi family in their great home, describing how they seem to inhabit a great decorative shell, migrating around the house according to the seasons. As I began looking for a house to buy myself, in the spring 2004, I visited homes of all shapes and sizes, I realized how true this migration within the home was, how simply most families lived. In a house just off Kettanine, shortly to be sold to German tour guide, a ruckus of blankets and cushions in an upper room indicated that everybody was still in winter quarters; in summer everybody would shift downstairs to the cool, dark rooms off the main patio.

Traditional Fassi homes may have been exceptional for their quality of ornamentation, they were modified according to the times and taste. At a house I visited down near Recif one summer afternoon, the family was comfortably installed on mattresses round the walls of the patio—in the shade of giant coconut palms. The blind wall of the courtyard was filled entirely with a giant poster of a South Pacific beach. The yellowed corrugated fiberglass covering the patio kept out the glare of the afternoon sun, the TV screen contributed a blueish glow. In another house, a billboard-sized patio wall was fully covered with a night shot of the Kaaba. On another occasion in 2005, I met a family shortly to relocate after their property, complete with 150m² of ruins, had been acquired by a foreign buyer. The American was in ecstasy over the traces of "really antique" tiling. In the former *hammam*, the family's student sons had produced their take on contemporary design: suspended Fanta cans gave the vaulted ceiling a mobile feel; the walls featured posters of boy bands and R'n B stars; stacked in a corner were naïve paintings of Fassi life (a money spinner?); a racing bike—slightly outlandish given the house's location in the depths of Guerniz—gave the room a sporty note.

Back to tradition was the leitmotiv for cosmopolitan neo-Fassis as they refurbished their property. Lengthy conversations discussed what sort of plaster rendering was most traditional, how exactly wood should be returned to its original state. However, whether they had converted their property for guest use or to live in themselves, the neo-Fassis produced homes as different as their origins. Though the target was authenticity, "the real Fassi style," the results differed hugely from one house to another:

> The most striking thing about Riad *Lune-et-Soleil* (Moon and Sun) is the emphasis, in what is actually a fairly small house, placed on museum-like displays. The tone is set right from the entrance, where a collection of terracotta food storage jars, arranged in a line according to size, is followed by the best (framed) collection of old maps and postcards of Fès I have ever seen. Old textiles are used as throws, there are arrays of traditional craftsmen's tools on the walls and low tables. No other house has such a range of historic items on display. It is almost the equivalent of a museum of local life—a contrast to the "great" riads which foreground the *ahl Fass* (authentic Fasi) style of the late

nineteenth century: needlepoint embroidered cushions, clocks (*lahrichiyet*), brocades (*dinarjet*), and wooden furniture (Field notes March 2005).

At Dar Seffarine the discourse of authenticity produced pared-down interiors, with smooth reddish-beige *madlouk* walls, cedar-wood shutters stripped down to the grain and architect-designed windows with a hint of Rennie Macintosh. Not all cosmopolitans are willing to return to an imagined eighteenth century, however. There is a standard authentic characterization of the traditional Moroccan house in Fès (and elsewhere) which typically brings together wrought-iron furniture, cushioned benches, and woolen textiles against a backdrop of mosaic tile work and carved plaster. Roof terraces are kitted out with terracotta plant pots, further wrought-iron furniture, and, on occasion, wooden sun loungers covered in doum-palm rope. Having survived the process of buying, fellow restorers are always ready with advice for the new incomer on how to transform their new home:

> Visit to [my] house with architects and Australian recent purchaser. Discussion of options for the future bathroom in 8m² old storeroom on mezzanine level. My worry: is the head-height sufficient (just about?). Local architect: "You could have a bath you step down into, you know a really big bath, over here. You can lower the ceiling over the downstairs toilet, and then you don't have the height issue to worry about." (Thinks: they'll certainly authorize that at the Municipality). Australian woman: ". . . that's a great idea. Think of it, you know, you're in your big bath and there's incense and candles . . . and you have room for a meditation space here." No, I can't quite imagine this, even as I type these notes. The neighbors filling up their orange plastic *bidons* (containers) at the local wall fountain probably aren't ready for a neighbor with a step-down bath (Fieldnotes August 2005).

In all the riads, decoration is carefully worked out for display, each home owner bringing in their personal touch—the antithesis of the fixed nature of the Fassi home as described by the Tharaud brothers in the early twentieth century. Plunge pools aside, the new mode of occupation is most clearly signaled in the minor, functional spaces: storage rooms and terraces. In addition to the great reception/sleeping rooms, Fassi houses have a multiplicity of tiny pantries (*buyout 'oula*), situated in the interstitial rooms generated in houses with irregular floor plans, rooms with four-meter high ceilings and multiple flights of steep, narrow stairs. The *oula*, the annually created food-stock, was stored in such spaces. Cosmopolitan Fassis convert them into bathrooms and lavatories. The teams of women who prepared the provisions for extended families have disappeared—and the kitchens, once places tucked into awkward corners of a house plan once the ceremonial rooms had been decided upon—have become places of display.

In this new scheme of things, kitchen activity becomes physically central, visible from the central patio: either through open plate-glass windows or through a great wooden door when an entire *sala* with five-meter high ceilings becomes a kitchen focusing on an immense marble-topped counter. Or the kitchen may be the first room one meets on entering the house, following a northern European model of traditional domesticity.

In a sense, the authenticity discourse of the incoming riad owners produces frozen domestic environments. The patio, center of the turbulent, occasionally ceremonious, and often raucous life of the Fassi family becomes a zone for aesthetic contemplation. Symbolic of this shift wrought by the cosmopolitan incomers is the fate of the *khabia*, the terracotta food storage jar, an item so indispensable to Fassi life that it is the subject of a proverb: "min qa'a el-khabia"—"from the bottom of the storage pot," that is, in the parlance of the *ahl Fas*, truly authentic, because the best pieces of dried, salted meat (*khli'a*) prepared after Aïd el Kebir and stored in a khabia would always gravitate to the bottom of the jar. So real breeding and prestige are not immediately accessible. Incomers recyle the khabia as patio plant pot and decorative feature to mask unsightly under-the-sink piping in the new bathrooms.

A GENTRIFYING DIASPORA?

Fès since independence has become a city of migrants, the vast majority of them poor, the very poorest confined to unsafe, unhealthy housing in the médina. But since the mid-1990s, a new, unexpected sort of migrant has taken up residence in the city. Often with considerable financial clout, these migrants from the North Atlantic world dislocate voluntarily to make new homes in Fès. Plans of returning "home" recede and the personal journey comes to predominate. No doubt these are very different narratives from the ones of loss yet to be told by *harraga*-s (migrants) heading for Europe. But like the young Moroccan men of limited means and education whom I have often met as I've traveled across the country, the desire to move begins young. The North Atlantic neo-Fassis dreamed of different cultural experience, learnt languages, migrated with their parents. While none of those interviewed came from interethnic marriage, some of those settling in Fès have a Moroccan partner. Perhaps their earlier lives, with parents who traveled or who wanted their children to travel, had predisposed them to take a partner with a different culture. Returns to the home country, be it in Europe or North America were experienced largely as an opportunity to recuperate, in a sense, and gain a perspective on life in Morocco. Despite new roots, a certain nomadism is an element of their lives. Having multiple homes is unproblematic.

There is, however, a paradox in the neo-Fassias' crossings to explore another culture. They come to a city that they identify as being authentic, pure in some way that their own cultures are no longer. Yet they hold fears for that very authenticity. The gentleman-restorer laments the "restoration" or rather destruction of a simple traditional home to serve as extra space for a tourist bazaar, is afraid for the delicate patina of the Aïn el Khaïl minaret as renovation works approach. "When there is too great a foreign presence, the magic goes," remarked another respondent. Said the owner of a large riad:

> It's a real dilemma for people like us—we want to be successful, we want to bring in tourists, but somehow there's got to be a way of limiting the tourists . . . but none of us can say "that's enough."

And as she described the migrations en masse of ex-socialites from London, Paris and Rome to cities like Marrakech, she prophesied: "It will be the jet-set here soon, and we'll be the forefathers."

POSTSCRIPT

From carnets, 30 August 2005: Far from Fès

It is now over a year since I bought the house on Zkak Roumene. Little by little my feel for the city develops. In March, I left the city after two weeks of supervising work on the house—exhausted. This time, after two months in Morocco, my language has come on considerably. A couple of days before departure, I was able to communicate with the builder far more effectively than I had thought possible. Certain terms had dropped into place, the process of refurbishing a Fassi *douira* is less of a mystery.

Little by little, I'm falling in with the way of doing things. From my eight months living in Marrakech, I took away the idea that communication was often difficult because I was constantly dealing with people for whom spoken Arabic was a second language after Tachelhit—and so they could not be expected to make the leap to understand my attempts to adapt my Tunisian spoken Arabic to Moroccan. Now when dealing with the workmen it is also a matter of dealing with people for whom the written word has a very different status. The builder reads my receipt from the RADEEF doubtfully and checks exactly what it means with a neighbor who works for them. Only then is he satisfied that everything is fine. In the whole, swarming mass of Fès el Bali, there are only a handful of news vendors. In March I left the country tired after my attempts to get an estimate of time (let alone money) needed to complete the works on the house. Now I just go with the flow. Problems are to be met as they arise. Why can't the builder explain why he does things in the way he does? Because he analyses and acts as needs arise.

Touring the twin old towns of Fès at a slow pace, visiting Marrakech and Casablanca this August threw the uniqueness of Fès into sharp relief for me. Each city is a world apart: it's as if you change country when you change city, a difference underscored by the long, slow train rides between them. The soundscape, early on a summer morning: cantilation from a distant mosque before sunrise, the call to prayer—not as synchronised as you might expect—then the birdsong, the doves whose cooing sets off at manic speed.

The interactions of everyday life. In the street, watching out for the sharp metal corners of the crate transporters wedged on the mules' backs. The neighbor appears in her doorframe with a tray of bread to baked, the child coming out of the door across the alley takes the tray automatically and carries it off down to the oven down Zkak Roumene. I catch snatches of conversation: "That tea was so good we nearly digested our socks," "Look at her, all painted up like a Marrakechi tambourine." In March, as I was buying groceries down at the crossroads of Aïn Khaïl and Nouaïriyine, I heard a voice say loudly, "Ech-cherif hada sakin maâ-na daba" ("This cherif (gentleman) is living here with us now"). Maybe I will be one day, but what might my contribution be to this place and society?

Far from Fès, I appreciate the generous and gentle way of going about things—but forget the hard edge and obsequiousness that leaves so many frustrated. Once north of the Mediterranean comes nostalgia for the mixed smell of coriander, mint, and mule dung in the souk and the flights of swifts over the médina terraces. But longtime friends in Casa, *cadres* (executives) with stable jobs in good companies are working out how to leave, Moroccans I meet on cybermen almost always tell me "mais je ne veux pas rester ici" ("I just can't stay here!") in March at the chicha-café on Boulevard Hassan-II, the conversations with Rachid, Youssef, and Amine turned on how to buy a work contract for Italy or Spain. As a non-Moroccan, I am aware of a new strain of small-minded religiosity—but only have to deal with its tyranny head-on occasionally: the *taxiste* in Marrakech who insisted that we ask for Youb and not Sidi Youb (no one but Islam's prophet can be called *sidi*), the rush-mat seller who refused to shake hands as "it's forbidden for Muslims to shake hands with *nasara* (Christians, foreigners)."

But as a cosmopolitan, I can dip in and out, learn something of the city's ways, enjoy the good things. A position of privilege in a major European city, a European nationality, and the falling price of air travel allows me to come and go. No longer a tourist, not even a posttourist, I'm an in-between sort of resident. I worry that the rurality of my neighborhood, the gritty touch added by trains of mules loaded with skins heading for the tanneries, the cheerful familiarity will disappear if the municipality pushes a road down from Aïn Zliten to Derb Lameur, bringing motor traffic in. And what if the city takes the same route as Marrakech, providing instant Moorish residence, previewable on the internet. Already an Australian woman has bought a place with notions of opening a little café. From my terrace, over at Chrabliyine, a foreigner's roof is instantly identifiable, glowing with terracotta *tadelakt* rendering in the surrounding jumble of cream, lichen gray, and dusty yellow walls.

I'm not really sure what this new way of living in the médina means. In the houses restored by foreigners and perhaps even more so by local notables, the stage seems to be set for exotic adventures. But *maison d'hôte*, "the house with a host," *dar edh-dhiyafa*, "house of hospitality" breaks with old ways of being in the médina: the very principle of hospitality is betrayed. The places where *ahl Fas* lived secure in their families are being given new identities. Restored, decorated, often stuffed with historical bit and pieces, the guesthouses of the médina are inhabited by people with new sets of commitments. Though I initially had thought to recover refurbishment costs through short-term lets to foreigners (see that future advertisement in the *London Review of Books* reading "thoughtfully furnished courtyard house with book-lined walls; accessible on foot and by donkey from Bab el Guissa"), this plan no longer seems so straightforward. On what basis do you reconcile a *dar* in an ordinary neighborhood and affluent visitors? For me, just another neo-Fassi, questions of home and away, motivations for movement and settlement remain difficult to formulate.

NOTE

1. Luxury, calm and voluptuousness, referring to Baudelaire's famous poem "l'invitation au voyage," "An Invitation to Travel," which is so often taken up in ads for travel to exotic locations.

REFERENCES

Bruner, Edward M. (awaiting publication) Tourism in the Balinese borderzone. www.nyu.edu/classes/tourist/bru-bali.dos, accessed October 2004.
Buck-Morss, Susan. 1987. Semiotic boundaries and the politics of modernity on tour: a village in transition. *New Ways of Knowing: the sciences, society and reconstructive knowledge.* Raskin, Marcus and Bernstein, Herbert (eds). Lanham, Md.: Rowman & Littlefield, 200–36.

Faubion, James. 1995. *Modern Greek Lessons: a primer in historical constructivism.* Princeton, N.J.: Princeton University Press.

Florida, Richard. 2002. *The Rise of the Creative Class* New York: Basic Books.

PRESS

de Dives, Alix. 1999. Fès en verts. *Côte Sud*, 57, avril-mai. Photographs by Bernard Touillon, 163–78.

Fadili, Rima. 1996. La sauvegarde du patrimoine architectural: la restauration de Dar Adiyel, Fès. *Architecte*, no. 2 summer 1996, 23–25.

Lamghili, Ahmed. 1976. Comment sauver Fès. *Lamalif* 78, March 1976, 18–20.

Msefer, Sabah. 2001. Les maisons d'hôtes à Fès. *Architecture du Maroc* 1, juillet-août 2001 (numéro spécial sur le tourisme de ville), 45–47.

Website. www.unchartedterritory.co.uk/pages/location_Morocco_Fez

8

Trilateral Touchstones

Personal and Cultural Spaces

Evelyn A. Early

I am finishing up this chapter on a sunny morning in the garden of the Mina Hotel in Tangiers, Morocco. I have just attended the 2006 American Institute of Maghrebi Studies (AIMS) conference on Ibn Khaldun, where I met friends connected to my research and seminars over the last thirty years. As I try to pull the many strands of my life together, I think of my encounters during the last three days. I watch Spaniards over on the ferry for the weekend from Al-Jeciras frolicking in the swimming pool. I realize that my daughter Amelia, born in Honduras but raised mainly in the Arab world, fits in better with the Arabic-speaking waiters than the Spanish-speaking tourists. In spite of a shared language, these tourists have nothing to do with the American-Latina identity that Amelia has forged most recently in Beltsville, Maryland, amongst Latin American middle-class immigrants.

At this AIMS conference our coffee break and meal conversation was cadenced by memories of when/where each of us had arrived in the Arab world. We remember where our paths had crossed over the years since then. One Moroccan professor and I had studied together in the late 1960s in Beirut; another and I had met in the 1990s at a Symbolic Anthropology seminar at Mohammad the Fifth University in Rabat. The American director of the AIMS Research Center in Tunis met me in the 1970s through Donna Lee Bowen, my coeditor for *Everyday Life in the Muslim Middle East*. They collaborated on research in the Tangrout *zawiyya* (spiritual center) in southern Morocco in the 1970s. Since then, my coeditor and classmate at the University of Chicago became my daughter's godmother. She was the person who first brought me to Morocco and introduced me to a whole new constellation of scholars. I traveled straight from Bulaq, Cairo, at the end of my research in 1977 to her traditional home in the medina of Marrakech, where I spent a week wandering back lanes with her, delighted to be led by someone else after three years of fieldwork where I had to focus on every move. An American archaeologist and I reminisced about visits during his dig at Sjilmasa, Morocco, in the 1990s, and compared notes on Moroccan Ministry of Culture officials with whom we both work. That elicited memories of a professor in Chicago, which sent us back to graduate school days and tales of the Great 1977 Blizzard in Chicago. That was when my car was snowbound for three weeks until a group of University of Chicago graduate students left their beers at the infamous Jimmie's Bar and helped me dig out my car. Those years in Chicago bridged my life in Egypt, where I had intended to establish roots and marry an Egyptian boyfriend and my Moroccan era where my daughter came home to live with me and where we returned when she was a teenager.

At breakfast in Tangiers, I bid adieu to academics with whom I had shared experiences in Egypt, in Sudan, in Syria, and in Lebanon. Yesterday, over rich pastry-layered pastille during an excursion to the medina of Tetouan, an American remarked how he arrived in Tunis for his first foreign experience in the Experiment in International Living program the same year a Tunisian at our lunch table was on a tour to the United States. Another American recalled his first trip to the Morocco; he rode the ferry to Tangiers in the fall of 1968. Another friend said he arrived in Cairo that year to study Arabic. 1968 was also the year I traveled to Lebanon to study for a master's at the American University of Beirut. Now, in 2006, all of these places are profoundly changed.

On a bus ride yesterday to the center of Tangiers, I listened as two Tunisian sociologists described their latest research on hybridity, commenting on the cacophony of hand-painted and commercial signs naming hole-in-wall shops for national heroes, or decorating modern shops with traditional designs. A woman in Western attire who should be eating continental cuisine smiles over a steaming couscous dish. A woman in a jellaba who should be washing dishes by hand admires Cascade dishwasher soap. At the sidewalk cafe near the hotel we viewed an amazing carnival procession in honor of the king's visit to Tangier. At first *gnawi* Sufis and traditional costumes and music signaled that this was indeed a Moroccan parade. But further down the column, Mickey Mouse and other fantasy cartoon figures appeared. School bands, a dragon shedding bright colored crepe paper along the way, and musicians dressed as Africans playing African music followed. This led me to think about where we were. Where else in the Arab world would we have experienced this mix? In the Levant, would we have seen processions with African music?

Sitting here in this cafe, I imagine all of the sidewalk cafes that tie me to different places and people. The Socrates cafe in Beirut across from the main gate of the American University of Beirut (AUB) was known for colorful characters such as the devout Muslim professor who drank his Johnny Walker out of a tea glass. One day a new waiter unintentionally exposed the professor's drinking by yelling out the order for scotch in a tea cup. And Uncle Sam's restaurant down the street, where I spent a summer buzzed on NODOZE writing my master's thesis in a strategic position under the air conditioner. In Cairo, there was Fishawi in the heart of the Khan al-Khalili tourist-trap bazaar. There were the other much more traditional cafes, tucked away in back streets, where I met Egyptian intellectuals. Many a bitter coffee drunk with writers in Cairo connected me back to their homologues in Beirut, whom I joined on return visits to Beirut at the Horseshoe Cafe on Hamra Street. Here in Tangiers, dawdling over coffee and savoring the carnival-like atmosphere, I think about the places of my life and how I maintain connections. Susan Ossman notes how serial migrants "do not have a stable institutional or national reference point that makes sense of their displacement" (Ossman 2004, 112). I wonder if or how my present career as a diplomat does indeed serve as a point of reference for me. Before I became a diplomat, I had already lived in Lebanon, Egypt, and Syria. Ever since 1968, I had formed relations with the arabesque of researchers and academics from North Africa, the Middle East, Europe, and the West who struggle with issues of development, state formation, and postcolonialism, and with whom I was enjoying the local Mickey Mouse/Gnawa scene here in Tangiers. Although my work has brought me to new places and new possibilities for encountering old friends, it is in fact my personal trajectory in which I have encapsulated myself that makes me willing to take on a job involving so much moving from country to country.

FROM PREACHER'S DAUGHTER TO INTELLECTUAL NOMAD

I was raised as a "PK" or "preacher's kid" in the small community of Sioux Falls, South Dakota. In addition to being a preacher, my father taught at the local Baptist College. My parents had moved to the Midwest from the South, since my father's commitment to models like Clarence Jordan's interracial Koinania Farm ill-fitted him to remain in Louisville, Kentucky. I vividly recall the missionaries who visited us and sent us exotic objects such as ebony figurines or shellacked coasters from around the world. My father counseled interfaith and interrace marriage candidates. I was accustomed to coming home from school to find what for a small town were quite diverse groups talking with my father in our living room.

After high school, I decided to go to Macalester College, which prided itself on international programs. The college awarded me a National Merit Scholarship sponsored by Readers Digest Magnate Dewitt Wallace. It was at Macalester that I met friends for whom the United States was their second country. My Iranian girlfriend came home with me for Christmas. She still talks about the marzipan cake we made as a family ritual, and the red rubber boots we lent her to walk through the snow. I invited a Yugoslav journalist Branko who was at Macalester's World Press institute, which sponsored fifteen international presses each year, to visit my family. When he accompanied me to the political party headquarters mounting the presidential campaign in my home town of Sioux Falls, Branko chuckled as he offered to contribute money to the parties—saying that would mean the parties could be accused of "being pinko."

All cool Macites chose an international program their junior summer. I eschewed the work aboard program that located us in Hilton hotels around the world in favor of SPAN, the Students Program for Amity among Nations study program. After reading Whitehead and other philosophers writing on the meeting of the East and West, I wanted to travel east. Israel was the Middle Eastern country chosen by the program that year. I decided to study how Sephardic Jews, who had come from Arab countries, assimilated in Israel. As an adult, I suppose I would have placed the line between East and West much further East toward China. But in the 1960s, I happily painted ying yangs on my notebooks, considering Israel to be Eastern. Imagine my surprise when I realized why I couldn't understand any of the Hebrew being spoken by the family from Baghdad living in the Or Yehuda suburb of Tel Aviv. It was not because I had only studied Hebrew on Saturday mornings for one year, but because the family was actually speaking Arabic. That moment of realization would become the defining moment of my life. For I discovered language trumps almost all in international communication. The realization moved me several years later to enroll in a year-long intensive Arabic program.

As a researcher, wondering about the Whiteheadian meeting of East and West, I focused on the recent Sephardic immigrants in Israel and when I moved to Lebanon to study for my master's in Middle East Studies at AUB, I picked the Shi'i southern migrants to the city of Beirut as a focus. I also studied one of the urban leaders, Rashid Baydoun, who founded a nongovernmental organization (NGO) that provided a school and other services to rural Shi'i migrants. I concluded that both groups remained peripheral to their societies but that in the first case of Sephardic immigrants, ideology and in the second case of Shi'i migrants, new kinds of leaders helped to bring the groups into the society. It never struck me that I too was a migrant, although I was a student and absorbing the Lebanese scene as an exotic "other country."

When I chose to spend the summer working on improving my Arabic, I moved in with a family who knew my Beirut friends in the small tobacco-growing village of Nabatiyya al-Fawqa. My host family rose at three in the morning to pick the tobacco leaves in the cool morning and to string them on the ceiling of my bedroom. I learned that the fragrance of tobacco drying bears no relations to the smell of cigarette smoke. These were dramatic times. The Phalangists and Arab nationalist/Palestinian students at AUB where I studied threw chairs at each other and went on strike while in the Palestinian camps real bullets were flying.

During my research on Shi'i NGOs I interviewed Imam Musa Sadr; within months he was to travel to Libya where he "disappeared." The last time I visited my southern Lebanese family in the mid-1970s the son's hand was bandaged from cuts sustained in a demonstration against the *Regie* tobacco company, which at that time, had a strangle hold on the southern economy. I felt then it was only the beginning of a tumultuous time, and it was. In a few years the Israelis would occupy southern Lebanon to a point south of the tobacco village. The Palestinian Intifada would rise. But by then I had moved my research to Egypt and entered a new phase of my life ushered in by the death of Gamal Abdul Nasser.

TWO COUNTRIES

I have lived in Israel, Lebanon, Egypt, and Syria as an academic; Sudan, Morocco, Syria, the Czech Republic (my "out of area" tour), and Morocco as a diplomat. But of all these countries, two feel most like home: Egypt, the country of my first true love, the boyfriend I did not marry, the home I thought I would establish; Morocco, where I brought my daughter home to live at eight months, and where I returned with her at fifteen years on a second tour to finish out her childhood. When I return to Egypt and Morocco after being away, I feel like I am coming home.

I arrived in Cairo to start Arabic language study the day before the funeral of Gamal Abdul Nasser. We sat on the plane as the dignitaries disembarked from the first-class section to loud announcements of their titles by Egyptian protocol. The next day my American friends in Maadi suggested we try to watch the funeral live, from downtown. In those days, cars were so scarce that we were able to park right next to the Shepherds Hotel. Few Egyptians were willing to pay Shepherd's prices so we easily found a seat in the roof restaurant from where we watched the mass of humanity swirl in grief around Nasser's coffin as it passed from hand to hand. Afterwards, we saw iron-grilled fences curved out of shape from the press of the crowds surging forward to touch Nasser's coffin. Shortly after my arrival in the country, I met Mustafa, who became my boyfriend. I also decided to pursue a career as a researcher.

My first year in Egypt was one of intensive language study. At night Mustafa and I attended plays and films, or drank tea with the family. We read classic texts including those of Ibn Khaldun for my "real class with Egyptian students" together as well as a variety of pulp fiction provided by my instructors. The idea was that reading such superficial items as the novel *Woman at Your Service* or the latest movie magazine would improve my speed at reading, getting my eyeballs moving right to left more swiftly. After Arabic study in Egypt, I enrolled in anthropology at the University of Chicago. After studying Lebanese Shia immigrants to Beirut for my master's, I turned my attention from migrants to Beirut to the rural migrants recently arrived in Cairo for my doctorate. I returned again to Egypt after these years in Chicago.

Diplomatic relations were severed between Egypt and the United States after the 1967 June or Yom Kippur war. But as one of a handful of Americans in the country huddled in the backyard of the embassy to celebrate July 4, 1973, I felt extremely happy and comfortable to be back after my sojourn in Chicago. I had a Fulbright grant of $2,500 that was going to have to last me a year. (It did thanks to a wonderful landlord who let me rent for 50 pounds a month because I was a rare foreigner wanting to live in a noisy downtown flat.) I picked up the check at the "American interests" section behind the former U.S. Embassy, now temporarily flying the Spanish flag until diplomatic relations would be restored. As I shopped for a possible affiliation to facilitate my research in Egypt, the lack of diplomatic relations was a roadblock. The director of the American University in Cairo's Social Research Center gave me the polite brush off, saying: "An American affiliation will do you no good in these troubled times." But I was ready to establish a life in Egypt as a person, not as an American.

Anti-Americanisms did not faze me. In Lebanon when I was a language student and anthropologist living in the south, I knew that most people assumed I was a CIA agent because I was an American, asking strange questions, in a place where no normal Americans visited. Anthropologist was not a category for southern Lebanese. I learned to live with an identity as "an American" to the general public versus "Evelyn the researcher" for friends and those intimately associated with my research. Years later as a diplomat, I still feel a divergence between Evelyn as "official American" and "Evelyn the person." Amazingly, it is now often easier to maintain a bifurcated identity.

My "American" job is my job as "diplomat," the job that the general public who sees me only as American can understand. My "Evelyn the person" identity is my anthropologist/researcher persona. Like Muslims who traveled to the West and thought they had gained a new (non-Muslim) identity, but after 9/11 found themselves, as Anar Ali puts it "Muslim Magnified," I do encounter situations when my identity as a cosmopolitan, as a person, and as an American collapse under the weight of world events. Then, except for close friends, my identity becomes "official American" not cosmopolitan or researcher. Anar Ali, a Canadian Muslim, writes of a similar collapsing of multiple identities into one: "After years of hard work (and thirty years in Canada) I finally arrived in a new geography. It was a cultural and psychological place, one that coalesced my identities into one and has given me a sense of hope. I called this place Canadian. September 11 changed all this. These events (September 11 and other terrorist acts) have all in one way or another expelled me from my new home. It was dismantled; my Muslim identity was teased out like code form a DNA strand. This is all you are, Muslim Magnified. . . . Terrorists and radical Islamists live in a different place from me, psychologically and culturally even if they were also raised in Canada" (Anar Ali 2006, 5). Anar has lost his "third space" in-between a native and a newly found culture. Most of the time, I can retain the luxury of finding that third space where I can be myself. But trying to maintain this space has caused me grief with my natal family. My brothers complain that I speak "special English" to them and that I have adopted an alien lifestyle, which makes them uncomfortable.

In any case, young and tough in Egypt in the early 1970s, I felt that my relationship with Mustafa bridged any opposition of nationality. I would carry out my research. We would marry and I would settle for good in Cairo. I was close to his family. I spent most nights keeping his mother company in her bedroom where we all gathered to watch television and talk over the day's events. I would regale them with my stories from the working-class, immigrant neighborhood where I was working. I worked in a traditional or *baladi* area whereas Mustafa's family lived in a modern or *afrangi* part of town. Through a string of personal relations that offered me referrals to influential Egyptian bureaucrats, I was able to conduct research at the Mother Child Health (MCH) clinic in Bulaq Abu Ala. This would provide opportunities to meet migrant women. The first day I visited the clinic I met the three women most critical to my entire three years of research. They were mothers who raised orphan children. They were, fortunately for me, at the clinic for their monthly food supplements provided by the ministry for the orphans.

In the clinic, I had a role that made sense in Egypt but that was also vague enough to afford me flexibility. Women in the clinic viewed me as they did the clinic social worker; they would explain to new comers that I was there "to understand how we raise our children." But unlike the Egyptian social worker, who disdained the traditional, country or baladi, women who frequented the clinic, I was interested in their lives and I welcomed their invitations to visit them in their homes. The social worker, like Mustafa's family, was in the more "modern" and afrangi stratum of Egyptian society. My baladi women friends were tolerant of the contradictions this raised for me. They accepted me as one of them although I was potentially allied with the "enemy afrangi clinic worker staff." I was also a non-Muslim, foreigner. I always let the women set the expectations for my behavior, and thus found that I could visit them at home at almost any time of the day although I avoided lunch time and evenings of course and that I could visit mosques and shrines with them, appropriately dressed, although I never prayed of course.

Anthropology fieldwork classes and diplomatic circles share the fear of "going native." I felt accepted by my Egyptian women friends during my three years of intensive fieldwork, but I always kept an outsider perspective although I adopted many of the typically baladi styles of greetings and interaction. In the book I wrote based on this research, I describe the day I "went native." It was a day when I had no friends with me. I reached out to my menu of social interactions and spontaneously selected a typical baladi woman and I used the same social standards that Egyptian baladi women do. As I was walking down the street a woman accidentally dumped her wash water on me. Tossing things from balconies is quite common and I knew she had not targeted me. Perhaps my surprise, and humiliation at being soaked, were the real reasons that I "leapt to the middle of the street, and, without reflecting, raised my fist and my voice simultaneously" and launched into a typically baladi string of curses on the woman for insulting me and my family (Early 1993, 20–21). I was socialized into baladi society but my greeting/ interaction styles did not change my perception of issues like health or economic well-being.

Although I did not go native, still my personal position in Egyptian society was, purposely, vague. I was a guest of Mustafa's family, who at times criticized "disgusting baladi habits" and at other times praised the virtues of the honest baladi folks. (This was in keeping with the multiple meanings of baladi, which allowed it to be used both positively and negatively in a similar way to the Western practice of both criticizing "honest simple folk" as uneducated or ill informed while simultaneously praising them for being hardworking and loyal to their families.) I was never comfortable either keeping silent or coming to the defense of my baladi friends. My structural position as foreigner was the one to which I usually fled; that allowed me to be a quiet observer, taking no sides in internal Egyptian matters. But I felt guilty when

I did that. I was the quintessential chameleon of whom Ossman writes in evoking the fears that serial migrants can provoke (2004). Here, the issue was not simply one of fitting into a homogeneous Egyptian society but of balancing the meaning of very different affiliations (researcher/friend and daughter) to different social groups.

At the same time Egypt was a country where I might live, albeit as an outsider, but where I would feel accepted by the peers of my husband-to-be, maybe. It was for that that I spend afternoons with my prospective mother-in-law watching her play croquet at Nadi Gezira, a posh club. It was for that that I drank endless tea with Mustafa's relatives and with all my new-found friends in Egypt. It was for that as well as my fear that the Egyptians might focus on my research and decide that the office director's letter of introduction didn't really give me research clearance, that I never talked about my research site to Americans I met at embassy and American Research Center in Egypt meetings or parties. I remained aloof from the ex-pat community, avoiding revealing that I knew English when I was in tourist areas with well-dressed but obnoxious American tourists.

As I sought acceptance by Mustafa's circle of friends and family, I found that language is both an integrator and an isolator. My aloofness was the ticket to integration into Mustafa's society. But it was also calculated. There were times I needed Western, American propping up. I sought it among American researchers who shared my love for the local culture and my tolerance for all the things that drove tourists to be testy: flies, dirt, beggars, sand storms, greedy street vendors hawking tourist trivia, the in-your-face nature of Egyptian society where any outsider in the street is fair game for conversation.

Years later after I had left Egypt and abandoned my plans of settling in, I found that my tolerance flip-flopped and I became an intolerant tourist with the best of them on a cruise down the Nile. No time for flies and flea markets. I wanted the white tableclothed, air-conditioned dining rooms. I was tired and older. This shift in my orientation to Egypt is best documented by my daughter Amelia. When I told her about this article she read parts about her, and then announced that she wanted to write about when she and I, on vacation in Egypt when we were living in Prague, met Mustafa and his new wife—a Hungarian woman who stayed in Egypt after her divorce from another Egyptian. Amelia remembered this trip vividly and wanted to put it in her own words. My daughter wrote this, speaking on my behalf, in the first person: "When we went back (to Egypt), to my surprise he (Mustafa) was married to a woman who was intellectually smart. But when you broke it down, it was a controlling relation that worked for both of them. One would organize the soap in the hotel, the other would be relaxing. Mustafa had never been an organized man and therefore he married a woman who would do things for him."

Inspired by memories of Egypt, Amelia continued—still speaking as though she were me—talking about another part of that trip. "On the same trip we went on a cruise. My daughter thought I was crazy and so demanding and uptight. My daughter was more of a nontourist than I was, even though I had lived in Egypt for so many years. She continually reminded me that I was making unreasonable demands."

What had happened? My daughter was embarrassed when I acted like a tourist, despite the fact that I lived in Egypt for many years. She couldn't see why I wouldn't enjoy the hot summer days, the flies buzzing in the air, and the nagging natives trying to sell her things. She and her godsister Victoria were having a great time enjoying our cruise. Victoria had never come to Egypt but was acting (in Amelia's eyes) "like a native." I went off on tours, while my daughter and Victoria chatted with Egyptians and mimicked the tour guide's stilted speaking style.

One can move in and out of degrees of being a chameleon, feeling at ease, and wanting to be something like a native. But some of the practices I adopted in the Middle East remain always with me and still, even today, I am startled if boyfriends do not act as considerately and conservatively toward me as Mustafa did. I am surprised when friends and neighbors do not treat me like my Egyptian friends did. Many Westerners who have lived in the Middle East find they share similar problems: cooking too much food for dinner thinking that at least ten extra people might show up, walking over to someone's home forgetting that the person would expect a phone call alerting them of the visit, or pouring out one's life history to someone before realizing that they just want to get down to the business at hand. I do not know if I became a native in Cairo. But it became my true second country in the sense that I had all intentions of settling there. It was only when my engagement to Mustafa didn't work out and I started to think of other life courses that I really set off on a path of serial migration that would bring me to my third home in Morocco.

MOROCCO'S MOVABLE SEMINAR

Just as Nasser's death marked my arrival in Egypt, the First Gulf War framed my introduction to Morocco. By 1991, I had abandoned the idea of trying to establish a family through marriage. I adopted my daughter in Honduras and brought her home to live with me in Rabat. The trip to Honduras to start the adoption and the trip to bring her home were split by the First Gulf War, which I feared would delay us. In Rabat, a monthly seminar became one of the sources of continuity in my life. The Symbolic Anthropology Seminar was started by my dear friend, the anthropologist and painter Abdulhai Diouri. I joined the group in the early 1990s and I faithfully attended most sessions for four years. This spring, in 2006, I returned to the seminar. It felt like I had never left.

It was at a seminar of Abdulhai's that I was first introduced to my friend Susan Ossman. So when she visited me in May 2006, I thought it would be fun to visit Abdulhai. On a sunny clear spring day we drove toward the sea, to Har Houra to Abdul Hayy's house where the bright blue front warding off the evil eye beckoned us. We creaked open the gate and made our way to the back stairs and climbed up past the petunias proliferating pink out of their pots. A cat scampered down the stairs as if to clear the way for us. The door was open. Abdulhai was home, but feeling quite ill. But an old friend was welcome.

In the early days I saw the Symbolic Anthropology Seminar as a chance to encounter rich cultural studies of the very country where I was still an outsider, as well as a chance to improve my French. I felt more comfortable talking anthropology in Arabic, my language of research for twenty years, but almost all Moroccan intellectuals I met used French as their language of intellectual exchange. I remember giving a paper to the seminar in Arabic in the mid-1990s. I can still see smiling faces of Moroccan historians and psychoanalysts as they exclaimed: "This is the first time we have discussed these kinds of issues in Arabic; we can actually do it!" This pointed out how very exotic I really was in Morocco. Part of me relished confronting the Moroccan sense of identity with their "national language," albeit my Egyptian-inflected version of it. But by 2005, speaking Egyptian in Morocco seemed less acceptable than ten years before, now that Moroccans were much more nationalistic about their Arabic. I resolved to purge my Egyptian and elevate my dialect to a standard Arabic peppered with expressions from the Moroccan dialect when a friend who met me early after my return in 2005 left a discrete message with my secretary: "Do not use Egyptian; it is not cute."

Morocco is an Arab, Berber, Muslim (Maliki sect), and Jewish, Moorish, African, Mediterranean "monarchy on the way to democracy." Moroccans disdain attempts to smash them into the "Muslim" or the "Levant" molds. Morocco may be producing some jihadists but the Muslim discourse in Morocco is not one of extremism. The government has assured a series of television talk shows that feature moderate interpretations of Islam and plenty of time for the youth to call in and ask questions. The Ministry of Religious Affairs has recently trained a class of women *morshidat,* or spiritual guides. The current minister for religious affairs is a Sufi from a major Sufi sect known for moderation and devotion. He is also a historian who attended the Movable Seminar a decade ago. The government is carefully monitoring all the Islamic movements and a recent political party law has excluded any parties of ethnic or religious affiliation. That said, the leading political party has a religious bent but one that is avowedly moderate. In the meantime the government is engaged in a rigorous roundup of any group that smacks of Salafist, extremist Islam.

Moroccans think of themselves first and foremost as Moroccans, not Arabs. Just as most resist any Saudi-exported Salafist movement, so they resist and resent the flood of Levantine music and soap operas. The French/ Moroccan owned Medi-1 television station scheduled to open this summer aims to have a cutting-edge news program with distinctively North African programming. In the meantime Moroccan TV stations, particularly the formerly almost exclusively French 2M channel, are increasing the local programming in Arabic. There has also been a significant movement to linguistically hybrid programs. On talk shows panelists move back and forth between Arabic and French depending on their level of comfort; a Saturday night disco's songs range from traditional Arabic in the style of Oum Khathsum (an Eyptian) to French romantic songs, to English rock.

Just as when Ossman speaks of how entering a city in different ways conditions one's understanding of the space, so the fact of coming to Morocco from the Levant and Egypt influenced my approach to things (1994). When I first lived in Morocco I was struck by what I thought of as schizophrenia between Arab and French culture. On my return ten years later I saw things more in terms of an attempt to balance the many aspects of Morocco with one face to Europe, one to Africa, one to the Levant, and one to the West. I traveled more widely and met lower-class villagers who reminded me more of the women I met during research in Cairo than of the educated Moroccans with whom I worked daily. I dabbled in the French/European side of Morocco that distanced me from my Egyptian days.

At home with Abdulhai, sipping tea, we spoke a mixture of English, French, and dialectal Arabic as we caught up on research and on art exhibits. Abdulhai . . . My thoughts again float back to the decade before when Abdulhai invited me (or did I invite myself?) to visit friends in the south for his yearly "getting in touch trip" related to his research on Sufism. We loaded my three-year-old daughter, her nanny, and ourselves into my Mercedes and took off for the trip of my life. It was a journey that coalesced family, fantasy, and frolicking. We arrived in small Kasbahs, parked the unhideable orange Mercedes bomb (which guaranteed that local security would visit, oh so casually, our host's house within the hour), and greeted our host family who immediately invited all of us to stay in the best two rooms of the house. Within minutes my daughter crawled into the lap of the father, babbling away in perfect children's Arabic. The following day we would visit all the Sufis and scholars of the area.

I interrupted my reminiscing, since Abdulhai and Susan were discussing her latest project about serial migration and cosmopolitanism. I needed to pay attention because I was going to write this chapter for the book! Abdulhai remarked that "the" (really "his") seminar had spent years looking at postmodernism and exploring alternative concepts to fit Morocco's current experience, and none had really fit. One of the lessons studying and living in Morocco teaches is that models and theories are easily disrupted. Morocco is a poster child for a study of postmodernism, a post "clash of civilizations" kind of place. In spite of its strong Islamist movement, it fits none of the prevailing conservative stereotypes of the Middle East or of a Muslim country. As we talked about cosmopolitanism and Morocco, my mind went back to a conference that Abdulhai had organized on different cultural conceptions of death. Susan and I had met at that seminar, which Abderrahmane Lakhsassi also attended. We quickly realized that we knew friends in common from graduate school days, exchanged cards, met for coffee, and then for lunch. Later, our paths crossed in Paris and in Washington D.C., and here once more, in Har Houra.

Here in Har Houra drinking tea with Abdulhai and looking at his paintings of his memories of the doors, lanes, and spaces of his childhood in Fez, everything came together for me. Not a boyfriend, but the man who had given my four-year-old her first painting classes and who had given me my first taste of Sufism and rural society in Morocco, Abdulhai anchors the "Movable Seminar" that helps hold together the arabesque that is my cosmopolitan "third space." This is the third place that "breaks the binary oppositions that have tended to inform how we think about migration, globalization and our own work as social scientists," the third place that "urge(s) the recognition not only for the 'other' but of 'others'" (Ossman 2004, 113). Abdulhai spent several years at Princeton. Like me, he has written a book in anthropology. When we talk anthropology we are not Moroccan and American but anthropologist and anthropologist. As he says in 2006, he does not feel like a native scholar, but rather a citizen of the world. Our world begins with our exchanges with one another, and with others at the Moveable Seminar.

MOROCCO IN AMERICA

Morocco was the country where I started my family. I brought Amelia home when she was six months old. One of the most treasured pictures in Amelia's baby album is the Moroccan maid and nanny meeting us as we arrive from the airport with the tray of traditional dates and milk. Today, although Amelia has a room decorated to her taste in Morocco, she is enrolled in a boarding school in the United States. When I visited her there this year, I remembered how she taught me about Moroccan children's dialect one day as we were sitting in the garden in Rabat. She was in her high chair bubbling out random words that I did not really understand. She used a word that signified something to the maid, but I didn't comprehend. She was quickly served a glass of water. Amelia learned Arabic quickly as that was the language of "goodies" that the maid and nanny understood well. If I had not had a child I would never have learned that Moroccan has its own set of words for children's activities: mimi to eat, nini to sleep, and so on—all delightful two syllable repetitions. Years later in Prague I would still ask my daughter if she wanted to "nini." Wherever we are, Amelia and my conversation is full of Arabic phrases and expressions. When we would speak Arabic on the street it was not only a code language for us but also a chance to show the special intimacy we share. Our use of another language distances us from the rest of my family, who criticize me for letting Amelia speak Arabic in front of them because it excludes them.

As we talked this spring in America, I read Amelia notes from the draft that would become this chapter. I asked her about her experience growing up in Morocco, the United States, Syria, and the Czech Republic before returning to the United States in tenth grade. She noted that in Morocco and Damascus she felt welcome, because she was able to speak to others in their own language. She was accepted, she said. In those places she felt her Latin American background made her "look like them and act like them." She was easily able to join a conversation and fit in, whereas in Prague she felt that she could not be herself in front of others. Unlike in Morocco or Syria, she felt that in the Czech Republic she was discriminated against because of her skin color. People often thought she was gypsy. I remember that she would come home unsure about whether she wanted to go out the next day. In our hotel room where we were having our reunion were pictures of Amelia's childhood in Morocco. She had fashioned them into a card for me to take back from America to Morocco with me. We always have some pictures and special, personal mementoes with us. For me it is the stuffed dog Amelia gave me to keep me company one time when I traveled, plus special jewelry and pictures. For Amelia, it is the pictures and the CDs that evoke the universal memory connector of music.

THE MANSION CAN'T MOVE BUT THE TRINKETS THAT TIE CAN

Recently on an airplane (where else do I have time?), I read an article about the lives of the rich people who move from one gated community to the next.

They also spend millions flying to remote places where they can meet one another without being seen. The author remarks that among his friends, it is not uncommon to meet on four different continents in as many months. He and his friend tried to calculate our average speed through life. So he took the number of miles he had flown in a year and divided it by the number of hours in a year for an "annual average velocity of 45.8 miles an hour. Of course there were times when I was going zero (fireside in Santa Fe reading Henry James) and times (Hong Kong to New York) when I was making nearly 800 miles an hours. I began thinking of my velocity in cockpit terms as a new V speed of sorts: Vpr-Personal Velocity" (Cooper 2006, 88). Ramo goes on to describe how his fast-traveling life has meant the loss of "the sense of connectedness to anything other than what you can take with you when you travel. And those things are your ideas, your dreams, your hopes, and your senses." Ramo notes that the "essential demand for a high-speed life is a kind of portable stillness," which he compares to the "damper that transmutes big shocks into small tremors" in Asian skyscrapers (Cooper 2006, 88).

When I feel dizzy from the speed of my moving every three to four years, I reach out to my earthquake-building damper—the network of friends who define my society. They are a kind of space capsule with me, a capsule made possible originally by the fact that we all moved around and facilitated more recently by the internet. Before internet I wrote countless letters and always kept the guest room ready for the transient scholar. It is not cultural values or national identity that determines who is a part of my networks, but rather the debates/discussions/research about society and values. Those personal debates are intertwined with memories of encounters captured in pictures and in mementoes of shared events. My daughter and I carry family trinkets as we travel. In our home there are special shelves dedicated to mementos that signal common experiences of the family or with members of our academic arabesque. The more generic, such as Islamic folk art from visits made with friends in Cairo, occupy public shelves in our living room. The more personal—such as pictures, or conference brochures, or silly trinkets such as a small plate or a hotel ash tray—reside on shelves in the personal spaces of our house.

At the Casablanca Book Fair this year, I retraced my steps through my different countries. Stopping by the Sudan stand I asked the representative about my academic friends in Sudan—all of whom he knew and promised to greet. I perused familiar Sudanese folklore studies and unfamiliar books on the Islamist government that came to power via a coup just as I left Sudan in the late 1980s. Next I visited the Iranian booth where I found a treasure trove of books in English on Iranian saints and shrines that I would read for information on folk Islam. The representative and I discussed in English the Iranians I met in Syria at the Shrine of Fatima (the sister of the Imam Ali) and how

Syrians questioned Shi'i Muslim pilgrimage practices. As a bonanza since I had bought a huge stack of books, the Iranian gave with a bronze plaque with Quranic inscriptions. That plaque joined a shelf crowded with similar sentimental memorabilia that remind me of people and places: a Turkish plate brought to me by a German friend, a mat with Allah woven in for me by a Sudanese woman, a wood carving from Honduras I bought when I went to bring my daughter home, an ornamental wooden egg from a Czech friend, a Quranic saying handsomely framed. Only I can understand the cacophony of my special ornament shelf. Amelia also has her own array, enriched by all the token gifts that school athletic teams from all over Eastern Europe brought to our house in Prague, but also marked by our Middle East sojourn especially in such pictures of her at age two with her Moroccan nanny who had dressed her up complete with mascara (to my horror) for her birthday party. Looking at my shelves evokes strong memories of connections ranging from those tied to the Quranic mat my Sudanese driver's wife wove for me to those associated with the Persian carpet bag a friend from graduate school who studied Iranian religious culture brought me in Cairo where I researched women's urban life. Trinkets are a material form of the academic arabesque that supports me in my migrations. They are a visual and emotional reminder of the more spiritual, personal support, the center of gravity provided by Mustafa's family in Egypt and by Abdulhai's Movable Seminar in Morocco.

CONCLUSION

My family's life has been profoundly affected by my mobile and cosmopolitan life. My daughter, born in Honduras and raised mostly in the Middle East, struggles with her identity as a Mediterranean culture-oriented Hispanic living with an Anglo mother. There are gray ambiguous areas in her life and identity. There are in mine too. In my second country of Egypt, I moved between becoming Egyptian as a (potential) wife of an Egyptian and remaining foreign as a researcher. In my third country, Morocco, I move between my status as official diplomat and as personal academic/researcher. My personal status splits between a Moroccan academic arabesque—the community of the Moveable Seminar, and a cosmopolitan academic arabesque—that encompasses my American contacts plus international scholars such as those I just met at the AIMS in Tangiers. I need not choose between the two arabesques because the two bleed into each other as individuals cross and recross lines between the two. It seems simple. Academic research is international. But in another sense it is profoundly personal. For instance, something like "Moroccan academic discourse" is interlocutor-specific and potentially fraught with controversy. The intermingling of researchers leads to links to different academic cultures. For instance, Americans and French meet more easily in Morocco than in either of their native countries. They share their very different approaches to the same object of research: Moroccan society and polity.

Living overseas has given me the advantage of learning many languages and teaching my daughter languages that will open careers for her. Amelia tells me that she plans to work in the UN or in a foreign country and she feels most at home living overseas. Sometimes when we live in the United States it is hard to raise a child rarely exposed to North American culture. For my daughter living in Boston and going to tenth grade was not a positive experience. Even though she has lived with a variety of students of varied cultures, it did not satisfy her need to be overseas. She told me that when she talked to students in Boston "they simply thought living abroad was awesome but they didn't understand the importance or impact it had on me." In a sense, Amelia remains "an outcast" in American schools and is now "condemned" to be an "international school child." Amelia is a bilingual child who, as Beck has said, moves "through the non-place of television and the Internet like fish through water" (Beck 2002, 31). Her "deterritorialization" means that she and I can celebrate family events anywhere as long as we are together. We have celebrated Christmas in four different countries in the past ten years. We celebrated her sixteenth birthday in a mountain lodge—neither at her school nor at our "home" in Morocco. When Amelia has time off between terms it is to Morocco that she begs to come. The day I completed edits on this article, Amelia was visiting Rabat and we lunched with Abdulhai on his porch with the pink petunias. Inbetween lunch and coffee, just as we were discussing Abdulhai's next project on new landmarks in a postmodern world, two moveable seminar participants dropped by. I had not met the professor of Berber studies from the school of oriental languages in Paris; as usual, I was meeting the French via the Moroccans. We exchanged mobile phone numbers as I was eager to continue our discussion, but I had promised Amelia we would not miss her friend's birthday party in Rabat. As we bid farewell, Abdulhai and I agreed to meet soon to view his paintings and talk about his plans for a conference on postmodern ideas of time and landmarks. My third space personal capsule of the moveable seminar was alive and well.

NOTE

This article is written by a professional anthropologist and represents the personal views of the author. It is not intended to represent any official views of the U.S. government.

REFERENCES

Ali, Anar. 2006. The Person behind the Muslim. *International Herald Tribune*. June. 17–18.

Beck, Ulrich. 2002. The Cosmopolitan Society and its Enemies. *Theory, Culture and Society* vol. 19 (1–2), 17–44.

Cooper, Joshua. 2006. Living at Jet Speed. *Newsweek*. May 15–22.

Early, Evelyn. 1993. *Baladi Women of Cairo, Egypt: Playing with an Egg and a Stone.* Boulder: Lynne Reinner Press.

Eickelman, Dale F. and Jon W. Anderson. (eds). 2003. *New Media in the Muslim World: The Emerging Public Sphere.* Bloomington: Indiana University Press.

Ossman, Susan. 2004. Stories of Serial Migration. *International Migration.* October. 111–21.

———. 1994. *Picturing Casablanca: Portraits of Power in a Modern City.* Berkeley: University of California Press.

Starrett, Gregory. 2003. The Great Chain of Buying. *New Media in the Muslim World: The Emerging Public Sphere.* Eickelman, Dale F. and Jon W. Anderson (eds). Bloomington: Indiana University Press.

9

In Search of Tangiers' Past

Leila Abouhouraira

One of my earliest memories is of taking the boat from Tangiers to Spain. As a child I learned Spanish by a kind of osmosis, from my family, people in the neighborhood, and from the television. The Arabic dialect of Tangiers is full of Spanish, as well as borrowings from English; Gibraltar is very close by. My father spoke Spanish fluently, as do my sisters and my brothers. Although my mother never learned to read and write, she can easily get by in Spanish. She certainly understands it better than she does newscasts in classical Arabic. French is also spoken by many people in Northern Morocco. "In the region where we lived there was the influence of both colonial powers (France and Spain). So we studied French and Spanish," Hamid explained to me.

> But more than this, it is more about Moroccans' attitudes. There is a certain attitude of openness because of being in a zone of transition and passage. . . . I don't see any attitude except this openness and movement toward others. There is an acceptance of the foreigner since so many foreigners transit via Morocco and there is a long tradition of migration.

Mokhtar, a middle-aged Algerian who grew up in Tangiers told me that

> Most of my adolescence, I lived in Tangiers. Tangiers is a very cosmopolitan city, you can find anything there. At the time it was even more of a tourist destination than it is today. We were drenched in a multiethnic milieu, speaking English or Spanish much more frequently than people in other parts of Morocco. In general, people from Tangiers speak foreign languages better than those from Casablanca or Rabat. Calling Tangiers "the door of North Africa" is very accurate.

Tangiers educated me to be mobile, multilingual, and curious about people different than myself. I am not at all a "cosmopolitan" in the way we usually define the term, either in terms of wealth or educational background. I grew up in a family that might be called lower middle class. My mother did not work outside the home. My father was a police officer. Today I am a translator and manger, not a famous "third world intellectual." That I am even writing here is really due to encounters along the path of migration rather than to my professional qualifications. Translation, migration, and meetings with people from afar—these are the keywords of my life. They were all given to me by my beloved Tangiers, my native city.

I always thought being born in Tangiers as a great privilege. But one day, everything changed. I realized that what has always been seen as an international city had suddenly been remapped to become a city of the Arab world. Tangiers, where we spoke so many languages, where no borders made any difference, the city to which people came from Rif mountains and from what is called the "interior" of Morocco as well as from all of the ports of the Mediterranean, my dear Tangiers was being abruptly closed, cordoned off from its natural setting. From Tangiers you cannot see Cairo or Jeddah, but Algeciras is clearly visible on the horizon. It is this geography of a Tangiers linked to these places that is natural to me. But Europe decided that the natural geography I grew up with simply wasn't right. In the 1980s visas were imposed for those who wanted to cross the straights of Gibraltar from the south. The map makers, border guards, and consulate administrators reconceived Tangiers as a kind of Western outpost of the Arab world. This set me on a path of serial migration. It led me to develop a kind of errant nostalgia for my city that has sent me out to search for a space resembling the one in which I was raised. I think of that memory place as a space of freedom. It is this freedom I want to explore in the following pages; through my own experience of serial migration, but also through the stories of friends, coworkers, and my family, other serial migrants whose paths have crossed mine in Morocco, France, or Canada and who have been kind enough to let me interview them for this study.

CLOSING THE DETROIT

I was in France at the university, studying English when I learned that a visa would now be required to cross the Detroit of Gibraltar. Easy trips to Spain were over for Moroccan nationals, or anyone with an Arab passport for that matter. This frightened me. I was apprehensive. I no longer assumed that I would return to Tangiers or even Morocco after completing my studies. It felt like someone was ripping apart my house, or separating my patio from the house. I could not rid myself of the impression that this challenge to the geographic and cultural landscape was totally unnatural.

I had never really thought of Tangiers as part of the Arab world. Or at least, not as exclusively part of that space. I was educated at the French lycée. It was a matter of chance rather than a family tradition or strategy. In my family, each sibling received a different kind of education. Some went to public schools, others to various private institutions. Unlike elite families, we approached education as a haphazard process. In any case, I ended up being much more proficient in French, Spanish, and English than in Modern Standard or classical Arabic. My family had always felt more connected to Spain and France than to the Middle East because of where we lived. But in addition to this, the fact of being a woman was certainly a part of why I so resented being confined and excluded from Europe by the imposition of the visa. Tangiers had been changing, I knew, with processes of "nationalization" and the spread of intolerant understandings of Islam. But I needed to think of myself as free and as having choices. Even though I was studying in France and I could obtain a visa, I saw my prospects for a future in Tangiers as compromised in important ways by the simultaneous imposition of the visa and the "Islamization" process.

Although I realized this, I did not immediately decide to remain in France after my studies. I still assumed that I would return to Tangiers. There seemed to be no other alternative for an unmarried girl. I was the first and the only girl in my family of five children to study abroad. I knew that after finishing my degree I would have to live with my parents. They would have never let me live by myself. I couldn't have my own place because of social pressures. In Morocco, at that time, a woman living on her own would inevitably be seen as someone with a bad reputation. Even a divorced woman is expected to go back to her parents, even if she is middle aged. The only other option I had was to stay in Europe or get married.

Morocco is not a country where it is easy to find someone to marry, at least, not in the way that I wanted to be married (Mernissi 1988). Some of my friends who studied in France returned to Morocco but remained resolutely single. Others accepted arranged marriages. Both tended to conceive as marriage as a privation of freedom. Especially for women, marriage was an escape from their parents' homes. Some women tell me that they are satisfied with this minimalist conception of marriage because "God wants it to be this way." Yet, they will be the first to ask me and other migrants to help their children to go abroad. At some level they recognize that there is something limited and crippling about a life lived as "destiny," or a life of eternal compromise (Aboumalek 1994).

In France, I chose friends with whom I had things in common. In retrospect, I see that the friends I selected mirrored the image of the ideal society I had developed as a child in Tangiers. I became close to Floresca who speaks Arabic ten times better than I ever will, as well as several other languages. I also got to know my friend Karen who is half Danish and half Italian, with an English grandmother. Like me, Karen grew up in Morocco. She could live there again if she pleased, or move somewhere else. I saw no reason that my life should be different than hers, nor did my Moroccan friend Amina. But as Amina told me recently, "it was just assumed then that you would go abroad for study and then return." Indeed, there was a kind of guilt associated with not returning, even if you thought you might have a better life elsewhere.

I seemed always to be surrounded by "foreign" friends. I took advantage of my studies to spend two years in England, where I taught French. Toulouse was not a wonderful place because of the large Moroccan community, or even because French habits are similar to those I am used to due to my education. Rather, it came to feel like home because it opened new doors for me to explore yet other parts of the world. Unlike my sisters, who were experiencing the closing inward of Tangiers each day, I was fortunate to be able to study and move about the world. In Tangiers, the society was becoming ever more "Islamic." Women who chose to wear shorts or go out alone were becoming the object of scorn and rumors. This was not the result of the visa in any direct way, but the rise of intolerance and a certain kind of religious rule making seemed to go along with closing the border. Of course, drugs and other contraband items had no trouble getting past the police and customs agents. But ordinary people spent their time looking across a narrow bit of sea knowing that they no longer had the right to cross to the other side that was so visible to them. This might not have been the justification for making my sisters live a kind of claustrophobic life in their home, but it cannot have been unimportant.

In 1985 I married a fellow Moroccan who was also studying in Toulouse. After we completed our studies we both wanted to stay in France. We easily found jobs and seemed to be starting to fit into the usual immigrant story. Even then, unlike so many immigrants, I didn't feel nostalgia for the place my parents continued to live. I loved to visit them, but the place I held in my memory, that I had known as a child was no longer. Little by little, I began to transpose my longing and memories unto the place I was living. The city of Toulouse and southwestern France started to feel like home. Even now, twenty years later, I think of it in that way. Whenever I meet someone from that region or see "Toulouse" written in a book, my heart skips a beat. I feel the same about Spain. Or at least, Andalusia. Like the Tangiers I grew up in, Toulouse is a city where connections to Spain are always apparent. So when I speak of Andalusia it is not simply in the kind of mythical way that some people nostalgically "recall" the lost Arab kingdoms, but instead, because it evokes a sense of familiarity.

My daughter was born in Toulouse, and we were content there. I found the kind of life I had imagined to be happy and fulfilled. But the pressures to "go home" were very strong. It was not a nostalgic feeling for the nation or the place that led us to decide to move to Morocco. It was strictly due to family ties. I was ambivalent about the move from the first; in fact, I was convinced that I wouldn't be able to stay in Morocco. My family is precious to me. But my living in Tangiers or even Morocco cannot make them happier. It cannot help them from feeling that they are being inspected and watched by the neighbors, who might decide that they are behaving in inappropriate ways. Even if I live next door to them, I do not have the power to make my sisters feel autonomous as women. Indeed, the idea that I might be able to find a way to do this sometimes makes me feel a little crazy. I imagine that my sisters would be happier if I could just get them across the border to Spain. There they could go about their business as they please. But Spain is now on the other side of the "great wall." So I dream about arranging to have them jump over it. I dream about the day we will meet in Andalusia.

In Morocco, my husband and I had good jobs. Our daughter attended private schools. Our "social standing" made it look like I had achieved a considerable amount of success. But I knew that at some point we would leave. Amina, who returned to Morocco after her studies in Toulouse as a matter of course, explained how she too she began to think of leaving again quite soon after getting resettled in Rabat.

> So, you imagine that France is not really your home and you go back to Morocco, the place you thought actually was your home. But then, after a little thought, it is not really your home either. I left with the idea of returning and the idea stuck. But once in Morocco I was disappointed. I could not see my future there so I started to look for something else.

At first, my husband and I thought of moving back to France. His "carte de sejour" (residence papers) was still valid. But in the course of discussing our future, we began to entertain the possibility of moving to Canada. We discussed the idea on several occasions with Amina and her husband, and with Susan. Susan moved from Rabat to Paris in December 1995. Amina left for Canada just a few months later. As I prepared to leave for Canada in 1998 I remembered the conversations we had had sitting around our mint tea in Rabat. I thought of how my life as a migrant had started when I was a student. I realized that times had changed. As young women we could live out of suitcases for months on end. Now I had all kinds of "baggage": an already long professional and personal story, not to mention all of the things that go along with having a family.

THE THIRD MOVE

The day has finally arrived. Here we are, sitting in the plane that will take us from Casablanca to Montreal. My son will be born in Canada, just like my daughter was born in France. I want them to move easily through the world, and yet I know that there is much more to this move than questions of visas and papers. When my daughter interrupts my thoughts asking: "Mama, why are we leaving when we have everything we need here?" I realize that she cannot understand what I "need." It was the need to remake the international city of my youth that led me to want to discover a new continent.

Today, I am pretty sure that my daughter understands the admittedly vague motivations behind our decision to move. We were searching for something. We thought we might find it in this far-off place, so totally different from Europe or Morocco. Sitting in the plane in 1998, eight months pregnant with my son, I was filled with hope and confidence. I did not really "choose" to go to Canada. It was the logical place to go next. Quebec wanted us because we speak French. The kinds of translation and management skills I have are very much in demand. So it was relatively easy to get a visa for immigration.

In Canada, I ended up encountering old friends. Amina now lived there. So did Assad and Hasna, who had started out in Alexandria, Egypt. When I interviewed Amina last summer, she had been in Montreal for eight years. Sitting in her backyard, I asked her where she felt at home. She could not even really understand my question. "Home, what do you mean, this is my home?" she began. "This is it. We're here." She then explained that although she said she sometimes misses her family, she really feels at home in Canada and has no feeling of regret or nostalgia for Morocco. "No I do not think of moving back to Morocco at all, I feel at home here, I will stay here for good." Do you feel lucky living here, I asked? "It is difficult to say that in these terms, but in some way, yes, we are lucky to be here. I feel comfortable here. I am at home. I am living my own life. There are problems though. The big thing is being so far away makes close contact with the family very difficult, it has almost disappeared."

Unlike Amina, Assad misses Morocco quite a lot. He explained to me his feelings about home:

I look at where I lived so far. I lived longer in Morocco than I lived in Egypt. Although I am Egyptian most of my professional life was in Morocco. It is dif-

ferent in Egypt. Egypt is home, yes, but perhaps these years (in Morocco) were
the best years I ever lived. . . . With no responsibilities, we felt at home, we knew
the country. But staying in a place forever, a place where you feel good
. . . that's the difference here (in Canada), feeling that we can stay here and what
we build will not be destroyed so that we have to start over somewhere else another time. This time, we are building something to stay longer, that is why I feel
at home.

For me, as a non-European foreigner in Morocco there could be no future. By
this, I mean, a future in which to settle permanently and raise my children. I
could not have Moroccan nationality to begin with. This meant that, at some
point, I might be obliged to go back to Egypt. That would be very difficult after
such a long time abroad. There is nothing left for me in Egypt. I started to think
that if I stayed in Morocco this would only become more the case. I wanted to
fix a point and make it home. Another point had to do with religion. Bringing
my children up in Morocco was somewhat detrimental to the kind of religious
upbringing I wanted them to have.

As someone who speaks many dialects of Arabic and who only speaks that
single language with his family, Assad has many friends in Montreal from
other Arab countries. Unlike me, he feels comfortable with this broader Arab
community. But in Morocco, the fact that he was an Arab and a Coptic Christian actually worked against him. In Canada, it is professional integration that
has been difficult. He had to study to "validate" his diplomas because his
Egyptian degrees are not recognized in Canada. There is a kind of professional protectionism. However, here he can raise his children in the way that
he wants. He told me that:

> We have done the best we can to get them to see that they are different from the
> others, but that they must learn to live with it. They are different, but they have
> to mix with everything and get involved in all kinds of activities. They know
> that they should preserve a certain image of themselves, a certain identity that is
> slightly different than the other children, in this way they can grow up in a kind
> of equilibrium among communities that is positive and healthy.

Mokhtar, who grew up in Tangiers and also lived in France, could have imagined staying in Morocco if he had not had children. He said:

> I left Morocco because I asked myself a lot of questions regarding my children.
> I kept asking myself questions about whether they could achieve the same level
> of education as I had, whether they would be able to find work in that country
> (Morocco) just like I had. You have to keep in mind that these are children with
> Algerian nationality. I tried to "marocanize" but it is very difficult. So I thought
> to myself that it might be more advantageous for me to actually take them some-
> where else. At first I didn't think of Canada. It meant changing my profession

completely, a real change of horizons but they will be in a place where they have more opportunities. If I did not have children, I doubt that I would be here.

Nadir, an Iraqi who lived in Morocco before moving to Canada, simply said, "If I had a choice between living in Canada or in Iraq, I would choose Iraq. And if it were between Morocco and Iraq, it would be Morocco." But he went on to say that Canada is his home, "If I say that Canada is my home it is because they recognize my rights, the people's rights. It is home in that way, even if for other issues that we cannot deal with picturing Canada as home."

While we often hear of the problems of illegal aliens in Europe, or the ways that developed countries discriminate against foreigners, these kinds of inter-Arab migration stories are not told. It is very interesting that while Moroccan serial migrants are ready to leave Morocco behind, serial migrants from other Arab countries seem to prefer Morocco to their current homes in many ways. This is particularly marked from those from Egypt or the Middle East. The reasons that led them to leave Morocco are related to the impossibility of becoming Moroccan nationals, or reconciling being an Arab and non-Muslim in a nation where that seems a contradiction in terms. The people I interviewed from the Middle East also said that they frequented other people from Arab countries in Canada; something that is not true of me, or of most of the Moroccans I spoke with.

It was interesting that most of the Moroccan serial migrants seemed not to be especially interested in meeting other immigrants from their country or other Arab countries. One man noted:

Over there (in France) there are many relations among Moroccans perhaps because the number of Moroccans is quite relatively high. There, there are people of every social group and category. So you can find people who correspond to yourself. Social relations are a little closer to what we knew before (in Morocco) when it comes to friendship, acquaintances etc. things are a bit clearer there when it comes to the kinds of values we want to have. Here (in Canada) it's just the opposite. It's more individualistic . . . and there aren't many Moroccans. I think that the motives for immigration are also different than what we find among Moroccans in France. The people who move here seek to integrate in their personal way in their own manner. And thus, they don't systematically seek out relations with other Moroccans.

Part of what many of those I interviewed had trouble with in Morocco was the sense of being "blocked" or "closed-in"—politically or personally. Mounir, for instance, noted that it was his ideological positions and conceptions of politics that made it impossible to live in Morocco; his first move to France was to avoid imprisonment, his second, to Canada, because he feels that here he can live freely, participate in politics, and have full rights. Nadir explained that his history of multiple migrations had made him more ready to speak out and voice his opinions. "Yes, after twenty-one years, I changed a lot. I am thirsty for culture. I am free. In the past, I was afraid to talk." As we have seen, he too appreciates his new life in Montreal because he feels it gives him the opportunity to have equal rights with other Canadians.

Abdelkader made another important distinction: between his own sense of self as someone who had moved several times and that of "regular migrants." In saying that he found his "own" way, he did not experience any ambiguity about his identity. He dismissed being caught in the push and pull between one country and another that Abdelmalek Sayad found among migrants who had moved from the Maghreb to France. He said:

> I would have to say there is a limit to this kind of ambivalent feeling of being in between, or the sense of belonging to two different situations that it the country of origin and the other and the one that you try to integrate, to live on. I think that I do not have this feeling. My real home exists in my mind. It will always be my country of origin. For me, nationality does not really reflect a deep belonging to this country (Canada). I feel sorry to say that but that is the way it is. So far, my priorities in my mind on a psychological and cultural level always point toward my country of origin (Sayad 1999).

This imagining of a Morocco that provides identity and direction needs to be interrogated in terms of its role in day-to-day life. So does the issue of how serial migrants might be similar or different from people who have moved from their country of origin to one new country.

Like Abdelkader the serial migrants I interviewed tend to distance themselves from "ordinary" migrants. They put the accent on the fact that they have known how to "fit-in" and not made the kinds of mistakes that those who have less experience in living in different places make. So it is not social origins that distinguish them from "other migrants." Obviously, my group was limited and biased by the fact that we met through personal relations. We had moved for personal, religious, and political reasons, not because we needed to find work. In fact, many of us had to go back to school or take lengthy exams to regain positions similar to those we had in Morocco. So we did not feel at home with the migration story of rags to riches as it is usually recounted (Green 2001).

TALKING IN TONGUES

Although I doubt I will ever move back to Morocco, I live with a certain notion of my own personal Morocco, a kind of reactivated memory of my Tangiers. I see this in how I use language in my home. Like other Moroccan and Maghrebian serial migrants I interviewed, I use languages in a very particular way with my family. All of the Moroccans, and indeed, the Maghrebians, I interviewed explained that they consciously try to "balance" the languages they use with their families. When Susan stayed with us in Montreal, she noted that while I made a point of speaking French to my daughter when I lived in Rabat, in Montreal I tend to speak to her in Spanish. Yet, I speak dialectal Arabic to my son who is younger. In fact, just like the other parents involved in this study, I try to help teach each child to improve on the language they don't get a chance to use much. Each child has their own language history, depending on where they were born and went to school, so I need to develop different languages with each of them. This is not only because I think about their careers, but because it has to do with establishing a kind of emotional balance. They need to be able to speak fluently with all of their relatives, and in Canada, I think they also need to know both national languages. It's not just a matter of adapting, but also a question of personal identity.

Among the people I interviewed who had grown up in Tangiers and more generally Morocco, I found that this approach to language seemed to be much more than a vestige of the colonial past. What might at first have been an imposed language becomes something a bit different for generations like my own, people born after Morocco won its independence in 1956. For us a multilingual society seems a bit dull, perhaps even unwelcoming. This does not appear to be the same for serial migrants from other Arab countries. Assad, my colleague from Egypt, speaks seven languages. But he speaks Arabic with his wife. He grew up in an essentially monolingual home an he speaks Egyptian Arabic to his children. Assad lived in Abu Dhabi as a child and he knows many Arabic dialects, including Moroccan. But it seemed he had no need to involve these many languages in his sense of himself. Many of the other serial migrants from the Maghreb said that, like me, they tend to speak in French or English with people from other Arab countries, because only a few of us feel comfortable speaking classical Arabic for very long. This is certainly the result of the fact that all of our paths have been similar: taking us between Morocco and France, and then at some point, from Morocco to Montreal. Perhaps it is also because Arabic is not the language of prestige in Canada, as it is in the Gulf, where Fatima Badry carried out her research. Yet, the men and women I interviewed showed the same willingness to adapt their speech in different situations as the Moroccan women she interviewed in the U.A.E. (Badry, chapter 10) However, we all speak Moroccan Arabic with our children. Although we do not want to live in Morocco, we do not want to have them forget the language.

REMEMBERING TANGIERS IN MONTREAL

The Tangiers of my childhood has been wiped off the map, but it lives in my heart. When I return to Morocco, I rarely stay long in Tangiers. Last time I stayed one night. When I think of my native city I dream of wandering around the old city, the medina. I imagine reliving memories, going back to my childhood. Yet, I flee all of this because I have always wanted to be independent and autonomous. The reality of Morocco is that fathers and even little brothers rule over women and girls. I run from this because even though Morocco is more liberal than most Arab countries with respect to women, there is an ever increasing social pressure there, a force trying to keep women in "their place."

So did I choose to move to Canada because it recognizes women's rights? Because it is a more democratic political system? I have to admit I did not exactly choose Montreal. I chose the idea of liberty. I felt the desire to move freely and that meant moving on. I wanted my new son to be born in a place where he would be able to have a passport that would leave the whole world open to him. As it turned out, I ended up finding another kind of Tangiers in Montreal. So many people have come to live here from all over the world. As Amina said, " It is a place where one can constantly learn from others, and about other countries and customs. It is rather like a kind of anthropology class without a school." The "Canadian" serial migrants I interviewed seem to be very content in their new homes. But then, most were not very unhappy where they were before either. Would they move again? I asked them. And they all said that they would, if the conditions were right and the opportunities alluring. It is important not to take the word "opportunity" in a kind of limited way. The reasons they gave for living anywhere had to do with pursuing ideals that were rather intangible, like freedom or particular political or religious values. Although I have rediscovered my Tangiers in Montreal, I too would be willing, even enthusiastic about moving again. My Tangiers lives in me and I can pursue it wherever I live. Indeed, it is impossible to be really at home in any country. No matter where we go, there will always be something else to look for.

ACKNOWLEDGMENTS

I would like to thank all of those who shared their stories with me, without them I could never have written this article. I also thank my good friend Susan Ossman who has helped me throughout the research, especially with the process of writing. Finally, I thank my husband Jamal Ouadahi, for helping me conduct the interviews and for his moral support.

REFERENCES

Aboumalek, Mostafa. 1994. *Qui épouse qui? Le mariage en milieu urbain.* Casablanca: Afrique Orient.

Green, Nancy. 2001. *Repenser la migration.* Paris: PUF.

Mernissi, Fatima. 1988. *Doing Daily Battle, Interview with Moroccan Women.* Trans. Mary Jo Lakeland, London: The Women's Press.

Sayad, Abdelmalek. 1999. *La double absence; des illusions de l'émigré aux souffrances de l'émigré.* Paris: le Seuil.

10

Positioning the Self, Identity, and Language

Moroccan Women on the Move

Fatima Badry

Like millions of people around the globe, I have found myself adapting linguistically and culturally to new contexts ever since I was a child. I believe that every time I crossed over into a new vernacular and culture, I have added a face to my identity that has made me different yet more aware of my previous selves.

I am told that, as a child, the first languages I was exposed to were Berber and Moroccan Arabic. Although I grew up in a Berber environment where my parents spoke Berber to everyone around them, the first language I remember speaking is Arabic because it was the language used by my Arab parents with their children. When I was six, my aunt decided to take me to school one day "because she didn't want me to play outside with other girls." All I remember is her dropping me off in a classroom where all the girls were much older than I was, with a French teacher who did not speak any Arabic. I don't know how I learned French, but I did learn it to succeed in school, fit in with the group, and to "be modern." My third linguistic transition came much later when I moved to the Anglophone world. Although I had learned English in school I really began to speak it when I lived in England and later in the United States. When I first arrived in California, I communicated with my American friends in my British English with a French accent. My accent gave me prestige among my American friends but I ended up losing that accent as well. I don't know when or how my accent gradually became American. Lastly, living in America, I met many Arabs from the Middle East who claimed they couldn't understand my Moroccan dialect. As the only Moroccan in the group, I learned to speak Palestinian Arabic, which was the dialect of the majority, and I became proficient enough to the point that some people mistook me for a Palestinian when I spoke.

My immersion in the different cultures and corresponding languages has often led others to position me outside all these cultures that I feel I belong to. Whenever I meet people for the first time and speak in Arabic, French, or English, the "natives" ascertain that I am not a "native" but they usually have difficulty telling where I am from. Where I position myself seems to be at odds with how others want to place me based on the way I speak. And my multilingual/multicultural background makes it difficult for me to answer the simple question: "*Where are you from?*" In fact, the answer to such question is problematic for many people on the move like me because it does not have a simple answer. What makes me who I am? Is it my citizenship? Does who I am depend on my birth place, regions or countries of my residence, my ethnicity, my education, my languages? I am the product of all these constituents and experiences, depending on what I want to project, who I am interacting with, and where I find myself.

In this chapter I adopt an interdisciplinary approach to explore the relationship between identity and language and examine psychological, social, and affective factors that may account for why in multilingual contexts, Moroccan women acquire new communicative competencies in other languages and/or dialects, and how such communicative practices shape their identity. Specifically, I examine possible reasons that lead Moroccan women living elsewhere to have little resistance to relinquish their way of speaking and how their linguistic and cultural adaptations affect their personal and social identity and their positioning within host communities. My academic background led me to consider these questions both from a psycholinguistic and sociolinguistic perspective and analyze the factors that make many migrant women successful in picking up the languages or dialects of the groups they associate with, contributing to construction of their identity. I depart from the general tradition of looking at migration as an act of economic necessity and the negative consequences on alienated minorities that it entails (for example, as described in the writings of Tahar Benjelloun). Instead I adopt a perspective on migration as an agent of personal transformations, by focusing on its impact on identity construction. My starting point begins with my personal experience and participant observations that revealed that Moroccans willingly learn new linguistic codes (languages and dialects) to communicate with others from different linguistic backgrounds with little expectation of reciprocity. Such adaptation is probably more pronounced in women than men because their motives for migrating are different. While men migrate chiefly because of economic reasons, women tend to migrate based on social motivations.

The question of language as a marker/maker of identity is debated from many perspectives in linguistics. From the strong Whorfian hypothesis that claimed that our perception and representation of the world, and therefore who we are, is determined by the structure of our language to the universalist approach espoused by innatist approaches which minimized the role of language as a shaper of our thought patterns, underlying our identity. The recent revival in psycholinguistic literature of the Whorfian hypothesis calls for the "need to [attribute] the origins of structure to interpersonal communicative and cognitive processes that everywhere and always shape language in its peculiar expression of content and relation" (Slobin 2001, 407). This new perspective, which is directed toward understanding how children develop grammatical categories of their native language, casts doubt on the universalist innatist conceptions of grammar. It opens the door to a more relativist position in psycholinguistics, where more importance is given to the particular language and culture being acquired as shaping the child's perception of the world through particular lenses and eventually tying his identity to the native language and culture.

While this position has appeal and seems to be supported by monolinguals' behavior, it runs into difficulty when bilingual and multilingual individuals are considered. If each language has its own windows through which we experience the world, how are different experiences lived through sometimes contrasting linguistic windows internalized and interpreted by those who are called on to weave through different linguistic and cultural communities in their daily interactions? How do transitions through interlingual situations impact their identities?

Possible answers to these questions will depend in part on how we define identity. In applied linguistics, discussion of identity and language is particularly predominant in studies of bilingualism/multiculturalism. Given the close relationship between language, culture, and identity we may expect that our identity is to a large extent shaped by our culture. The question then is how a person (or a community) deals with speaking more than one language, each with its own representation of the world? How do these different representations affect personal and social identities? These are central questions for the sociolinguist. From a variationist paradigm, identities are considered to be an expression of the self based on demographic attributes which include social class, gender, age, and location. Such a framework has however come under strong criticism because of its failure to recognize that

multiple identities are constructed and negotiated through language and are themselves in need of explanation, and that secondly, linguistic forms and strategies have multiple functions and cannot be directly linked to particular identities outside of interactional contexts. Finally, several studies . . . persuasively demonstrated that on many occasions people do not at all sound the way they are expected to . . . thus researchers need to pay more attention to local and constructed—rather than expressed—aspects of identity (Blackledge & Pavlenko 2001, 244).

Researchers have come to recognize that languages in contact situations peoples' linguistic identities are not static. A careful analysis of a single person in different interactions shows that depending on the characteristics of the exchange, she does not always sound the way we expect her to sound based on demographic affiliations. In response to the view of identity as a fixed and predetermined attribute of the person, the socio-psychological approach examines social identity as an outcome of language contact, which is negotiated within the group. In this paradigm, identity is constructed as a reflection of a desired self-image and communicated by the individual within a particular context. In familiar cultural contexts where they are at ease with the norms of social interaction, people feel safe and understood by others. In new and unfamiliar environments they tend to feel vulnerable and threatened. When someone perceives a threat they try to adapt to the new situation by adjusting their behavior and trying to belong. From this perspective successful negotiation of identity provides security in those unfamiliar contexts because of the "feelings of being understood, valued, supported and respected, despite the intercultural differences that may surface in the process" (Blackledge and Pavlenko 2001, 244).

However, critics have argued that looking at all unfamiliar situations in terms of this "adaptive" approach fails to see identity as a social construct. Differences among individuals or even groups have to be taken into account to understand how people react to new social situations. Social differences within a given group must also be considered in assessing strategies of adaptation or efforts to belong. Faced with a new environment some individuals may seek to stay within their original linguistic group while others may adopt the out-group ways of speaking and behaving. Still, in other cases, individuals change group membership when they are dissatisfied with their group identity. More important, this model of linguistic adaptation suffers from a monolingual bias. It assumes that one has to abandon one's first language/ culture and integrate into the second one in order to belong. It cannot allow us to theorize about individuals who are members of different multilingual communities. Another assumption in this model is the existence of two identifiable, durable, and discrete cultures: the native and the target or host culture and language. Today, such a distinction is hard to maintain as cultures and languages in contact do influence each other and the influence is not always unidirectional (Blackledge and Pavlenko 2001).

The ethnographically oriented approach developed by Gumperz (1982) captures the actual hybridity of identity because it considers identities as "fluid and constructed in linguistic interactions" rather than the fragmented conception derived from a dichotomous approach. Individuals move through an identity continuum and position themselves and others to produce common and coherent interactions. Once subjects have positioned themselves within an identity as their own, they are likely to see the world from that position (Davies and Harré 1990 in Blackledge and Pavlenko 2001). But such positions are not stable and are subject to continuous change because "[s]elves are neither made or changed in isolation. Rather the process of identity formation is dialogical in nature. Who we are and what we become is tied very closely to the social circumstances in which we find ourselves" (Ryan 1997). Along these same lines, Thesen (1997) suggests that when we study identity, we need to look at what activates "new allegiances and choices that distance oneself from old ones," or as Hall (1990, in Giampapa 2001) remarks, identity is as much about "being" as it is about "becoming." Identity refers "to how people understand their relationship to the world, how that relationship is constructed across time and space, and how people understand their possibilities for the future" (Norton 1997, 410).

Norton Pierce states: "It is through language that a person negotiates a sense of self within and across different sites at different points in time, and it is through language that a person gains access to or is denied access to powerful social networks that give learners the opportunities to speak" (quoted in Giampapa 2001, 284). To signal our transition from one act of identity to the other, we use language to mark our positioning. However, our positioning is not always accepted and may be challenged by others who try to reposition the individual or even the group to which the individual belongs. This is particularly the case when we are moving across languages and cultures. In their discussion of the relation between language and culture, Hamers and Blank stated that language is not only the vehicle through which our culture is transmitted, it is also the medium through which it is internalized by the individual (1998, 116). Although members of the same culture share symbolic systems and behaviors, their transmission is "only approximate in the sense that they are equivalent rather than identical for any two individuals and are unevenly distributed in the society" (ibid, 116). Still, language defines group membership, ethnic and social identity, and delimits boundaries between them. Language is one of the most salient markers of identity. Consequently, people from outside the group may try to change their ways of talking in order to become part of the host society. Linguistic adaptation becomes a prerequisite to auxiliary changes in other aspects of cultural behavior. In this sense our linguistic identity becomes a commodity that we construct according to the social setting in which we find ourselves. It is a fluid, rather than a fixed, construct where using different vernaculars to respond to different communicative needs calls for performing "acts of identity" which reflect one's positioning in response to various facets of social life. It is in this sense that the multilingual person's identity moves along the continuum of identity performance by combining elements from the multicultural/multilingual repertoire at one's disposal with the outcome of identity being a hybrid rather than a fragmented construct. According to Morgan (1997), "Identity is not so much a map of experience—a set of fixed coordinates—as it is a guide with which . . . [people] negotiate their place in a new social order and, if need be, challenge it through the meaning making activities they participate in." In order to achieve this language also becomes a market commodity rather than a symbol of ethnic or national identity (Block and Cameron 2002). Nonetheless, self-identification must necessarily express the diverse experiences drawn from the multiple contexts within which we live. From this perspective, it is reasonable to expect that resistance to adopting new ways of speaking becomes low because people do not see their performances in different vernaculars as a threat to their identity. To the contrary, not performing to expectation may constitute more menacing to one's self image.

As a multilingual migrant living in the UAE myself, my own experiences have been important in formulating the questions I have raised and will undoubtedly influence my interpretation of the answers. My starting point stems from the major question that has always preoccupied me based on my observation of Moroccans' linguistic behaviors in contact situations. Why do Moroccans so readily give up their dialect, one of the most prominent markers of their identity, when they meet others? I have seen men and women in Morocco struggle to communicate in the other's dialect/language and wondered why it is always the Moroccans that make the biggest effort? When Moroccans meet other Arabs, I have observed that even when the other is trying to communicate in Moroccan Arabic, Moroccans insist on speaking some form of Egyptian picked up from movies or resort to the standard form when that fails. If Moroccans behave that way at home, how would they act when they live outside their country?

Interviews were conducted with ten Moroccan women (ages twenty to forty) living in the UAE, both professional women and housewives, to investigate the effects of migration on language as a marker of identity and to understand how they negotiate their personal and social identity to become part of, or distinguish themselves, from UAE society. In what ways are their linguistic repertoires a manifestation of who they are and how do they use language as a market commodity to achieve their goals? The questions were designed to elicit the participants' evaluation of their own linguistic and identity repertoires. I asked about how these women identify themselves while living in the UAE (Arabs or Moroccans first). I enquired into what determines their choice of language/dialect when they need to communicate with others in different socio-linguistic contexts. I also explored how their thoughts about how their choice of linguistic codes affects their representation of others. I was particularly interested in finding out how linguistic adaptation affects their identity and sense of belonging to different groups. Before discussing the findings, a few background notes on the UAE are necessary to contextualize the findings and discussion.

Since the 1960s, the UAE has witnessed what some refer to as a silent revolution, thanks to its oil exports. Since its establishment as a federation of seven Emirates known as the United Arab Emirates in 1971, the country has gone through major socio-economic transformations that have led it to have the fourth highest per capita in the world (FDI magazine 2004). The federal government has used its oil resources to build the country's infrastructure from roads, to schools, hospitals, modern villas, and high rises to some of the most luxurious hotels in the world. This modernization has been accomplished by a massive influx of guest workers. UAE citizens make up less than 20 percent of the total population of 3 million. The UAE relies heavily on the migrant work force at all levels and in all sectors. Generally speaking, 50 percent of the population is from South East Asia and provides most of the un-skilled labor force, while Arabs and Iranians (23 percent) and Westerners (17 percent) occupy positions in the service, trade, white collar, and managerial sectors. Despite governmental efforts to encourage population growth of nationals, the expatriate communities remain essential to sustaining the booming economic development of the country (FDI magazine 2004).

Moroccan migration to the UAE is a recent phenomenon compared to migration from other Arab countries such as Egypt, Syria, Lebanon, and other states. It was encouraged in the 1980s as a by-product of the close ties between the two governments and the tightening up of migration regulations toward Europe. Moroccan men came to the UAE to serve in its army, National Guard, and police force. Women's migration did not pick up until the 1990s although many women came to the UAE as second wives to Emarati husbands before that. Gradually, Moroccan women came to the UAE to work. Today, although statistics are not available, a significant number of women live and work in the UAE. Informal information I acquired from bankers suggests that more than 70 percent of remittances to Morocco are sent by women. With the development of tourism and trade, major UAE companies opened recruiting agencies in Casablanca and Agadir in the 1990s and recruited hundreds of jobless young university graduates to work in the service sectors in hotel chains and retailing. Other women have migrated on their own, often buying their visas, to work in beauty salons, Moroccan couture, and the trendy Moroccan baths. Generally speaking, Moroccan women do not enjoy a good reputation in the UAE. Although some of them fit that profile, as do many others from other nationalities, most work long hours and live in groups to save money to send back home.

Although the UAE is an Arab and Muslim country, its social dynamics, its history and contemporary culture are quite distinct from those of Morocco. The official language is Arabic but one cannot get buy without some knowledge of English. Given that most shopkeepers and business employees are non-Arabs, everybody has to know some English to conduct daily business. To communicate with the Asian or Indian cashiers at the supermarket or shopkeepers in the *souk* (market), people use a pidgin form of English with Arabic and Hindi or Urdu influences. This linguistic situation provides Moroccan women with their first communication challenge since neither French nor Moroccan Arabic are very useful in daily interactions with the outside world. Their first priority is then to learn enough English together with a mixture of Middle Eastern Arabic dialects, a sort of "dialect franca," which combines vocabulary from Levant dialects (Lebanese, Palestinian, Syrian), Egyptian Arabic, and some words from the Gulf varieties of Arabic.

When I encounter Moroccan women in different social contexts in the UAE (waitresses in restaurants, receptionists in hotels, clerks in shopping centers, social gatherings, work related circumstances, etc.), it is only my linguistic training that enables me to identify them as Moroccans by their accent since they do not use Moroccan Arabic in their interactions with others but rather speak in the dominant dialect. In contrast, it is easy to recognize the country of origin of other Arabs from their dialects in similar encounters. When asked why they choose to speak in some other dialect than Moroccan, they explain that it is for ease of communication as other Arabs don't understand Moroccan Arabic. Ease of communication may be one determinant but other factors may also play a role in their choice. Moroccan women are also willing to set aside their dialect of Moroccan Arabic and pick up other Arabic dialects spoken in the UAE because they share the perception with other Arabs that Moroccan Arabic is not only hard to understand, but also they feel that it is not expressive, has limited vocabulary, is rough, and even sometimes rude. There is a prevalent assumption among lay Arabs that the Moroccan dialect is somehow not "real Arabic." One woman was unwilling to speak Moroccan to her Egyptian prospective employer because according to her, "it is not real Arabic and he [the Egyptian employer] wouldn't understand it." She preferred to use French because she felt uncomfortable speaking the Moroccan dialect to another Arab and didn't know how to speak "real" Arabic. Such negative perceptions explain why Moroccans give up their dialect altogether and replace it with another dialect, or mixture of dialects, perceived as closer to Modern Standard Arabic (MSA). They conceive MSA as a "real" language, although it is actually itself a simplified version of classical literary Arabic that facilitates communication among people who speak different dialects of Arabic. In extreme cases women go so far as to block Moroccan Arabic from their repertoire and not speak it even in interactions with other Moroccans. I tried to conduct interviews in Moroccan Arabic, but conversation tended to employ code-switching between Gulf Arabic, a Levant dialect, and Moroccan Arabic or French. One of the participants pointed out that when her two-year-old daughter uses Moroccan words, her Emarati father cannot understand her because "nobody understands Moroccan Arabic." As a result the mother speaks Gulf Arabic with her children. She feels that this enables them to make friends at school and communicate with those around them. For her the importance of integrating her children into the linguistic community in which they are living overrides all other considerations.

Moroccan women seem to travel through a kind of linguistic identity continuum where Moroccan Arabic occupies the lower end of the scale. This is due to the prevalent perceptions associated with it as being not real Arabic. Standard Arabic is situated at the highest end of the scale but nobody really attains that level in day-to-day interactions. A hierarchy of spoken varieties of Arabic places Middle Eastern varieties (Levant dialects) in prestigious position for they are considered as "most Arab." Since Arab identity is a valued commodity in the UAE, Moroccan women are willing to make the effort to show that they are Arabs by changing the way they talk. Women married to locals are quick to point out that their responsibility to their children requires of them to speak Gulf Arabic. Nevertheless, in settings outside the home involving interactions with Westerners they put forward their French or English language skills and downplay their Arab identity. This code shifting reflects different acts of identity and can be explained by instrumental motivations toward language use as a market commodity (Bourdieu 1982). Moroccan women want to use forms of speaking that allow them to be part of the discourses that hold power in society. Yet the women I interviewed maintained that adopting another language and another mode of living has not in any sense diminished their sense of being Moroccan. While they are first and foremost Moroccans, speaking another dialect of Arabic does not contradict their national identity. They still cook Moroccan food, wear Kaftans at home, follow Moroccan traditions of hospitality, listen to Moroccan music, and visit Morocco every year. Indeed, for them these other markers of Moroccan identity seemed to matter more than what language or dialect they speak. As they see it, language is an instrument to accomplish certain goals.

Not all women are as attached to their country of origin, however. Among those who received a French education the sense of national belonging seems to be weaker. For this group they feel that it is only their families that connect them to Morocco. Amal, one of the participants in the study, responded to the question about where she belongs the most by stating: "Je suis terrienne, La où je suis bien, c'est mon pays" (I am an earthling. Wherever I feel good is my country). When it came to identifying herself, she clearly recognized a hybrid identity constructed from predetermined and determined features. The predetermined self was the sum of being born a Moroccan, Arab, Muslim woman, and having received a French education that resulted in French acculturation. There were all characteristics of herself that she did not choose. Her determined self or chosen identity was composed of how she thinks of herself as a "Canadian from Montreal" because that's where she feels at home. Although she left Canada more than five years ago and is enjoying her life in the UAE, she still identifies herself as a Canadian because she feels it is the closest to her French cultural identity. She likes living in the UAE because it is in harmony with her Arab predetermined identity and using another Arabic dialect reinforces her Arabness.

Another reason why many Moroccan women do not want to speak Moroccan Arabic in public is to avoid being fitted in the dominant negative stereotype about Moroccan women in the UAE. Moroccan Arabic is a salient marker that may lead others to pigeonhole its female speakers. Women do not want to be perceived as Moroccans from first sight and thus be judged negatively. The problem of perception of Moroccan women in the UAE is a serious one as many young Moroccans were brought in the 1980s and 1990s by local men as mistresses or second wives. As a result, many Arabs living in the UAE are quick to judge Moroccan women as easy and "men stealers," a task which it is believed, they accomplish through the use of black magic! This negative perception is particularly strong among Emarati women.

Moroccan women's desire to assimilate into the established circles through the adoption of another medium of communication other than their native vernacular is at variance with the linguistic behavior of other Arabs in the UAE. In listening to people in the street, or on radio or TV programs for example, it is easy to recognize whether speakers come from Egypt or Lebanon. Palestinian and Iraqi women speakers are also readily identified by their speech. On the part of these groups there is no attempt to alter their speech to speak the Gulf dialect of Arabic, or the dialectics of people from other Arab countries with whom they interact. Such assimilatory behaviors can be interpreted within the accomodationist convergence approach proposed by Giles and used by Suleiman to explain the different direction of code switching between men and women in Jordan after the Jordanian-Palestinian clashes of 1970. Suleiman (1999) draws on the power of symbolism of language to account for Palestinian males' adoption of a more Bedouin pronunciation of some speech markers (g instead of k or q). He ascribes this shift to Palestinian males' desire to become invisible and blend in the Jordanian society after their defeat. Such explanation corroborates the importance of ethnic and national variables in bringing about sociolinguistic changes (ibid. 16). Suleiman also identified the different variables at play in the opposite direction. He looks at code switching of men and women in Jordanian society. While he found that males' convergence toward Bedouin pronunciation is politically motivated, both Jordanian and Palestinian women's convergence toward urban Palestinian pronunciation is motivated by social variables. Suleiman maintains that women's marginal position in a strongly patriarchal society makes the shift of Jordanian women toward urban Palestinian pronunciation insignificant in the overall balance of power, because "female speech is regarded as a less valuable commodity in the overall linguistic economy" (ibid. 23). He supports Ross's position that "subordinate 'roles and identities may be highly stressful and frustrating to many of their holders' who may choose to escape from their position by adopting the speech patterns, among other things, of the dominant group" (ibid. 18).

The readiness of Moroccan women to adopt other's ways of speaking in interactions with other Arabs may be assigned not so much to a willingness to give up markers of their Moroccan identity but rather as an indication of what they consider as Arabness. The geographic position of Morocco, its ethnic makeup, and its history all contribute to making it a nation at the periphery of the Arab world. Although Morocco declared itself an Arab nation when it won its independence from France in 1956, and although its official language is Arabic, its claims to Arab identity are often questioned by people from the Middle East. This is partly due to the perception that the Moroccan dialect is a mixture of Arabic, Berber, and French. The fact that this description of Moroccan Arabic does not rest on objective linguistic characteristics is irrelevant. What counts are peoples' perceptions and attitudes. All of the women I interviewed share the feeling that their dialect of Arabic is just not equal to other dialects. They see it as deficient in terms of facilitating communication with others in the Middle East. By adopting the others' dialects they feel that they can affirm their Arab identity. Clearly, this implies accepting the positioning of Morocco as marginal in the schema of Arab identity. This identification corresponds to what Gill (1999) described as a "denial of ethnicity" in favor of the "collective ideal" of Middle Eastern varieties of Arabic as symbolic of "national unity and authenticity." We must not assume, however, that they make this movement along the identity continuum without apprehension. Our choice of identity projection, through our linguistic behavior, is governed by our perception of the added value that social identity will bring us in the interaction (by assessing its position in the identity hierarchy). However, we are also constrained by personal identity values that may in certain instances resist and conflict with the desired social identity. In such cases, hybridity becomes apparent, which results in feelings of not belonging, disorientation, and in-betweeness, even something we might call "identitylessness."

In interactions, the conflict between personal and social identity is often resolved in favor of the latter. The women interviewed look at language as a capital that is likely to bring high returns for them. They are able to engage in interactions and challenge the prevalent social order by constructing and asserting social identities of their own choice. According to Pierce "learning is successful when learners are able to summon up or construct an identity that enables them to impose their right to be heard and thus become the subject of the discourse" (cited in Ellis 2002, 42). These women are successful in learning another dialect of Arabic because they are socially motivated to do so. It is generally accepted that learners are willing to make substantial cultural and linguistic investments when they see their value as enabling them to successfully function in the targeted social contexts. Speaking the other's tongue challenges the stereotype of the woman as the weak link and the Moroccan as not the Arab. The women interviewed have left Morocco because they were dissatisfied with their lives there. They felt they were not recognized as full citizens, they were frustrated by the limitations imposed on them because of their sex by their families and the society at large. Most of them left knowing little about where they were going. Sometimes a relative or friend was already living in the UAE and encouraged them to come. By leaving Morocco, they seem to have made a commitment to themselves that they were going to make something of their lives and do what it takes to succeed. But upon arriving in their new home things were generally not that easy. Women often felt frustrated and disoriented, but they quickly understood the value of flexibility and the necessity of adapting. Free from the family and the "what will people say" that constrained them in Morocco they were often willing to take risks. This included engaging with people in the new setting and learning to adapt their speech. What made these migrant women successful in learning to fit in in the UAE was often the result of a strong sense of rebellion against the family and social constraints. Their desire to prove something to themselves and to the people back home made it imperative for them to adapt quickly. This brings us back to the issue of remittances. If women send more money back to Morocco than men, it is perhaps because of their heightened sense of family responsibility but it is also because they are proud to demonstrate that they have been successful. They seem to want to show that Moroccan society's low expectations of women are wrong.

To understand the ease with which Moroccans learn to speak in the other's tongue, it is important to remember some historical and geographical considerations. Historically, the French colonial enterprise in Morocco was built on the civilizing mission of the French culture of the indigenous population. In order to value the French language and its culture, the Moroccan dialect and Berber had to be denigrated. The fact that the dialect is after all not the written language made it easy to accomplish this. In addition, Morocco's location at the crossroads between Africa, Europe, and the Middle East has resulted in Moroccan peoples' tolerance and openness for other languages and cultures. Multilingualism is seen as a plus that opens doors for better economic opportunities rather than a threat to one's authenticity.

Although language is the expression of our identity, identity and language cannot be superimposed. My study of Moroccan migrant women shows that although they might decide that the Moroccan dialect will not get them what they want in their interactions in the UAE and they willingly give it up in favor of another language or dialect of Arabic, they still maintain other markers of Moroccan identity. This was particularly clear from my observations of social interactions involving people I had interviewed. For instance, during the interview Amal had no hesitation declaring that she had become Canadian. But at a party she was the first one to get up and dance to the Moroccan tunes, declaring how much she missed the atmosphere of Morocco. Indeed, perhaps Amal needs to be Canadian and live in Dubai to be able to revel in this "Moroccan ambiance." Adopting a different way of communicating and alternative identities not only serves instrumental purposes, it also serves to free these women of the constraints imposed by the society they left behind. As Sadiqi writes, discussing language and gender in Morocco, "women's linguistic agency is part and parcel of women's struggle for self-assertion. In all cases, women's linguistic agency is presented as creative and powerful; it is constituted of strategies of communication that women use to maximize their chances in achieving gains in real life contexts" (2003, 1).

REFERENCES

Baker, Colin. 1995. *Attitudes and Language*. Clevedon, UK: Multilingual Matters Limited.

Bartlett. T. 2001. Use the road: The Appropriacy of Appropriation. *Language and Intercultural Communication* 1, 1, 22–39.

Blackledge, Adrian and Pavlenko, Aneta. 2001. A Negotiation of identities in Multilingual contexts. *The International Journal of Bilingualism* 3, 5 September 2001, 243–57.

Block, David and Cameron, Deborah. 2002. *Globalization and language teaching*. London: Routledge.

Bourdieu, Pierre. 1982. *Ce que parler veut dire: l' economie des echanges linguistiques*. Paris: Fayard.

Coupland, N. 2003. Introduction: Sociolinguistics and Globalisation. *Journal of Sociolinguistics* 7, 4, 2003, 465–72.

Crawshaw, R., Callen, B., and Tusting, K. 2001. Attesting the Self: Narration and Identity Change During Periods of Residence Abroad. *Language and Intercultural Communication* 1, 2, 101–19.

Eckert, P. 2003. Sociolinguistics and authenticity: An Elephant in the Room. *Journal of Sociolinguistics* 7, 3, 392–431.

Ellis, Rod. 2002. *Second Language Acquisition*. Oxford: Oxford University Press.

FDI magazine. 2004. www.fdimagazine.com. CIA yearbook UAE Ministry of planning. UAE Department of Economic Development.

Giampapa, F. 2001. Hyphenated identities: Italian-Canadian youth and the negotiation of ethnic identities in Toronto. *The International Journal of Bilingualism* 3, 5, September, 27–315.

Gill, Helene. 1999. Language choice, language policy and the tradition-modernity debate in culturally mixed postcolonial communities: France and the Francophone Maghreb as a case study. *Language and society in the Middle East and North Africa*. Suleiman, Yasir (ed.). Richmond, Surrey, UK: Curzon.

Gumperz, J. 1982. *Language and Social Identity*. Cambridge, MA: Cambridge University Press.

Hamers, Josiane and Blanc, Michel. 1998. *Bilinguality and Bilingualism*. Cambridge: Cambridge University Press.

Heller, Monica. 2003. Globalization, the New Economy, and the Commodification of Language and Identity. *Journal of Sociolinguistics* 7, 473–92.

Morgan, B. 1997. Identity and Intonation: Linking Dynamic Processes in an ESL Classroom. *TESOL Quarterly* 31 (3), 431–50.

Norton, B. 1997. Language Identity and the ownership of English. *TESOL Quarterly* 31, 3, Autumn, 409–29.

Rampton, B. 1999. Styling the Other: Introduction. *Journal of Sociolinguistics* 3, 4, 421–42.

Ryan, J. 1997. Student Communities in a Culturally Diverse School Setting: Identity, Representation and Association. *Discourse: Studies in the Cultural Politics of Education*. 18 (1), 37–53.

Sadiqi, F. 2003. Gender and language in Morocco. University of California International and Area Studies Digital collection. *Women and Gender in the Middle East and the Islamic World Today*. vol. 4 repositories.cdlib.org/uciaspubs/editedvolumes/4/1061.

Slobin, D. 2001. Form-Function relations: How Do Children Find Out What They Are? *Language Acquisition and Conceptual Development. LCC3 Language, Culture and Cognition*. Bowerman, M. and Levinson, S. (eds). Cambridge: Cambridge University Press.

Suleiman, Yasir. 1999. Language and Political Conflict in the Middle East: A study in symbolic sociolinguistics. *Language and society in the Middle East and North Africa*. Suleiman, Yasir (ed). Richmond, Surrey, UK: Curzon Press.

Thesen, L. 1997. Voices, Discourse, and Transition: In Search of New Categories in EAP. *TESOL Quarterly* 31, 3, Autumn, 487–511.

11

From Tribe to Virtual Tribe

Abderrahmane Lakhsassi

As a child, walking beyond the walls of my hometown for the first time, I watched herds of camels moving up from out of the deep south of the Saharan. They were heading north. It must have been a year of drought in the desert. I was scared by the huge number of these strange animals preparing to spend the night just beyond the walls in front of our house. Even more frightening were the few nomad shepherds dressed in dark blue clothes held together with a belt, garments that left their legs completely bare. These were the aàrabn (the nomad Arabs) who are alleged to steal children and hide them in their leather hanging bags (aqwrab). Mothers in Tiznit used images of these men as icons to frighten naughty children. From my child's eyes the world was divided by the coming of the camel herds. There was my hometown surrounded by its defensive walls and the rest. Apart from my birthplace the whole country, if not the rest of the world, was inhabited by these ugly, terrifying nomads. This was my first representation of the Other.

It is always difficult to talk about the self and even more of oneself. Whether as a reaction to primitive positivism, or an attempt to chart alternative self formations, narratives of self and subjectivity have become a part of academic discourse over the last decades. I am still somewhat uncomfortable with this kind of writing. Putting aside *pudeur* (cultural decency), exposing one's life experience and submitting it to analysis can be a difficult task for two reasons: first, studying one's own experience is by no means easy. The underlying assumption here is that some sort of *distanciation* (representation at a distance) is necessary for theorization in social scientific discourse (Lakhsassi 2005). Secondly, it is not so easy to make one's personal life into subject matter that will be of interest to anyone else. Are certain kinds of selves more worthy of writing about? Are some authors more talented at making themselves into interesting fictions? These are just two questions that I asked myself as I prepared to write this essay about my experience of moving from a small Berber town in southern Morocco to Marrakech, Beirut, Paris, Manchester, and Casablanca.

Here, I will describe three stages of being and belonging that I have moved through in the course of my life. My analysis does not rely on formal fieldwork. Nor do I draw on interviews, questionnaires, or even comparative studies to develop my three-stage model. I draw only on personal and biographical data. Tiznit of the 1950s, Lebanon of the 1960s, and Paris of the early 1970s exist now only in memory. So although I will be concerned with an individual's life, my own, and the confrontation of the self with different cultural and political structures, I do so in the knowledge that these experiences are now historical. The places involved in my story are far from me now, not only in space, but in time. It is by reference to this temporal distance that I might argue for the validity of my analysis. Indeed, any discussion of the self has to take place in time. Throughout its peregrination through geographical space and different socio-cultural milieus, the self shapes itself by confronting the Other. But this Other is never still. Other and others are ever changing. Linguistically, racially, religiously, the self is challenged by different Others at different points in time as well as in different places. A constant process of readjustment and redefinition is fundamental to identity that is a result of a set of evolving relations and connections. Today, from the point of view of my mother and family, I am a Westernized person. An Arabic-speaking Moroccan will call me a Berber, whereas for someone from the Middle East I am a Moroccan (a *berbari*). For Europeans I am an Arab and for my American colleagues I am a Muslim. None of these identities is false, indeed, all of them are at the same time true—according to context.

But how did I come to live in so many places in the first place? Where did this constant desire to move to different places and speak different tongues come from? It is impossible to answer this question definitively. I can point to my first experience of encountering people who seemed totally different, absolutely Other. As a child in Tiznit in the 1950s it was the shepherd nomad who embodied alterity. He was utterly different from my parents and family members and other people of the village. When I was a small child the nomad and his flocks incarnated the possibilities of lives lived outside the walls of my little town. Like other people in my village, I saw the nomad as ugly and uncivilized. Yet, I also felt that he appeared to me as a messenger to tell me about the world beyond my doorstep. Thinking about the nomads and their travels led me to begin to experience an uncanny feeling of suffocation when I was at home. I sensed the limits of the village walls and village society. I was not sure I wanted to be a settled city dweller—so set in place, so unlike the ever-moving shepherd. The image of the nomad evoked in me a desire to travel, a thirst to know the world, and a feeling of guilt for wanting to leave home. These paired sentiments that have never left me.

So a feeling of being "out of place" (Said 1999) and the urge to move on has haunted me since I was a boy still living in that then-little town in southwest Morocco. What pushed me to get out of the "hole" I was born in to encounter different places and people was no doubt due to an irresistible yearning to constantly search for something.[1] But what was it I sought? That is what I will never know. What I do know is that normality is generally represented in terms of settlement and stasis. So while I was studying at AUB (the American University of Beirut) in the late 1960s, I remember coming across some phrases in a book that said something like: "the natural state of a body is to be in movement." I vaguely associate the sentence with the British philosopher John Locke, but what was important was not the academic consequences of the words. What was important to me was the emotion I felt when I read them. I suddenly remember feeling very warm and comfortable inside. I had needed some reassurance, some indication that the continuous longing for motion within me was legitimate. Reading words in a book that considered movement to be normal reassured me. One must remember that especially at that time ideas about the nation, belonging, and indeed, village prejudices, all agreed that too much movement or adherence to various communities was absolutely abnormal. What sense of belonging and connections to others were possible for a village boy set on wandering so far from home?

MY LIFE IN MOTION

Although my very first representation of the Other was developed by observing the shepherd nomads and hearing the dreadful tales my mother told me about them, I soon learned that there were yet other kinds of people in the world, that this image needed to be changed or amended. When I was a boy I was sent to a school with a French *maître* (schoolmaster). Leaving Koranic education system to join public school was not in any sense a parental plan. When a new public one-room school opened in my uncle's empty house, right next door to ours, I was sent there as a punishment. Having failed to meet my father's expectations in terms of Koranic learning, he left me as a kind of a sacrifice with the Christian teacher next door. This was how I ended up with Monsieur Leclerc who taught us to sing "O! Les matelots" (O! Sailors). His classroom had colorful pictures of boats and ships on the wall, in total contrast with the dark Koranic schoolroom I came from and where my elder brother continued to go to without me. For our class, Mr. Leclerc bought two balls, one blue, the other red. Coming home that first morning from my first French class, my mother wanted to know what that *arumi* (Christian-European) taught us. When I told her that we were singing and playing football during class breaks, she was, naturally, disappointed. For my part, it was a rather pleasant encounter with difference. Unlike the first picture of the nomad outside the town walls, the image of Frenchness our teacher projected was not frightening, on the contrary. He contributed to forming my second image of Otherness.

Two years after the end of the French Protectorate, Morocco joined the Arab League after years of discussion with the other members. As Fatima Mernissi notes:

> In 1945 the Arab character of Morocco was far from evident, and Allal al-Fasi had to plead his cause to persuade the first members of the Arab League to define Arab in such a way that not-so-Arab Morocco could fit the definition. History has proved Allal al-Fasi to be correct in his predications. His party's wishes became those of the Moroccan state. Morocco, as an independent nation, became a member of the Arab League on 1 October 1958. It affirmed its Arab identity in the *Loi Fondamentale de Royaume* (June 1961), which became the basis of the 1962 constitution:
> Article 1. Morocco is an Arab and a Muslim country.
> Article 2. Islam is the official religion of the state.
> Article 3. The Arabic language is the official and national language of the state (Mernissi 1987, 17).

Thus, theoretically, Arabic became the only official and national language. This choice had a tremendous impact on our primary school education. As a matter of fact, the school program launched by the Istiqlal (Independence) Party in the late 1950s was intended not only to thwart the French *mission civilisatrice* but also to accelerate the elimination of the Berber dimension of the country. Schoolbooks used in class reflected this Jacobin notion of nation building. The few sentences on the Berbers in the history books refer only to their being the first inhabitants of the country. The image this educational system propagated was Middle East centered, one might say Arabocentric. Pre-Islamic Arabia, its history and culture became the starting point of this system in constructing the national self-image of the ordinary citizen. Not a word was written about the pre-Islamic history and culture of North Africa. Ancient Morocco was not a subject of study. Our part of the Mediterranean world came into history only with the Arab-Islamic conquest, according to our text books. Thus "the school system acted as a machine to fabricate Moroccans, which means in this precise context Arabs for the nationalists" (Aboulkacem 2006, note 28; see also Aboulkacem Thesis, 2005). The whole curriculum was disconnected not only from our everyday reality in Tiznit but also from the national reality as a whole. I remember an example from my days in primary school. I puzzled over a picture of a ram in a text book (*al-tilâwa al-musawwara*). I was not a city kid, so I knew about animals. But this animal looked strange. In the place of a tail it had some kind of strange growth. I was profoundly disturbed by this strange looking creature, but I never dared to ask the teacher what was wrong with the ram in the picture. The picture was supposed to illustrate a poem we had to learn by heart called, "*al-waladu wa-l-kharûf*" ("The Boy and the Ram"). I lived with that puzzle throughout my school years in Morocco. It was only later, when I once was traveling in the Lebanese countryside that I realized that our book had been printed in Lebanon and "their" sheep have a different kind of tail than "our" Moroccan sheep!

As a child I was taught that inside the classroom and its intellectual universe, the self becomes the Other. In school I spoke French or Arabic. The Arab nationalist movement was then at its peak. The 1956 Suez Canal crisis fueled the Arabocentrism of the classroom; our Arabic teachers had their eyes turned toward Cairo and Damascus. Those who were politically minded were always fiercely competing with their French colleagues. For instance, to counteract the initiative of Mme Foucault who used to keep a piece of soap in her closet so that students could wash at school, Mr. Al-Manqush suggested that we should change socks three times a week so we would not need to wash our feet at school. In a school like mine where many pupils came to school barefoot, he did not realize that people without shoes would not have socks!

Yet, outside of the space and time of the classroom there was no schizophrenic experience of public space. The language of our town remained and remains Berber. It was only later, during my high-school years in Marrakech from 1963 to 1966 that I realized that linguistic considerations could create a feeling of "us" and "them" among Moroccans. Until high school my social and cultural life took place in the Berber tongue. French and Koranic (classical) Arabic were simply bookish languages for me. They were good enough in formal situations such as the classroom. But in public space and natural situations they were of no use. Edward Said noted that "everyone lives life in a given language" (xiii), and my everyday experiences were assimilated in the Tashelhit Berber dialect. This was the language of my self. It was the language that tied me to the people who counted most in my life. If needed, I would easily translate knowledge from my studies into the common tongue of public space. But all of this changed once I moved to Marrakech where public space was monopolized by the colloquial Arabic known as *darija*.

There is no question that at the time being a Berber meant feeling somehow outside of the nation. Until quite recently it was not unusual to hear that in

Morocco there are "Moroccans" and then there are "Berbers." The location of Berbers outside of the emerging modern nation had been working beneath the surface of nationalist discourse since before independence. Nothing could better summarize that situation than the answer of the leftist leader Mehdi Ben Barka who defined the Berber as someone who has not been to school yet.

> The supposed Berber problem is just a residue of the cultural policy of the Pro-tectorate. It is the product of these "schools for notables" reserved for a well-in-tentioned urban oligarchy. *The Berber is simply a man who has not been to school.* It's a problem of instruction and social evolution, of intellectual equip-ment and the technical development of the countryside. (S. Ossman's transla-tion, quoted in Lacoutre 1958, 83)

In Marrakech my image of the other as being either a nomad or a French missionary teacher vanished. The image of the Arabized city dweller came to overshadow both of these Others. Public linguistic borders outshined other considerations in defining identities. If a requirement of getting out of one's provincialism is "the willingness to engage with the other" (Hannerz 1992, 239), I was more concerned with protecting the self than anything else. I did this through silence and avoiding interaction with the new Other. My first two years in the boarding school were spent listening rather than speaking. Yet, I did not go as far as some. The *Berber Manifesto* relates the example of a worker who pretended to be mute to avoid being ridiculed when using either his mother tongue or Arabic with a Berber accent.[2]

Only after a couple of years, once I felt comfortable in using colloquial Arabic, could I engage with the Arabized city dweller. Appreciating and shar-ing jokes with Arabic-speaking colleagues was a signal to me that I had en-tered the *darjia* speaking world. Before that phase, I never thought for a sec-ond that I could express humor in a language other than my native tongue. The self, my self, was increasingly being encapsulated in "national bound-aries." It was at this time that I started to listen to the national Arabic radio, and to appreciate Moroccan Arabic and Egyptian music. Berber radio pro-grams were produced for illiterate males and particularly for women. Even when programs were available on the air, their diffusion was limited in geo-graphical space and time. So since everything was done to base the new na-tion on one unique language to the detriment of the multilingual and multi-cultural dimensions of the country, I internalized the idea that Berber is a private language to be used in intimate circles. I implicitly accepted that the colloquial Arabic of the region around Casablanca was the language of the national public sphere. It took me a long time and painful efforts to be able to join this national linguistic realm. I felt that belonging to a public language and culture must give someone the best feeling imaginable because one could be a member of a wider group. So, although I knew Moroccan Jews or Blacks were minorities, I never thought they could experience the same frustration and exclusion that I did, so long as they could speak colloquial Arabic.[3]

There is no doubt that people belonging to a stigmatized and a publicly despised culture, whether religious, ethnic, or linguistic, are inclined to move toward cosmopolitanism and universalism whenever they can. For me, learning a prestigious language like French, and later on English, was a way of making up for my cultural and linguistic deficit. It was certainly a way of hiding my stigma, consciously or not. Somehow, at this stage in my life, participation in the culture and language of the public environment was an ideal goal to achieve. At the same time there was a reinforcement of my awareness of the particularity of Berber poetry and art. This rendered the private sphere even more valuable to me. I began to oppose this cultural world to the public domain in my mind. I became conscious of the beauty of my intimate language. Berber songs and music increasingly attracted my attention. They began to occupy even more of my private time as if to compensate the fact that they were excluded from the public realm. In Marrakech they became my secret garden.

When I moved to Beirut in the late 1960s as a scholarship student at the American University it took me as long as in Marrakech to appreciate the distinctive humor and way of life of my Middle Eastern colleagues. For instance, I only gradually came to appreciate Lebanese cuisine. Indeed, like jokes, openness to new foods is a kind of signal of readiness to encounter alterity. Refusal to appreciate foreign cooking can denote the lack of readiness to be open to difference. Once, when I was living in Paris, I received a businessman from my hometown. I decided to take him to an unusual restaurant for the sake of tasting some exotic food. To my disappointment, he was not excited about the French food for it was new to his palate. But he was not unhappy either. But when I accompanied him to London and I suggested that he might enjoy eating Chinese instead of European food he adamantly refused. "My dear Abderrahmane," he said, " I will eat Italian food even if I do not like it, since we are still within *ahl al-kitab* (People of the Book) but Chinese. . . .[4] If "competence with regard to alien cultures itself entails a sense of mastery, an aspect of the self" (Hannerz 1992, 24) the importance of playing on accepted borders and interdictions is not always pointed out in treatises on cosmopolitanism. The first time I went to France, it was a *jambon de Paris* (ham) and a beer that I craved. Tasting pork and alcohol was not simply a transgression of a religious taboo; it was also an indication of my desire to meet the Other through his gastronomy. "A state of readiness" to try new things and transgress borders was something I prepared inside myself before I even stepped across the French *frontière*.

It was through sharing jokes and enjoying Levantine cuisine that I encountered Middle Eastern people in Lebanon, but on the AUB campus, it was American culture with its protestant ethic that began to fascinate me. I experienced a cultural shock between two Western approaches to education. I could not help but compare Mrs. Allen, my first English instructor in Lebanon to Mme Foucault, my French teacher in Tiznit. Mrs. Allen, an American woman, was so very relaxed. She usually dressed casually. On rainy days, she used to come to class wearing black rubber boots. The same was true of Mr. Buckingham, the director of the orientation program. He got "close" to students. I appreciated this informal attitude, which I never experienced with my French (let alone my Arabic) teachers in Morocco.

At AUB more than thirty nationalities shared the same campus in a country that was itself multiconfessional, multiethnic, and multilingual. Junior year abroad students from the United States were part of its scenery. One of these undergraduates suggested that changing geographical locations might actually be a solution to problems at home. In an open letter to the university magazine he wrote "the problem is not where I am but within me." Did I really grasp then what he meant? Indeed, I did believe that changing places could appease some kinds of malaise. Looking out at the world from the Middle East, Paris eventually became my new Mecca.

My move to Europe, to Paris, in the 1970s was not primarily for my studies. University studies were an excuse to live abroad and to avoid going back home. One could live cheaply in Paris at that time. I enrolled to do a second university degree at the Sorbonne. Cosmopolitan cities like Paris or London can feel like a desert for anyone without a network of social relations. But because I was a student, Paris was a warm and welcoming place. Paris was politically as well as socially stimulating: political activism was an easy avenue to socialization. Perhaps this is why it remained my compass point even after I left to do my Ph.D. in England. I liked England, particularly London. I visited London often even when I lived in Paris. There, I discovered the British Commonwealth and became aware of people from completely different horizons, New Zealand, Australia, East and South Africa, and particularly the Indian Sub-continent. People from these places were few and far between in Paris at the time. But I enrolled to study at the University of Manchester, and for some reason I was never really able to make that city a home. Perhaps by the time I arrived in Manchester I just "ran out of gas" after all of my travels. Maybe my desire to be on the move was extinguished. I was tired of always being a stranger. I was not homesick, but I developed a new interest in Islamic philosophy as a way of finding a place in Manchester.

THREE STAGES OF MIGRATION

There are basically three phases in my peregrinations. The first, which I would call a "tribal" one, began at home and finished in the campus of AUB. The second, characterized by a search for some universal belonging, ended up at Manchester where I had the feeling of being totally detached with no point of reference whatsoever apart from work at my university. The third and last phase started when I realized that deepening the particular is probably a more secure road to the universal than denying it or looking for a ready-made universalism. Let us call it "rooted cosmopolitanism" to use Ulrich Beck's expression (Beck 2001, 19). During the first phase my mental and emotional efforts had to meet the Other in his relative multiculturalism. Studying languages and Western literature and philosophy for instance was a way to get involved intellectually with Others or at least some kinds of different Others. In this precise case, these were those that are dominant throughout the world—varieties of a Western model. This period was also, paradoxically, a time during which I was holding tightly to my own tribal perspective. It was in Beirut that I first started to transcribe Berber oral poems during my leisure time. I used to listen to Berber music with friends and started to translate some of the songs into French. Curiously enough, it was a Lebanese teacher who kept encouraging me to pursue this work. Mr. Samaan was one of my first English instructors during my orientation program at AUB in 1966. Once he learned that I was a native Berber speaker, he kept suggesting that I start working on a Berber-English dictionary.

It seems to me in hindsight that all my learning about the Other was something of an intellectual sport. My beliefs and values appeared to remain the same even though some doubts started to creep into my worldview. It was really in Beirut that the gap between intellectual belief in humanism and universality on the one hand and my Berber particularism on the other blew wide open. I could not then see how they could be reconciled. I was trapped on a see-saw between what I saw as universal and my own particularism and sense of self. I felt like I had an impossible choice: to hold on to my mother tongue no matter how it was seen by others or sacrifice the deep belief in the kind of universalism I was taught.

Arab nationalist ideology with its antiminority attitude was sweeping AUB at the time (al-Shawaf 2006). Nothing illustrates its intimidating overtones better than the image of a Sudanese student from the deep south who stood up one afternoon in the campus speaker's corner to cry out, "I am an Arab! I am an Arab!" although he didn't speak a single word of Arabic! Unlike this south Sudanese who no doubt broke under pressure and tried to denying his particularism, I was caught in-between Arabs and non-Arabs in this struggle as a Berber from an Arab country who had been educated in classical Arabic as well as French and English. It was only later on in my journey that I realized that there was nothing incompatible between the two positions, that for me one could not exist without the other.

The second phase coincides with the time when I became aware that Western universalism is one among other universalisms. I questioned its power and egocentric tendencies. I started to take interest in Islamic culture and civilization. In the 1970s I was faced with a situation that for me was symptomatic: many of my peers then found it awkward and even absurd that I decided to travel to Europe to study about Islam and Islamic philosophy. Yet, for me it was a way of holding to a certain kind of identity within this so called universalism—even at the cost of being exposed to some obsolete Orientalist ideas. Perhaps I was trying to integrate myself within the Arabo-Islamic entity as a way of making up for the drawback of the lack of public face given to Berber culture. I was not trying to hide or cover up my origins, local culture, or language, but it seemed it could not be extended outside of private, intimate circles. One needed to find other arenas and ways of speaking for that.

The third phase began at the point when I returned to Morocco, a home that was no longer so much home to me anymore after sixteen years abroad. I was not the same as when I left as a young student—if only for the passing of time. To say the least, I had developed a certain distance toward my early environment. But I also continued to orient myself with respect to my earliest experience. I came to place the study of Berber cultural forms at the center of my intellectual interests. An anthropological approach to the study of Berber poetry—accompanied with a disposition and a readiness to understand its significance and values at a more general level—helped me to set a kind of compromise if not reconciliation with this native world of mine. With my mother I discovered a passionate subject of discussion about Berber poetry and oral tradition in general (Lakhsassi 1988, 1989a, 1989b). Returning to Morocco, I knew it would be difficult and challenging to communicate with some members of my family and old friends. The tribal world I came from no longer looked quite the same. The nomad I was so frightened of as a child had probably settled down in a shantytown. Tiznit is no longer a little town. Its mushrooming neighborhoods have swallowed the walled paradise in which I grew up (N'Ikhsassiyn 1987).

Mine has been a story of a long *detour.* How did I tolerate living in Rabat and Casablanca and being accepted by those in my hometown without giving up my acquired sense of cosmopolitanism? In the midst of the process of return the feeling of belonging to a universal sect or society started to overtake me. It was stronger than any other collective sentiment I could feel. I realized that the tribal world has vanished now, leaving room for a *virtual* tribe that I share with all those who can no longer live only within the boundaries of their own places of birth. We must stretch beyond given linguistic, regional, and national borders. In this space of belonging, my original tribe can appear as one representation of the particular. It can be subject to analysis on a far larger scale than has usually been done by anthropologists or historians. Some of its values and achievements can be considered as an authentic contribution to the human legacy. As I have become an anthropologist at home, I have worked to make the particularities of my original tribe a part of a more general conversation about the human condition. This is part of what I can exchange with my virtual companions (Lakhsassi 2005).

There is no question that we are far away from the 1960s and 1970s when any particularism, whether religious, ethnic, or linguistic, was seen as a conspiracy against the Arab nation. Public space is not monopolized anymore by such ideologies. The Berber movement that has taken advantage of transnational spaces over the last decades helped to keep alive our language and culture, and by extension, Berbers' self-esteem. Berber studies has ceased to be the domain of colonial scholarship. Maghrebi scholars started doing research in this area from the early 1970s. Their work prepared the ground for social and political Berber movements within national borders. The growth of these movements has coincided with the growth of ethnic rights and human rights movements around the world. The impact of these new transnational connections has had a profound impact on how Berber/Amazigh expressions are viewed in Morocco. Today, the intense sense of exclusion I experienced in Marrakech during the 1960s is no longer possible. Personally, the fact of going through a series of other places, languages, and ideas influenced my attitude about events in Morocco and how I perceived my own language and culture. The new atmosphere of the country makes it possible for me to live in Casablanca in a way that keeps me connected to my self as I have been shaped by the places I have moved through. My passages through many places was a kind of rite of passage into my new virtual tribe that allows me to live in Morocco as a member of my tribe of birth.

CONCLUSION

"Césaire and Senghor rediscovered the sentence of the German philosopher Hegel who stated that "it is not by negating the singular that one moves toward the universal, but by deepening the particular." And Césaire added: "You see, the more we are Negroes the more we will be men."[5]

My two quests—going from one place to another looking for something I could not identify, and progressively creating a personal world that I carry with me wherever I went are not incompatible. As a matter of fact, they are two sides of the same coin. From my first glimpse of the herds moving north from the Sahara, I have been attracted by the unknown. Ever since my days at school with Mr. Leclerc I have been learning new meanings and values in order to get out of my native cultural abyss—but not at any cost. The fear of being trapped in a new system or another "hole" has always haunted me. Perhaps it is a form of claustrophobia. Yet, the feeling that there must be something more interesting and more appealing somewhere else, in a life different than the one I am living persists. It never left me throughout my travels. My life has thus developed in a kind of *du provisoire permanent* (temporary permanence). In the first phase, the world in which I was living was not the universal one I ended up with. I tried to protect myself from the assaults of ways of living that challenged—instead of enriching—my own. From Tiznit to Marrakech where I discovered the low status given to my mother tongue and local culture, to Manchester, where I was not afraid but felt no sense of direction, the circle was closed. Now I am back "home" in Morocco, in Casablanca, far from Tiznit, which is not a home to me in the usual sense anymore. I see that my willingness to travel and to know others implies never getting totally involved with any one place. This has both advantages and disadvantages. On the one hand, it prevents me from going deeper into becoming assimilated to any one way of life. It also keeps me contented with life as it offers itself to me. I am perhaps more an interested and curious tourist than a serial migrant who becomes totally involved in each place he lives. The kind of distance I always have with the people and places, languages, and ideas I encounter means that I can maintain my own, slowly evolving, sense of personal meaning. I do not get caught up in any new alien system of meaning without careful reflection. Thus, I avoid the regret or sorrow some people who "go native" feel if their hopes of transformation through moving and becoming Other are dashed (which inevitably occurs). My distanced approach facilitates my ability to take displacement lightly. I never took another culture or place as "a package deal," I try to draw on my various experiences selectively to build the self.

For a long time, there must have been some sort of fear of taking root that prevented me from remaining in a particular place. I never knew quite what I was running from or what I was trying to find. As I mentioned, I often experienced a kind of suffocating feeling resembling a nightmare (*baghrar* in Berber/*bu-tekkay* in Moroccan Arabic). But as time has passed, I have forgotten that fear, that striving to move beyond the claustrophobia of place. I have increasingly come to appreciate the places I have lived. Locations of our past are not so much the disappearing old places as such, the way they once were, but the moments we spent there, vanished times now gone forever. My childhood hometown still stands as ever in my mind in contrast to the actual town that exists today—a place devoid of that gone-forever time. It has taken me all of these years, these many voyages with their detours to understand that the kind of universalism I was probably looking for could emerge from that small place I was born. Instead of running from the particular, I now seek to create a dialectic or a bond between the different moments, memories, and questions I ask my many places. It is perhaps once we achieve this point that we are cosmopolitans. Perhaps cosmopolitanism is not just about not being local, but of developing a kind of productive universalism of the kind suggested by Aimé Césaire and Léopold Senghor.

ACKNOWLEDGMENT

I would like to express my gratitude to Susan Ossman for her encouragement, suggestions, and help in preparing the final version of this paper.

NOTES

1. On the metaphor of the "hole" in Moroccan literature as related to village life, see Ossman 2002, p.19.
2. The *Berber Manifesto* was published on 1 March 2000. It sixth demand reads:

When a poor Berber speaker leaves his village to go look for work, usually in cities, it is only with enormous difficulty that he is integrated into the working-class society of his peers: his poor knowledge of Arabic barely allows him to ask his way and earn his pitifully small wages. He is perpetually embarrassed at work in his relations with his employers and colleagues. He comes to believe that he is cursed: a result of being Amazigh. Over the last thirty years, it has been recorded that at least 60 percent of construction workers in large cities are Berber speakers. They may use their hands to construct beautiful buildings and sumptuous homes but they are reduced to living in the greatest material and psychic misery. One of the charitable Berber cultural associations that took an interest in their lot discovered that *one of them took on the role of a mute so as not to suffer the sarcasm that his incapacity to express himself in Arabic inspired* (my italics). Add to this the incredible number of Berber speakers who go to the totally Arabized city centers to beg with a mere twenty to thirty words in the language of dâd [Arabic language]. www.mondeberbere.com/societe/manifeste.htm (Accessed May 17, 2006) Susan Ossman's translation from French.

3. Some Moroccan Jews were Berber speakers, and others who received a French education could not converse easily in Arabic. On Berber-speaking Jews, see Lakhsassi, "Pourquoi la langue première des juifs berbères n'est pas Amazigh?" a paper given at the International Conference on *Morocco Today* (Marocco Oggi) organized by the Uni-

versity Ca' Foscari Di Venezia (Italy), 26–28 January 2006, to be published by its Department of Euro-Asian Studies.
  4. Muslims, Christians, and Jews are "people of the book."
  5. martinique.rfo.fr/article10html (accessed 10 May 2006), translation by Susan Ossman.

REFERENCES

Aboulkacem, El-Khatir. 2006. De la négation nationale à la construction identitaire; le cas des Amazigh marocains. Unpublished article.

——. 2005. Nationalisme et construction culturelle de la nation au Maroc: processus et réactions. Thèse de Doctorat, Paris, EHESS.

Beck, Ulrich. 2001. The Cosmopolitan Society and Its Enemies. *Politologiske Studier*, arg. 4, NR2, May.

Césaire, Aimé (and Senghor), Aimé Césaire. martinique.rfo.fr/article10html (accessed 10 May 2006).

Hannerz, Ulf. 1992. *Cultural Complexity, Studies in the Social Organization of Meaning*. New York: Columbia University Press.

Hart, David. 2000. Scratch a Moroccan, Find a Berber. *Tribe and Society in Rural Morocco*. David M. Hart (ed). London: Frank Cass.

Lacouture, Jean and Simone. 1958. *Le Maroc à l'épreuve*. Paris: Seuil.

Lakhsassi, Abderrahmane. 2006. Pourquoi la langue première des juifs berbères n'est pas Amazigh? International Conference on *Morocco Today* (Marocco Oggi) organized by the University Ca' Foscari Di Venezia (Italy), 26–28 January 2006.

——. 2005. Anthropologue at home. Limites de la 'distanciation' et piège de l'empathie. *La Méditerranée des anthropologues. Fractures, filiations, contiguïtés*. D. Albera and Mohammed Tozy (eds.). Paris: Maison méditerranéenne des sciences de l'homme et Maisonneuve & Larose.

——. 1989a. Réflexions sur la mascarade de Achoura à Tiznit. *Signes du Présent* no. 6, 31–39.

——. 1989b. Injustice et résistance dans la poésie berbère. *Revue du Monde Musulman et de la Méditerranée* no. 51, 111–20.

——. 1988. Présence de la poésie berbère. (Dossier: Regards sur la culture Marocaine). *Librement* (édité par Kalima), no. 1, Casablanca. 57–61.

N'Ikhsassiyn (Abderrahmane Lakhsassi). 1987. Tiznit. *Lamalif.* Casablanca, no. 191, 58–70.

Mernissi, Fatima. 1987. [first published 1975]. *Beyond the Veil: Male-Female Dynamics in Modern Muslim Society*. Rev. ed. Bloomington & Indianapolis: Indiana University Press.

Ossman, Susan. 2002. *Three Faces of Beauty: Casablanca, Paris, Cairo*. Durham, N.C.: Duke University Press.

Said, Edward. 1999. *Out of Place: A Memoir.* New York: Vintage.

al-Shawaf, Rayyan. 2006. A Foolish new attraction to oppressive Arab nationalism. *Daily Star*, March 23, 2006. www/dailystar.com.lb/article.asp?edition_id=10&categ_id=5&article_id=23162

12

Linked Comparisons for Life and Research

Susan Ossman

The facile mobility of such an apparently ethereal, privileged figure as the cosmopolitan offers little guidance about which ways of moving through the world are most efficacious or beautiful, which resting points along one's way might involve unacceptable subjection, or prospects for liberation. Ulrich Beck suggests that cosmopolitan living includes "rival ways of life in the individual experience, which makes it a matter of fate to compare, reflect, criticize, understand, combine contradictory certainties" (Beck 2001, 18). Yet, he does not tell us how, where, and when the cosmopolitan gains this fateful ability to identify distinctive ways of life and melt the sharp edges of contradiction. Why indeed should we be interested in the cosmopolitan minority at all, when it is so obviously more urgent to develop a worldly perspective that leads us to extend hospitality to nomads, immigrants, or otherwise displaced people (Derrida in Borradori 2003)? Or might paying attention to "lived cosmopolitanism" lead us to question the separation between the citizen of the world and those who seem to require his aid (Appiah 1997, Calhoun 2002)? If it is apparent that we need fresh means to compare "rival ways of life" in a world situation where national borders and cultural markers are increasingly blurred, we might imagine that a global vision inspired by all kinds of people on the move might help us to see more clearly. In this chapter, I suggest that that people who live transnationally do have something quite particular to say about meaningful social locations and significant contradictions. One of the first things that my conversation with people who have lived in several countries shows is that we need to pay more attention to the work of time and the different paths taken by people on the move. Refugees can turn into immigrants, displaced people, like political exiles might come to demonstrate "cosmopolitan" proclivities. As people move through time, or from place to place, they take on new faces according to different regimes of identification. They come to comment on these in deciding which places to include in their lives.

Take Alice. As a multilingual, highly educated child of a diplomat, she seems the picture of the cultivated cosmopolitan. She seems like the kind of person ready to go anywhere, for a while. We would probably imagine her living long-term in a global city (Sassen 2002). Still, when I mentioned to her that I recently moved to London, she told me that she would never live there. While she would happily return to live in New York, and is content for now in Paris, as the child of an Italian mother and Venezuelan father, London was off her list of possible places to settle from the time she left high school. She attended British schools, and it would have seemed natural for her to attend university in England. But when she visits the United Kingdom, she is mistaken for an Indian. This is why she decided to study in the United States instead of the UK, because she had sensed that being placed in that category meant she would be exposed to racism. She lived in Guyana in her youth, where her South Asian friends and involvement in the Caribbean region made her attentive to the history and vestiges of British colonialism. Alice understands the diverse methods of producing statistics and counting immigrants employed by various national bureaucracies, indeed, as an anthropologist she has become a specialist of immigration and ethnicity. She explains, for instance, that conceptions of people from other places, or assumed to be foreign born, are extremely rigid in France. But what matters with respect to her personal choices is how she herself might be captured in the particular nets of one or another system of categorization. Although her American education and fluent English might lead her to have professional opportunities in London, her looks limit her willingness to include that city in her possible futures. When she imagines herself in England she does not envision the world at large, but rather, specific forms of ignorance and erasure of herself in a particular place and time. She locates rival ways of life in terms of a calculus of acceptable limits of the way that social categories obscure what is fundamental to what makes her a singular individual.

Majid was born in Morocco. He moved to France when he was in his twenties and lived there for a decade as a political exile. Thanks to an amnesty in the 1980s, he was allowed to return to Casablanca. But after only a couple of years, he decided to move to Montreal. Although he says that he has never wavered in his loyalty to socialist ideals, his political engagements have been very different in his two adopted countries. In France, there are many possibilities to maintain connections to Moroccan political organizations, as well as Maghrebi immigrant associations. In Quebec, Moroccans and Maghrebis are not visible as a particular category, nor are they perceived as a particular social or political problem. In Canada, Majid has not joined immigrant organizations. Instead he has chosen to join groups engaged in what he calls "more universal struggles." It is not that his ideas or motivations for political action had changed, he said, but that the history, number of migrants, and manners of organizing identities in each country offered him different opportunities for situating himself politically. In France, Majid felt as much a Maghrebi and a Moroccan as he did a political exile. In Montreal, on the other hand, one might imagine him as something more of a world citizen. He emphasizes that both kinds of engagement are the same to him since contributing to building the kind of world he hopes for requires different modes of engagement in different nations. It was in Morocco that he had trouble acting on his political ideals. He says that he is emotionally connected to his country of origin, and he could live there comfortably. But he said he has "made the choice to adhere to more open, more rational and democratic ideals." This "differentiates me from my compatriots of my country of origin. When I am with other Moroccans I feel something like a base-line culture that I have in common with them. Yet, there are these differences on the ideological plane, these different values, if you like. I've adopted values that cannot be applied in my country of origin and that I cannot always share with my compatriots of my country of origin."

Although Alice says that she feels she is a "fake native" in all of her homes, there is a line of self-continuity or social authenticity that she is unwilling to cross. Majid affirms his emotional connection to Morocco, but has chosen to live in places where he feels able to live according to his political values. Both Alice and Majid make comparisons that depend on seeking continuities and connections in their lives in ways that limit and divide the globe. They implicitly comment on social and political spaces by their willingness to include them in their personal geographies. One might see them as developing the kind of "considered freedom" that James Faubion points to as an important, if often ignored, aspect of Michel Foucault's ethics. He writes, "For Foucault, ethical practice requires not simply a repertoire of technologies but also an 'open territory,' a social terrain in which a considered freedom might actually be exercised" (2001, 85). Alice and Majid can be seen as creating open territories through their motions, territories that are "considered" in ways that generalized accounts of cosmopolitan life do not allow. Their refusals to live in particular places are at odds with conceptions of the globe as limitless, the spaces of the world as equally proportioned. Their judgements about different countries are made in terms of their individual aspirations and personal convictions, but this does not mean that they have no broader social or political message.

Like other people who have lived in several countries, those I have called "serial migrants," Alice and Majid think about the world through the precision of limited social and political terrains. National borders figure prominently as terms of comparison. They use recognized frontiers to trace their movements and gain distance from the selves of other countries that are subject to other modes of categorization, other forms of governmentality. They play on the gaps between these and the actual geographies of their lives, which appear as moving images or perhaps, as musical compositions. Their practical reflection on the location of "rival ways of life" can only be understood as a process, which means that it is not possible to identify contradictions in static terms.

Here, I will explore how moves of serial migration have led me to develop particular ways of working through comparison in order to develop something like a considered study of globalization. I will draw on interviews with other people of many countries to comment on the stages by which I became a serial migrant myself. This will lead me to examine what mobility might mean not only for freedom in general, but for the kinds of considerations we bring to trying to actually experience moments of liberation, interludes that might lead us to alter how we think about ourselves and our societies. Although I will introduce biographical details, I will not dwell on anecdotes about famous people or the intimate dramas that make a singular life into the stuff of best sellers. Instead, I will try to explain how the kind of work I have done as an anthropologist might be related to a particular experience of immigration, which led me to settle (for a while) in Morocco. I will try to show how moving through social categories and political terrains tends to encourage people to perceive comparisons not as "fated," but as knowingly conceived. I will suggest that following connections across countries often leads to recognizing unexpected points of contradiction.

LIFE IN-BETWEEN

In 1980, after completing my first degree at Berkeley, I went to Paris as a *jeune fille au paire* turned waitress turned insurance clerk. I married and gave birth to a son. During these first years in France, I often felt like I was sitting with "my ass between two chairs" as the French saying goes. The two terms between which I was situated could be used to politely explain any opinion I expressed, any *écart* (distance) between my behaviour and prevalent social expectations (Ossman 2002, 152). "Yes, of course you must think that, you had an American upbringing." "But of course, you cannot be expected to know how to do that, not being from here." If in France my foreign birth provided explanations, in the United States, my increasingly long residence abroad conveniently excused my idiosyncrasies. When one lives between two countries, this kind of overidentification along national lines seems to infiltrate every action. I found this exasperating, although I know other Franco-Americans for whom it seems not to be a problem. One might comfortably inhabit in-betweeness by deciding to occupy one or another of the positions more gracefully, that is, more entirely. "Why not return to school to become a specialist of the history or politics of *one country or the other*, or study the history of relations between the two?" friends suggested. A doctorate in American literature, others said, might be a way to find a good job in France. Or perhaps I could "pursue my study of French history and, eventually, apply for a job in an American university?" others kindly proposed. I was aghast at these reasonable propositions because I was unwilling to see myself as simply a representative of a particular language, culture, or country. In my youthful naiveté, I supposed that one should chose one's areas of study or expertise according to more personal or intellectually compelling criteria. Perhaps I was inhabited by some inchoate cosmopolitanism, having imbibed the utopian notion of an international intellectual community that transcends bodies and borders. In any case what was clear is that I had to work through what I was in order to move toward an understanding of what might be worthy of passionate engagement. One thing I was in France was an immigrant, albeit, of a very particular kind. It was by working through and around a term that included me bureaucratically, but not socially, that I felt like I could move toward becoming something more of a citizen of the world.

When my friend Hisham applied for French nationality in the early 1980s he was interrogated about his "feelings" toward the Imam Khomeiny, although it was a matter of public record that he was a prominent member of a left-leaning Moroccan student union. When I went to my immigration interview, my political involvements or ideas were considered irrelevant. I had to answer the questions printed on a series of standard forms. How long had I lived at my current address? What was my profession? How many siblings did I have? "Will your five sisters join you in France?" the friendly woman behind the desk inquired, not even trying to suppress a smile that grew broader as she read off the questions. "If one of them does want to move to Paris," she giggled, "let me know, since I'd be more than happy to take their place in California!" Hisham was from a wealthy family, whereas I had worked as a waitress *au noir* (without papers) and then held a low-level office job while I was in graduate school. But my appearance, education, and lack of connection to colonial history meant that I could never be a real *immigré*. The chasm between how I looked, where I came from, and the assumptions written into every official form and law to which immigrants are subject could only inspire laughter or suspicion. At least, this was the case when I was face to face with someone in an office, if they possessed information about my place of birth, or what in French is referred to as one's "family situation." In situations where people had only my name to represent me, for instance, over the telephone, the gap between my looks and my status as an immigrant was filled in. My blue eyes no longer made my interlocutor hear my "Eastern" accent, leading him to scribe my name as Suzanne Haussman and ask about my connections to the illustrious Alsatian family. In exchanges mediated by telephones or faxes, often in spite of the information on my CV, I tend to become Sawsan Osman, just another immigrant whose family must live in Sfax or Oran.

Being always a little out of place can lead people to want to point out some of the contradictions, inequities, or absurdities of national identification. Alex wrote to me about his own decision to have only one passport:

> A long story would be the changes I observed within Europe during my back and forth voyages that started in early 1990s, especially those regarding nationality. I was carrying a Romanian passport, and while in the beginning of my travel I was permanently regarded with suspicion by the authorities, now it turns out that people in Western European countries do not even know if Romania is in the EU or not. I made a point not to apply for or change my citizenship, a personal political stance in order to bring to the surface the absurdity of the "national order of things." However, I sometimes feel stopped in accomplishing many things because of the passport I am holding.

It might seem that someone like Alex would be the first to acquire several nationalities. He could easily pass as a "real" French Frenchman. Yet, in spite of his flawless accent, he chooses to flaunt his passport to display Europe's internal hierarchies. The way in which he draws attention to his Romanian nationality is reminiscent of Emmanuel's explanation to Shana Cohen concerning his decision to live as a Jew in Morocco. His simple presence in Casablanca, his expression of his own opinions was, he explained to her, a kind of critical action against stereotypes (Cohen chapter 5). I suppose that I could have made a point of being an immigrant American in Paris. But the way that I was transfigured into a Muslim or a rich Alsatian according to whether I met someone in person or over the phone led me to envisage new possibilities for achieving the same kinds of objectives as Alex and Emmanuel.

With no strong personal connections to the immigrant suburbs and, in spite of my name, no family connections to any Arab or Muslim country, the academic interest I began to express in issues of immigration was generally seen by my friends as evidence of my attachment to issues of human rights and universal values. As a scholar, I could seek to understand the immigrant's suffering and exploitation (Sayad 1999). As an activist, I might hope to ameliorate his condition. But in neither of these positions was I expected to make a connection between the immigrant and myself. Yet, when I became a French citizen, I did so for many of the same reasons as any migrant laborer. I wanted to insure my right to have a say in my son's future, especially since I was in the process of divorce. I also wanted to be able to apply for jobs that required applicants to be nationals or Europeans. Perhaps other less tangible aspects were also involved in my story of immigration.

When I interviewed Ricardo last year, he told me about how his life had taken him from Venezuela to the United States, to France, and finally, to Dubai. He explained his willingness to move as "typically American." Indeed, the historian Nancy Green has pointed to the role that the narrative of American immigration plays in how scholars study migration everywhere (although she focuses on North America: see Green 2002). Ricardo explained his life in terms of the tales of migration to South America with which he had been raised. My own interest in immigration was surely related to the prominence of the image of the melting pot in my early education as well as the constant references to immigration and "the old country" in my family. Given my family history, one might have imagined that I could have examined Polish immigration to Western Europe, a particularly interesting topic in the heyday of Solidarność. But while "finding one's roots" was in keeping with the social climate of the early 1980s, I saw this tendency as both narcissistic and theoretically flawed. It seemed that it was neither through the depth of rootedness nor a dream of unlimited flight that I could get out of my double bind. Instead, it was in the process of displacement that some solution seemed possible to envision. It was by following the most tenuous and problematic connections, those that seemed least able to place me in a known category, that I found the freedom to define the places and topics that would lead me back to academic study. It was through the thin and misleading category of myself as immigrant that I moved into the Maghreb.

Initially, I studied colonial history, focusing on cinema and notions of aesthetic national authencity. After completing my DEA at the Université Paris VII, I traveled to Morocco over the summer. That visit led me to move from analysis of the way that independence was projected to take aesthetic form toward a broader study of the role of media in the development of contemporary Moroccan society. I envisaged the possibility of engaging in fieldwork and participant observation, which led me beyond the disciplinary bounds of history, toward media studies and anthropology. In France at that time, I saw no way to pursue this topic, since anthropologists there were not quite ready to become interested in modernity, and media and communications was only beginning to become established in French universities. Ironically, my quest

to transcend my double life as a Franco-American led me to pursue the
Maghreb in North America.

MOVING HOME

Some Moroccans of my generation studied abroad because certain subjects
simply were not taught in Moroccan universities. Others did so because degrees from France or Belgium, the United States or the USSR were considered more prestigious than those of national universities. Some simply
sought to take advantage of scholarship funds to travel and discover new
places. Whatever the reason for leaving Fez or Agadir, most say that they always assumed that they would eventually return home. Having been brought
up in the years just after independence, influenced by the nationalism of the
1960s and 1970s, many Moroccans who studied and then worked abroad
eventually returned home because they felt that it was ethically and politically imperative for them to do so. Yet, in Morocco by the 1980s, the initially
high demand for educated workers that had followed independence had
given way to a slow job market (Cohen 2004). Even highly educated people
found it hard to find work. And even those who were able to secure positions
often considered moving back to their second country. Talking with people
who had studied or lived abroad and who lived in Morocco in the 1980s,
I was struck by how conversations tended to compare Morocco to that other
home, which was often France, the former colonial power. The kind of positively reconfigured home that includes a series of transnational and virtual
communities that Abderrahmane Lakhsassi has been able to create seemed
difficult to envision by people caught in the clutches of this binary opposition (chapter 11). This was a pattern I knew only too well, and like me, some
of these returnees ended up deciding to move to yet another country.
(Abouhouraira chapter 10)

    However, I came from the most powerful country in the world, which was
one of the reasons it seemed impossible for me to be an immigrant. While my
Moroccan friends generally thought that they were returning home for good
after their time in France, I expected my return trip to California to be short
term. I returned to the United States not to settle, but because it offered the
perfect place to prepare for my departure to Morocco. By enrolling at Berkeley, I commenced an academic career that I expected would transcend national territories, involve me in international networks of people and lead me
into new fields of intellectual debate (Early chapter 8). My journey to Morocco via America was not about settling down. It was about keeping my options about place open. Yet, if I ended up in Berkeley, it was also due to practical and familial factors. In the San Francisco Bay area, my parents and

sisters could help me out with my infant son. The University of California provided subsidized childcare, something not available to graduate students at many American universities. Even once I was "in the field" I could easily return to Berkeley for long periods should I need to confer with my professors or seek out rare books in the library. I was happy to return home, but I envisioned it more as a particular region and set of relationships rather than through the prism of the nation.

As I concentrated on the particularity of place and the networks of personal connections that tied me to the cities of Paris and San Francisco, I found the Maghreb growing somehow vaguer and more general. My project was pulled in the direction of Middle Eastern studies, or set in the context of the Islamic world. In California I found that other students of Arabic tended to be mainly interested in religion or preoccupied with Palestine-Israeli relations. Everyone in the entire university seemed passionate about Orientalism. But only a few people seemed to take the time to examine how particular colonial policy actually led to distinctive modes of subjection (Fuller 1988; Rabinow 1989). Of course, Morocco has been the subject of many important anthropological studies published in English since the early 1970s. They led me into village settings and made me aware of debates on segmentation. They also led me to wonder whether the Maghreb that I had gotten a glimpse of in France or Casablanca still actually existed. While human rights organizations pointed to the number of political prisoners in the Cherifian kingdom, the approaches to anthropological fieldwork current at the time favored cultural critique rather than direct political participation. Although I was much inspired by work in the interpretative, culturally critical vein, I found it difficult to fully engage conversations in their critical spaces because they tended to separate home and field in ways reminiscent of the double bind I was running away from. After the outward journey, anthropologists were still expected to return from the field not only with data, but with a new viewpoint. I had no qualms about personal or epistemological transformation, but I had trouble envisioning the Maghreb as radically disconnected from the places I had lived previously and would probably live again. I failed to see myself as someone who might someday return from a year or two of study to better comment on the strangeness of my home (Ossman 1999). To which home would I return, by what route? I wondered.

THE THIRD STEP

The anthropologist arrives in the city by foot, the sociologist by car and via the main highway, the communications specialist by plane (Garcia Canclini 1995, 4).

When I met with Abderrahim in 2005, he spoke of how moving to his third country led him to develop a more complex view of the world and, especially, more confidence in developing his own perspectives. He grew up in Saudi Arabia and moved to the United States in his twenties. He studied and then worked on the East Coast for many years, then moved to London for professional reasons. He explained that during his years in North America, he was always comparing Saudi Arabia to the United States. Each country expanded in his mind to represent the Middle East and the West, an opposition that was put to the test by his move to London. There, he says, his comparative habit of mind was upset, which opened up new perspectives not only on "his three countries" but the world at large. This meant not only that he added the UK into the mix, he also became increasingly aware of *how* he was generalizing about what he observed. The move to England made him more cognizant of the unevenness of both "the West" and the "Middle East." One might have imagined that this could be confusing, but instead, he says that it led him to clarify his opinions and be more able to develop his own opinions, more capable of taking a stand on important issues.

I moved to Morocco in the company of the many definitions of the country I had collected in my previous travels. There were many fewer accounts or set images of Casablanca to refer to, but I had plenty of personal and professional connections to my new city. These strings of relation pulled me in different directions. I sometimes felt like a marionette brought to life by the hands of several masters. In casual conversation, my tongue had to set off in different directions to keep up with the Casablancan mix of tongues. One can follow the argument or line of expression in this multilingual talk, but it is not always easy to predict which word from what language will be used to designate a particular object or emotion. The significance of the words we find highlighted in anthropological texts points to their cultural resonance or the lack of an adequate translation in the language of the writer. In Casablanca, I assiduously studied Moroccan Arabic, but it was the play on different languages that exhilarated me and tested my linguistic aptitude. I sometimes felt that the elements of my mind were being rearranged according to seemingly random games that reassembled the syncopated style of Casablancan exchanges. Eventually, this led me to focus less on a general landscape of ideas or the depth of meaning in any single world, but instead on the way that lines of thought or ways of thinking are constituted through interaction with others. I wrote of how the connections among the discourses and people of my life led me to take "strong positions" to steady my line of research and questioning (1994, 16). This was as much a social imperative as it was the result of my efforts to devise a thesis for my doctoral dissertation. Perhaps because of the obvious ways in which the lines of my life tied me to others I met in Morocco, or because I was seen by others as having an identity that mixed places and languages like a Casablancan conversation, I was no longer politely excused for any unwelcome opinions based on my place of birth. Like Abderrahim, I found that the move to my third country led me to be better able to articulate my thoughts. Living in the closely surveyed society of Casablanca in the 1980s and early 1990s, I experienced a sense of freedom. In the midst of people who said I was a heathen in need of conversion, saw me as a divorced woman in need of protection, or considered me as a colleague they might confide in, I found myself becoming increasingly able to find my balance as I moved through the city's moving social terrain.[1]

I was inspired by Pierre Francastel's affirmation that "images exist only in motion," and I sought to see how the continuities of my life might extend beyond my personal story. This led me to explore how the media intervene in shaping transnational political spaces and conceptions of participation through research in Paris and Casablanca during the French presidential elections of 1988 (1994). Transnational imaginations were also the object of study in another project that looked at how elsewhere is pictured among people living in three Moroccan cities with special relations to Italy, France, and Spain (1997). As I worked through fields that crossed national borders, I read proposals urging anthropologists to follow people, things, and images in order to address processes of globalization (Appadurai 1988). I thought further about the different ways that pictures, people, and things lead us to follow particular paths. I paid more attention to how the precise steps of the ethnographer relate to the pursuit of particular objects in motion and how this leads to delineating a field of study (Silverstone 1998).

As Garcia Canclini notes, "one's entrance into a place influences how and what and for what reason one studies it." If I wanted to work as an anthropologist studying communications in order to (eventually) propose an ethnographically based sociology, I needed to travel via several routes, trying out various kinds of vehicles. I also needed to think more carefully about the way that specific movements involve different kinds of fuel and particular kinds of repair or rest (Ossman 2002a).

When I took a position at the Rabat center of the *Institute de Recherche sur le Maghreb Contemporain* (IRMC, now the *Centre Jacques Berque*), I had the opportunity to developed a collaborative program to explore the relationship of moving media to sites of social interactions across the Maghreb. Organizing this project involved inciting connections and developing places of for collective thought in several sites. It required a kind of fieldwork preparation so that we could get together to exchange ideas about our research on football stadiums, nineteenth-century cities, and fast food restaurants as they related to the circulation of media (Ossman 1998). My personal topic of research for this project developed a comparative study of beauty salons as a place where media images are embodied.

LINKED COMPARISONS

While moving to my third country involved multisite projects from the start, the project on beauty could be seen as actually mimicking the steps of the serial migrant.[2] After an initial article on salon visits in my neighborhood, I began to notice how the magazines, soap operas, and talk about actresses one encounters there originate not in some "anywhere" global space, but in identifiable places (Ossman 1991). Sketching the paths of these images and objects out of the salons of Casablanca, thick lines lead to the catwalks and production studios of Cairo and Paris. So I traced a triangular field of study from Casablanca toward these cities, crossing Europe, the Mediterranean, the Arab world, and the Middle East. Merit Melhuus has recently written, "there are significant differences in the ways contexts are established (in this case by anthropologists) and that these differences depend fundamentally on the ways in which data are generated. In other words, the new sites for fieldwork not only demand new methods, they also require other forms of contextualization in order to make sense" (2002, 83). By shaping the context of this project according to beauty exchanges, I identified terrains that methodological nationalism and the borders of area specializations obscured. This was in keeping with the most forward-looking demands for dynamic sociology and multisite ethnography (Marcus 1998; Urry 2000). In practice, working through the contexts already established by existing academic sources came to be one of the more demanding aspects of this work. Much as Abderrahim suggested that when he was living in the United States, he tended to generalize about Middle Eastern culture based on his experience of Saudi Arabia, so many works about Arab beauty or beauty and Islam generalize about a vast region based on detailed ethnography in a single place, or engage in the kinds of textual exegesis that critics of Orientalism have convincingly denounced (for instance, Chebel 1984). Research on various aspects of politics, social organization of the three cities involved in my study is rich, precise, and varied. Indeed, it is not so much the limits of assumed national or local contexts that made moving among these texts rather difficult, but rather the fact that once a context is set, it tends to take on a life of its own and incite scholars to engage with particular kinds of questions. While the situation of poor urban women has been the subject of extensive study in Cairo, similar explorations are more likely to be found on the Paris of the nineteenth century than today.

That the study of Parisian fashion is well developed might be predictable, but works about fashion, design, and studies of the visual arts and architecture are also very present in literature on Morocco. Cairo is the location for many studies on cinema and television. The list could go on. The point is that making up a field for linked comparative research involves crossing scholarly as well as national lines, not to mention the frontiers that separate national traditions of scholarship in and about each site. The crossings and contradictions among these thickened the context drawn out by the initial research triangle.

Like so many of the serial migrants I have spoken with, I am particularly conscious of what each move erases from who I am. I often actually feel how the continuities I experience in my life are denied by static ways of establishing identity. Linked comparative research involves attention to what is forgotten when connections are obscured. It involves "importing" the ways that a topic is treated according to one map and placing it into another (Oakeschott 1995, 309). Yet, the critical potential of this kind of comparison is not exhausted in the recognition of connections and continuities uncharted on standard maps, or even alternatives to these drawn up by financial markets or flows of capital (Sassen 2002). It was because the comparative project involved long moments of rest in a strategically selected spaces that I came to identify points of continuity and contradiction that cosmopolitan living leaves undetected. It was through the comparisons of salons of the triangular field that the project gained its critical momentum.

Salons seem more or less the same around the world. This is part of what made them worth investigating, since any good social scientist will know that behind such apparent similarity must lurk the source of cultural divides and social difference. The grounds for the first are often located in distinctive national or ethnic conceptions or practices, The second rely on national measures of income or analyses of class position. Ethnographic research led me to see that salons can be categorized according to whether their clients get to them by foot, by car, or by plane. They can be classified further by the ways in which they rely on distinctive patterns of social interaction and ways of making the media part of judging and producing beauty. A proximate salon is usually within walking distance of one's home. There, individual appearance is a matter open to discussion for all who enter. People tend to know one another's families, and looks tend to be judged according to how they correspond to how the person is perceived in the neighborhood. Fast salons, on the other hand, are often located in commercial and business districts. People drive to them or walk to them on their lunch break or after work. There, the relationship of the client to the hairdresser is central. The competence of hairdressers is judged according to how they can produce beauties based on menus. They thus differ markedly from elite salons, where Jacques or Marco turn their clients into unique works of art. Such elite salons can be so attractive that people will travel by plane to get to them. But however people arrive, they are fit into a geography of networks of celebrity and fame. Their relationship to the body and social geography could not be more different than the fast salon that is often part of a franchise promising that its services will be the same anywhere. These three kinds of salon with their different arrangements of space and conceptions of society exist in different measure in Casablanca, Paris, and Cairo. So do the social and evaluative worlds that they are a part of. Some people are able to pick and chose among different kinds of salons, just as they play on different modes of evaluation in their lives. Others are confined to one or another kind of beauty parlour, which I have suggested indicates limitations in terms of mobility, both physical and social (2002). It is by noticing the differences behind the apparently similar modern woman as she is elaborated in what appear to be essentially similar salons that three parallel worlds with profoundly different criteria of evaluation came to my attention. Together they worked to create what we experience as the distinctive realities of Casablanca, Paris, and Cairo.

Through linked comparative research, I came to rephrase the question of contradiction in ways that take into account the relationship of mobility to social interaction, lived experience to ways of arranging conflicting modes of thought. By moving through a space traced by a particular topic, a space where a particular site where I could sit with others was everywhere apparent, I gradually came to draw on the works of others in ways that allowed me to shift context. By extending the worlds of judgment I found in salons beyond their walls, I relocated points of contradiction as well as social difference. How do worlds of face-to-face proximity, image-driven legal rationality, and celebrity intermingle? What kinds of gaps and freedoms, object importations, and strategic decisions can be better understood by taking into account this ethnographically derived model? These questions can only be answered through further research through other terrains. But already based on the study of practices of beauty, we can begin to glimpse how more "serious" areas of political and social research might be submitted to the proximate/fast/elite model. One might imagine crossing into contexts that are so built up and apparently impenetrable that to try to implement new ways of moving through them is practically impossible.

Linked comparisons can be configured in many sequences that break down and build context to work toward a dynamic, mobile sociology. When we design projects that do more than follow things or people, but trace the paths we take to reach them and note the rhythms through we which engage them, it becomes possible to establish an idea of the modes of production of the contexts we take as significant. This can lead to meeting up with emerging modes of subjectivation and freedom that depend on the regulation of ways of moving and the identification of distinct mobilities.[3] Instead of seeking to smooth out contradictions by occupying some middle, or perhaps, higher ground, we come to see how contradictions and connections among rival worlds are precisely what shape nations, places, and certainties that cannot be combined.

GLOBAL VISION

Simon was born in the UK, then moved to Canada when he was eighteen. After a brief stint in London for graduate school, he began to wander from job to job, teaching in English-language schools in Asia and the Middle East. When I met him in Bahrain, he had just celebrated his forty-eighth birthday. He told me that he has never tried to learn foreign languages beyond what he needs to ask for a drink or find a hotel. It is not that he lacks linguistic ability but because he actually likes not having to get too involved with anyone (Tandogan and Onaran 2004). He says that he likes to envision the world through his camera. Is it this photographic view that leads him to criticize the English and American institutions where he has worked because they "do not give enough attention to the specificities of students' "local cultures"? He thinks that it is wrong to lead people to adopt "Western ways" and manners of thought and he feels some qualms about participating in this process. "We should respect each way of life," he tells me, as I remember lines from books of what we now call classic anthropology. Of course, anthropologists always make a point of demonstrating their local knowledge and readiness to adapt. It is for this, some say, that our knowledge is grounded, or at least more precise than Simon's. Besides, we have always sought contact, tried to come to know the people. Does this mean that anthropologists can never be quite cosmopolitan?

It is interesting that serial migrants and anthropologists alike show particular hostility to the cosmopolitan, even when he is figured as more engaged than Simon. Both groups balk at the distance that Simon revels in, seeing it as related to a position of privilege and the kind of hedonistic lifestyle promoted by the magazine *Cosmopolitan*. Yet nearly every serial migrant I have encountered points to the ways in which motion across borders and beyond social barriers allows for modes of thoughtful freedom. What distinguishes their accounts of this dream from Simon's implementation of his is that they seek to create liberty in the gaps that their cross-country experiences make in their lives. Simon moves on, he says, to avoid tearing his heart or feeling pulled down. But most serial migrants develop their cross-country spaces through personal obligations and a sense of responsibility and loyalty to each of their homes. The problem with the cosmopolitan, their testimony seems to argue, is that he seems to run from the more significant ways in which his displacement might, however slightly, alter the balance of the world. He smoothes out contradictions to ease his way, avoiding the snags and miscomprehensions of what they see as reality. Significantly, all of the serial migrants I have interviewed or questioned over the internet say that they feel like world citizens. The apparent difference between themselves as citizens and the cosmopolitans they view with disdain might be conceived in terms of questions of consideration—not only of others, but of freedom itself. It is not simply their interaction with others and commitment to all of their homes that shapes their ethical problems with the cosmopolitan, but how they problematize and place the interplay between these engagements and possibilities for liberty gained through renewing one's relationship to oneself (Faubion 2001).

In reviewing how I displaced the spaces of my own moves through life to work through linked comparisons, I see that I began by challenging borders by focusing on links among cities. Maps were rapidly replaced by dynamic spaces where images were embodied and played on, places marked by particular social networks and conceptions of social ties (Lewis and Wiggen 1997). Salons spanned Casablanca, Cairo, and Paris in this field in motion, fracturing and forming each city, and leading me to explore coexisting social realities. Because these worlds depend on how people relate to one another, which in turn has to do with how they move from place to place, exploring how they pass among these coexisting realities opens up paths for envisioning dynamic sociology (Urry 2000). However, it is doubtful that such study can lead to anything like a cosmopolitan vision (Beck 2006). For it is in the considered freedom that frees up spaces for thought and ethical practice by admitting to the necessary persistence of contradiction that a sociology of motion can emerge. It is precisely because it is a study in the limits of encounters with actual others that the embodied and dynamic paths of ethnography opens horizons for cosmopolitics.

NOTES

1. Much more could be said about the position of the researcher and the ethnographer in particular. Many of the papers presented at the ASA's Diamond Jubilee conference held in Keele in April 2006 explore the place of the anthropologist as related to debates about cosmopolitanism My aim in this chapter is much more modest. I try simply to analyze how my ways of working through ethnography might be related to a life path that may or may not be considered cosmopolitan. My research on serial migration is ongoing, so I expect to write more on these topics in the future.

2. This is obviously a turn on the usual assumption of the foreign body as the one who mimics, see Bhabha 1994; Taussig 1993.

3. Roger Silverstone inspired my way of thinking of divergent paths through similar spaces in the elegant presentation of his research on museum visits that he gave at the conference on mimesis and the media organized by the CELSA and the CNRS in Paris in 1997 (1998). I recently had the pleasure of reading his latest work on "contrapuntal cultures," which further pursued the study of coexisting social realities. In the midst of writing this chapter, I was shocked and deeply saddened to learn of his death. I dedicate what sparks of inspiration or creative thought these thoughts on comparison and mobility might provoke to his memory.

REFERENCES

Appiah, Kwame Anthony. 1997. Cosmopolitan Patriots. *Critical Inquiry* 23, no. 3. Spring. 617–39.

Appadurai, Arjun (ed). 1988. *The Social Life of Things, Commodities in Cultural Perspective.* Cambridge: Cambridge University Press.

Bhabha, Homi. 1994. *The Location of Culture.* London: Routledge.

Beck, Ulrich. 2001. The Cosmopolitan Society and its Enemies. *Politologiske Studier* arg. 4, NR2, May.

———. 2006. *Cosmopolitan Vision.* London: Polity.

Borradori, Giovanna. 2003. *Philosophy in a Time of Terror: Dialogues with Jurgen Habermas and Jacques Derrida.* Chicago: University of Chicago Press.

Calhoun, Craig J. 2002. The Class Consciousness of Frequent Travelers: Toward a Critique of Actually Existing Cosmopolitanism. *South Atlantic Quarterly* 101, 4. Fall. 869–97.

Chebel, Malik. 1984. *Du corps en Islam.* Paris: PUF.

Cohen, Shana. 2004. *Searching for a Different Future: The Rise of a Global Middle Class in Morocco.* Durham, N.C.: Duke University Press.

Faubion, James D. 2001. Toward an Anthropology of Ethics: Foucault and Pedagogies of Autopoiesis. *Representations* 74, Spring. 83–104.

Francastel, Pierre. 1983. *L'image, la vision et l'imagination, de la peinture au cinéma.* Paris: Gonthier.

Fuller, Mia. 1988. Building Power: Italy's Colonial Architecture and Urbanism, 1923–1940. *Cultural Anthropology* 3, 4. 455–87.

Garcia Canclini, Néstor. 1995. *Hybrid Cultures: Strategies for Entering and Leaving Modernity.* Minneapolis: University of Minnesota Press.

Green, Nancy. 2002. *Repenser les migrations.* Paris: PUF.

Gupta, A. and Ferguson, J. 1997. Discipline and Practice: "The field" as Site, Method, and Location in Anthropology. *Anthropological Locations, Boundaries and Grounds of a Field Science.* Gupta, A. and Ferguson, J. (eds). Berkeley: University of California Press.

Hannerz, Ulf. 1992. *Cultural Complexity, Studies in the Social Organization of Meaning.* New York: Columbia University Press.

Levitt, Peggy. 2001. *The Transnational Villagers*. Berkeley: University of California Press.

Lewis, Martin W. and Wigen, Karen E. 1997. *The Myth of Continents. A Critique of Metageography*. Berkeley: University of California Press.

Marcus, George E. 199. *Ethnography through Thick and Thin*. Princeton: Princeton University Press.

Melhuus, Merit. 2002. Issues of Relevance. Anthropology and the Challenges of Cross-Cultural Comparison. *Anthropology, By Comparison*. Gingrich, Andre and Fox, Richard G. (eds.). London: Routledge.

Oakschot. Michael. 1995 (1939). *Experience and its Modes*. Oxford: Oxford University Press.

Ossman, Susan.1991. Les Salons de beauté au Maroc. *Les Cahiers de L'Orient* no. 20, printemps.

———. 1994. *Picturing Casablanca: Portraits of Power in a Modern City*. Berkeley: University of California Press.

———. 1997. Partir: Ou la proximité entre 'ici' et 'là': émigrations imaginaires depuis trois villes marocaines. *Egypte/Monde Arabe* no. 30–31, autumn/hiver.

———. (ed). 1998. *Miroirs Maghrébins, Itinéraires de soi et Paysages de Rencontre*. Paris: CNRS Editions.

———. 1999. Parcours et partages: pérégrination sur le savoir pratique des anthropologues. *Parcours d'Intellectuels Maghrebins*. Kadri, Aïssa (ed). Paris: Karthala.

———. 2002. *Three Faces of Beauty. Casablanca, Paris, Cairo*. Durham, N.C.: Duke University Press.

———. 2002a. Anthropologie of the Armchair. *Newsletter.* American Anthropological Association, November.

Rabinow, Paul. 1989. *French Modern: Norms and Forms of the Social Environment*. Cambridge: MIT Press.

Sassen, Saskia. (ed.). 2002. *Global Networks, Linked Cities*. New York: Routledge.

Sayad, Abdelmalek. 1999. *La double absence; des illusions de l'émigré aux suffrances de l'émigré*. Paris: Seuil.

Silverstone, Roger. 1998. Les espaces de la performance: musées, sciences et rhétoriques de l'objet. *Mimesis: imiter, représenter, circuler*. Ossman, S. (ed.). *Hermès* 22, 175–88.

Taussig, Michael. 1993. *Mimesis and Alterity: A Particular History of the Senses*. New York: Routledge.

Tandogan, Zerrin G. and Incirlioglu, Emine Onaran. 2004. Academics in Motion: Cultural Encapsulation and Feeling at Home. *City and Society* 16, 1, 99–114.

Urry, John. 2000. *Sociology Beyond Societies. Mobilities for the Twenty-first Century*. London & New York: Routledge.

Index

Abdel Rahman, Sheik Omar, 30
academic identity, as precluding being
    an immigrant, 147
academic research: ethical dilemmas,
    29, 118; personal aspects, 5, 79,
    99–102, 158, 178, 187–188,
    206–207, 210
academy, divisions within, 5,
    58–59,159; as a community, 151,
    205
acts of identity, 178. *See also* identity
Afghans, 21
AIMS (American Institute of Maghreb
    Studies), 11, 143, 158
Al-Ghazali, 74
al-Qaeda, 8, 27; members in U.S.
    custody, 38; and Zaccarias
    Moussaoui, 34–37, 40
al-Qaedism, 29
Albania, 101–102, 108
Algeria, 47–49
Algerians, 107; in France, 51, 53
Amador, Dr. Xavier, 30
Amazigh. *See* Berber
America, and theories of migration,
    207
American, universities, 58
Andalusia, imagination of, 164–165

anthropologist, as cosmopolitan, 215,
    216n1
anthropology: collaborative, 4, n.1;
    concepts, popularization of, 215;
    fieldwork, 209; going native, vies on,
    150, 203; at home, 197; and
    immigration, 204; modernity, 206
anti-Americanism, 148
Arab World, 12, 144, 153 162;
    migration within, 168
Arabic: dialects, 12, 48, 153, 156, 173,
    180; dialects in U.A.E., 180;
    hierarchies within, 12–13, 180–181;
    study of, 121, 126, 144 192, 210;
    taught in French schools; 50
Arabic and identity, 183. *See also*
    language and identity
Arabocentricism, 190–191, 196
Arabs: racism against, 31. *See also*
    immigrants and beurs
architect, as intermediary, 129
area studies, conceptual limits, 60
assimilation, 14; in USA, 82; serial
    migrants refusal to, 199. *See also*
    migration and immigrants
asylum seekers, 18
AUB (American University in Beirut),
    144, 189, 194, 195

219

About the Contributors

Leila Abouhouraira is a communications and translation specialist who has worked in corporate settings in Morocco, France, and Canada. She is currently working on a study of language, migration, and globalization. She is also involved in programs for the *Régie Régionale des Services Sociaux* in Montreal, an agency that helps needy immigrant families.

Fatima Badry is professor of English and linguistics at the American University of Sharjah. Her research interests center around first and second language acquisition, Arabic morphology, and Arabic socio-linguistics. Her current projects explore the linguistic practice and migration experience among Moroccan women living in the countries of the Persian Gulf. She is the author of *Acquiring the Arabic Lexicon: Evidence of Productive Strategies and Pedagogical Implications* (2003).

Shana Cohen has conducted extensive research in Morocco. She has written two books, *Searching for a Different Future* (2004) and *Globalization: A Moroccan View* (2006). She is currently working and conducting research with voluntary sector and nonprofit organizations in Morocco, the UK, and India. She is a lecturer in sociology at the University of Sheffield in Sheffield, England.

Evelyn A. Early is currently Counselor for Press and Cultural Affairs at the American Embassy in Rabat. She has conducted research in Lebanon, Egypt, Syria, and the United States on topics ranging from Islam in kiosk and electronic media to the informal economic sector, to ephemeral art to the role of art and film in culture. She has published widely on medical anthropology and acted as a consultant for programs on women in development. She is the author of *Baladi Women of Cairo: Playing with an Egg and a Stone* (1993) and coeditor (with Donna Lee Bowen) of *Everyday Life in the Muslim Middle East* (2002). Before serving as a diplomat in the Sudan, Morocco, Syria, and the Czech Republic, she taught at the Universities of New Mexico, Houston, and Notre Dame.

Nabiha Jerad is an associate professor at the University of Tunis. Her current research is on language and identity in the postcolonial Maghreb and among North Africans in France. She has published articles on language and North African literature, with particular attention to the way that the two shores of the Mediterranean have been involved in exchanges of various kinds ("La Méditerranée a travers les récits de voyageurs des deux rives de la Méditerranéan," *Revue Littératures frontaliéres* 2003). Her article "The Maghreb between the two Rims of the Mediterranean" will be published this year.

Smaïn Laacher is a sociologist at the Center for the Study of Social Movements of the Centre National de Recherche Scientifique (CNRS). He has examined many aspects of immigration, asylum, and population displacements in Europe. His publications include a study of the history and legal aspects of nationality (*Questions de nationalité. Histoire et enjeux d'un code*, 1987), an account of the Sangatte detention center (*Aprés Sangatte? Nouvelles immigrations. Nouveaux enjeux*, 2002), and a book on alternative systems of economic exchange (*Les systémes d'échange local. Un utopie anticapitaliste en pratique*, 2003).

Abderrahmane Lakhsassi teaches Islamic Thought at Mohammed V University in Rabat, Morocco. He received his B.A. from the American University of Beirut and his Masters in Philosophy at the Sorbonne. His Ph.D. thesis (Manchester 1982) focused on Ibn Khaldun's epistemology. He was a visiting professor at Hartford Theological Seminary in Connecticut in 1991 and at Michigan State University in 1997. He was twice a Fulbright Scholar-in-Residence in the United States: 1994–1995 at Centenary College and Morris County College and 2004–2005 at Davidson College and Wake Forest University. He has published extensively on Islamic thought, Berber poetry, and popular culture. His most recent book was published in collaboration with A. Sebti, and is called *From Tea to Mint Tea: Custom and History* (in Arabic) (1999).

Nick Mai is Research Fellow in Migrations and Immigrations at the Institute for the Study of European Transformations of London Metropolitan University. His current work is young migrants from Morocco and Romania within the EU. He has studied migration between Albania and Italy, Morocco and Spain, and Cuba and the United States. He also directed a project to set up and manage four youth centers in central and southern Albania. His articles include "Albanian Masculinities, Sex Work and Migration: Homosexuality, AIDS and other Moral Threats," in *National Health: Gender, Sexuality and Health in a Cross-cultural Context* (1994) and "The Albanian Diaspora in the Making: Media, Transnational Identities and Migration" (*Journal of Ethnic and Migration Studies* 2005). He is co-author with R. King of *Out of Albania: from Crisis Migration to Differential Inclusion in Italy* (forthcoming).

Justin McGuinness is an assistant professor at the American University of Paris (AUP). His academic interests include urban planning, ethnography, media, and the study of professional communities. Justin is the author of the Footprint Guides for Morocco, Tunisia, and Libya—the latter under the pseudonym of James Azema. His most recent book is *Tunis 1800–1950, portrait urbain et architectural* (2004), co-authored with Zoubeir Mouhli. At the AUP, Justin is currently developing a multidisciplinary course on the history, material form, and spatial practices of the Islamic City.

Susan Ossman teaches at Goldsmith's College, University of London. She has also worked as a professor and researcher in Morocco, France, Belgium, and the United States. Her work examines how transnational media contribute to shaping nations and regional identities. She has developed new comparative methods for the study of globalization, leading to the integration of issues of mobility into discussions of social distinction. Her publications include *Picturing Casablanca, Portraits of Power in a Modern City* (1994), *Miroirs Maghrébins, Itinéaires de soi et Paysages de Rencontre* (1998), and *Three Faces of Beauty, Casablanca, Paris, Cairo* (2002).

Nadia Tazi is a philosopher and publisher. She is active in contemporary political and social debates through her writings and editorial activity on architecture, the body, human rights, and most recently, on questions of gender and Islam. She authored *Mutations*, in collaboration with Rem Koolhaas (2001) and was a coeditor of *Fragments of a History of the Human Body* and *For Rushdie* (1994). She also edited a book on Islam and virility with Fethi Benslama (*La virilité en Islam* 2004), a subject she further develops in an upcoming book.

Susan J. Terrio is a cultural anthropologist and associate professor with a joint appointment in the French department and the sociology/anthropology department at Georgetown University. Her research interests center on youth, adolescence, immigration, delinquency, juvenile justice, France, and Western Europe. In 2005–2006 she was a resident fellow at the Radcliffe Institute at Harvard University where she is at work on a book-length monograph of the Paris juvenile court based on four years of ethnographic and archival research conducted there between 2000 and 2005.